Building Really Annoying Web Sites

Building Really Annoying Web Sites

Michael Miller

Hungry Minds™

Best-Selling Books • Digital Downloads • e-Books • Answer Networks • e-Newsletters • Branded Web Sites • e-Learning

New York, NY ♦ Cleveland, OH ♦ Indianapolis, IN

Building Really Annoying Web Sites

Published by
Hungry Minds, Inc.
909 Third Avenue
New York, NY 10022
www.hungryminds.com

Copyright © 2001 Hungry Minds, Inc. All rights reserved. No part of this book, including interior design, cover design, and icons, may be reproduced or transmitted in any form, by any means (electronic, photocopying, recording, or otherwise) without the prior written permission of the publisher.

Library of Congress Control Number: 2001092893

ISBN: 0-7645-4874-3

Printed in the United States of America

10 9 8 7 6 5 4 3 2 1

1O/RZ/QZ/QR/IN

Distributed in the United States by Hungry Minds, Inc.

Distributed by CDG Books Canada Inc. for Canada; by Transworld Publishers Limited in the United Kingdom; by IDG Norge Books for Norway; by IDG Sweden Books for Sweden; by IDG Books Australia Publishing Corporation Pty. Ltd. for Australia and New Zealand; by TransQuest Publishers Pte Ltd. for Singapore, Malaysia, Thailand, Indonesia, and Hong Kong; by Gotop Information Inc. for Taiwan; by ICG Muse, Inc. for Japan; by Intersoft for South Africa; by Eyrolles for France; by International Thomson Publishing for Germany, Austria, and Switzerland; by Distribuidora Cuspide for Argentina; by LR International for Brazil; by Galileo Libros for Chile; by Ediciones ZETA S.C.R. Ltda. for Peru; by WS Computer Publishing Corporation, Inc., for the Philippines; by Contemporanea de Ediciones for Venezuela; by Express Computer Distributors for the Caribbean and West Indies; by Micronesia Media Distributor, Inc. for Micronesia; by Chips Computadoras S.A. de C.V. for Mexico; by Editorial Norma de Panama S.A. for Panama; by American Bookshops for Finland.

For general information on Hungry Minds' products and services please contact our Customer Care department within the U.S. at 800-762-2974, outside the U.S. at 317-572-3993 or fax 317-572-4002.

For sales inquiries and reseller information, including discounts, premium and bulk quantity sales, and foreign-language translations, please contact our Customer Care department at 800-434-3422, fax 317-572-4002 or write to Hungry Minds, Inc., Attn: Customer Care Department, 10475 Crosspoint Boulevard, Indianapolis, IN 46256.

For information on licensing foreign or domestic rights, please contact our Sub-Rights Customer Care department at 212-884-5000.

For information on using Hungry Minds' products and services in the classroom or for ordering examination copies, please contact our Educational Sales department at 800-434-2086 or fax 317-572-4005.

For press review copies, author interviews, or other publicity information, please contact our Public Relations department at 317-572-3168 or fax 317-572-4168.

For authorization to photocopy items for corporate, personal, or educational use, please contact Copyright Clearance Center, 222 Rosewood Drive, Danvers, MA 01923, or fax 978-750-4470.

About the Author

Michael Miller is a successful and prolific author with a reputation for practical advice, technical accuracy, and an unerring empathy for the needs of his readers.

Mr. Miller has written more than three dozen how-to and reference books over the past twelve years. He is known for his casual, easy-to-read writing style and his practical, real-world advice — as well as for his ability to explain a wide variety of complex topics to an everyday audience.

Mr. Miller is also president of The Molehill Group, a strategic consulting and authoring firm based in Carmel, Indiana. As a consultant, he specializes in providing strategic advice to and writing business plans for Internet- and technology-based businesses.

Credits

Acquisitions Editor
Chris Webb

Project Editor
Eric Newman

Technical Editor
Matthew Haughey

Copy Editors
Jeremy Zucker
Maarten Reilingh

Editorial Manager
Colleen Totz

Project Coordinator
Ryan T. Steffen

Graphics and Production Specialists
Joyce Haughey
Gabriele McCann
Jill Piscitelli
Betty Schulte
Brian Torwelle

Quality Control Technicians
Andy Hollandbeck
Carl Pierce
Marianne Santy

Proofreading and Indexing
TECHBOOKS Production Services

Cover Design
Michael Trent

For my brother, Mark, and sister, Melanie, both of whom grew up much less annoying than I did, for some reason

Preface

How does one get to be annoying?

I came up with the idea for this book after a somewhat protracted encounter with a seemingly never-ending series of pop-up windows, generated by a Web site that shall remain nameless (primarily because my publisher doesn't want to invite any possible legal action from the site in question). After muttering a curse under my breath and finally managing to close the last of the pop-ups, my curiosity took hold. Yeah, those pop-up windows are annoying — but how do you create them? Not that I wanted to integrate annoying pop-up windows into my Web site (the thought that anyone would want to *deliberately* annoy visitors to a site was foreign to me, then); it's just that I was curious. Something that annoying had to be pretty complex, I figured. I merely wanted to find out how it was done.

Discovering the code to create a pop-up window was relatively easy. All I had to do was view the source code for the aforementioned nameless Web site, and there it was, nothing more than a few lines of JavaScript. I decided to verify the code by searching some of the better JavaScript code libraries on the Web and found that I was right — generating an annoying pop-up window was actually a fairly easy thing to do.

While I was browsing the code libraries, I got more curious. If popping up a pop-up was that simple, what about some of those other maddening "special effects" you find on so many Web sites these days? Just how *do* you add self-playing background music to your site? How do you make the background flash and colors shift and graphics float around the page? How do you change the shape of the cursor and the color of the scrollbars — and, more important, *why* would you want to do these things?

It was then that I had the vision. If *I* was interested in the tricks behind all these annoying effects, lots of other users probably were, too. Might there not, in fact, be an audience for a book that showed how to do all these irritating things — kind of a step-by-step guide to the most annoying tricks you can add to a Web site?

As I contemplated this question, I kept thinking of all the other things that go into a truly annoying Web site. Why stop at pop-up windows and self-playing background music — why not produce a guide to building the most annoying Web sites imaginable? The book could present details on everything from bad color choices and bloated graphics to the animated graphics and hijacked cursors that we all love to hate. Given the huge number of truly annoying sites that are already on the Web, there *must* be a lot of users deliberately trying to make their sites as irritating as possible. Otherwise all those annoyances would be accidental, and the odds against that are . . . well, it just couldn't be, could it?

Besides, I tried to convince my high-minded publisher a few days later, this book would only *pretend* to show users how to do all those annoying things. What it really was, under the surface, was a book that demonstrated what *not* to do on a Web site—what tricks and techniques to avoid if you want to keep your visitors happy and definitely not annoyed. Yeah, that's the ticket, I said—this is a subversive guide to *good* Web site design. The instructions on how to execute all those nasty tricks are there purely for reference; the main goal of the book is to point Web site developers down the straight and narrow path that avoids annoying or frustrating their users.

That's why I know that *you* will never implement any of the maddening tricks and techniques presented in this book (which ended up with the title *Building Really Annoying Web Sites*—slightly less offensive than my original suggestion, *How to Tick Off People Online*). You want to learn what all the bad Web designers are doing only so you can be sure not to make the same mistakes on your own pages. You definitely don't want to add a pop-up window that appears when someone tries to leave your site, or a small version of your company logo that is visible as a nonscrolling watermark at the bottom of every page, or (my biggest pet peeve) a totally useless Flash animation that visitors must endure before they can enter your site. All that is beneath you—right?

In any case, that's what my high-minded publisher thinks, so if you *do* decide to try the pop-up window gag (it's in Chapter 5, by the way), don't tell anyone you learned it from this book. I wouldn't want anyone to think that I actually *encouraged* this sort of irresponsible behavior!

How This Book Is Organized

Building Really Annoying Web Sites contains more than one hundred different annoying tricks, organized by type into twelve chapters. Here is what you will find as you thumb through the book:

+ Chapter 1, "Bothersome Backgrounds," discusses how to pick the most annoying background colors and graphics, as well as how to create animated, nonscrolling, and fading backgrounds. You'll also learn how to use page transitions to irritate your site's visitors—and how to create the infamous falling objects background effect.

+ Chapter 2, "Tedious Text," presents a number of ways you can use the text on your page to annoy visitors. In addition to the obvious bad font, size, and color choices, you'll also learn some really neat text-based tricks—including blinking, glowing, fading, growing, and scrolling text.

✦ Chapter 3, "Loathsome Links," addresses the issue of bad addresses (otherwise known as dead links) and presents a variety of mouseover effects — including one that makes a user open a link without clicking!

✦ Chapter 4, "Senseless Scrolling and Frustrating Frames," delves into the issue of framed pages and how to use those frames to irritate other users. In addition to basic frame annoyances, you'll learn how to ensure that your pages are always framed — and how to put your own frame around any pages linked to or from your site.

✦ Chapter 5, "Pointless Pop-ups and Worthless Windows," is sure to be the main event for many readers. You'll learn how to create a variety of annoying pop-up windows, including full-screen windows, always-on-top windows, windows without menus and scrollbars, frameless windows, and the ever-popular window-that-can't-be-closed. You'll also learn some other irritating window effects, including shaking, jumping, and sliding windows.

✦ Chapter 6, "Crazy Cursors," shows how to change a boring cursor into something much more annoying. You'll learn how to change the shape of the cursor as well as how to add various cursor effects — including trailing cursors, trailing stars, and trailing text. As a final bonus, I show you how to generate some onscreen fireworks whenever users place their cursor over a link — it's pretty neat!

✦ Chapter 7, "Grating Graphics," discusses how to use Web page graphics in the worst possible ways. Not only will you learn to present graphics that take forever to load, you'll also learn how to make pictures fade in and out, how to turn a graphic into a nonscrolling watermark, and how to create an automated slideshow — the kind that the user has absolutely no control over.

✦ Chapter 8, "Maddening Music and Senseless Streaming," presents step-by-step instructions on how to add background music to your pages — and how to make that music play automatically, with no way for the user to stop it. You'll also learn about MP3, MIDI, and other audio formats, as well as how to place movies and scrolling media on your site.

✦ Chapter 9, "Aggravating Animations and Purposeless Plug-ins," is where I rant and rave about self-playing Flash animations. (I *hate* those things!) Of course, I'll also tell you how to add Flash to your pages, how to use JavaScript to emulate a Flash animation, and how you can avoid being annoying (if you so wish) by automatically redirecting users to other pages, based on browser capability.

✦ Chapter 10, "Nonsensical Navigation," discusses different ways you can confuse users with your site's organization and navigation. You'll learn how to hide your home page, how to create virtually untypeable URLs, and how navigation bars and menus can help to reduce your site's annoyance factor. You'll also learn how to nag users into either bookmarking your page or making it their default home page.

✦ Chapter 11, "Rage-Inducing Registrations," tackles all the forms and dialog boxes you can use to prequalify — and "pre-annoy" — visitors to your site. You'll learn how to make users answer a variety of annoying questions before they can enter your site, as well as how to completely block specific visitors from your site.

✦ Chapter 12, "Painful Purchasing," discusses all the things that e-tailers can do to alienate their customers. You'll learn a number of ways to discourage sales, including how to screw up the checkout process and leave customers in the dark about product availability and shipping. (The sad thing is, most of the annoying tricks in this chapter are standard operating procedure at far too many Web retailers!)

There's More on the Web

If you want to see examples of some of the best tricks in this book — as well as download accompanying graphics and code — check out the *Building Really Annoying Web Sites* Web site, at www.annoyingwebsites.com. All the tricks are arranged by chapter, and you'll even find some tricks that we didn't have space for in this book. (I apologize in advance if you find the site itself a little irritating; it uses some of the tricks I present in this book!)

I'd also like to acknowledge some of the major Web-based code libraries, which contain a large variety of really neat Dynamic HTML and JavaScript tricks. If you're interested in learning more annoying (and even some non-annoying) tricks you can add to your Web site, I recommend you take a look at the following sites:

✦ Dynamic Drive DHTML Code Library (www.dynamicdrive.com)

✦ EarthWeb.com JavaScripts Archives (webdeveloper.earthweb.com/pagedev/webjs)

✦ JavaScript Source (javascript.internet.com)

✦ Kurt's Free Original DHTML (website.lineone.net/~kurt.grigg/javascript/)

✦ Nic's JavaScript Page (www.javascript-page.com)

What You Need to Know to Use This Book

This book doesn't assume that you're a big-league JavaScript code jockey. In fact, you don't need to know any JavaScript at all to use this book — although you shouldn't be intimidated by the thought of copying some basic scripts into the HTML code of your Web pages. I do assume that you're somewhat familiar with HTML coding, and that you're comfortable with manipulating raw HTML code. You should also have some type of HTML editing software installed on your system and know how to use the program to edit basic HTML code.

Beyond that, you need to have your own Web pages or Web site, of course, and access to those pages via FTP or some other method. After all, if you want to employ any of the techniques presented in this book, you'll want to be able to upload newly edited versions of your pages.

Finally, you need to understand that HTML and JavaScript are constantly changing languages. When new versions or new commands are introduced, these new approaches might not work with older Web browsers. For that matter, code that works with Internet Explorer might not always work with Netscape, and vice versa. Most of the tricks in this book are designed to work on all versions of all browsers, but don't be disappointed if some scripts don't work on your particular browser. That's just the way things work—or don't, as the case may be. For the best possible results, use the latest and greatest version of your particular Web browser to experience how these tricks really work.

Conventions Used in This Book

Each chapter in this book begins with a list of the tricks presented in that chapter and ends with a summary of what you should have learned by reading the chapter. Between the start and the finish are the tricks themselves, numbered in order of appearance.

You'll also find icons in the book's margins that highlight special or important information. These icons look like this:

 Note This icon means that the text that follows is an aside to the main point.

In addition, the following formatting and typographical conventions appear throughout the book:

✦ Code examples appear in a `fixed width font`.

✦ File and function names, as well as World Wide Web addresses (URLs), appear like this: `www.mywebsite.com`.

✦ The first occurrence of an important term in a chapter is highlighted with *italic* text. Italic is also used for placeholders—for example, `<body onLoad="genericPopup('`*popup-url*`')">`, where *popup-url* is the address of the page you want to load into your pop-up window.

✦ Menu commands are indicated in hierarchical order, with each menu command separated by an arrow. For example, File ➪ Open means to click the File command on the menu bar and then select Open.

✦ Keyboard shortcuts are indicated with the following syntax: Ctrl+C, which means to press the Control key and the C key at the same time.

Contacting the Author

I always love to hear from my readers. If you want to contact me, feel free to e-mail me at annoying@molehillgroup.com. I can't promise that I'll answer every e-mail, but I will promise that I'll read each one!

If you want to learn more about me and any new books I have cooking, check out my main Web site at www.molehillgroup.com. Who knows—you might find some other books there that you'd like to read.

Acknowledgments

First of all, I'd like to thank my old pals Joe Wikert and Richard Swadley for being receptive to this idea and greenlighting the book project. I'd also like to thank all the folks at Hungry Minds who helped in the creation of this book, including Chris Webb, Eric Newman, Matt Haughey, Jeremy Zucker, Maarten Reilingh, and Ryan Steffen.

My special thanks go to the folks who gave permission to have their code adapted for the various tricks presented in this book, in particular Kurt Grigg and Marcin Wojtowicz. (Make sure you check out Kurt's Web site at `website.lineone.net/ ~kurt.grigg/javascript/` for more neat tricks!)

Contents at a Glance

Contents

Bothersome Backgrounds

You can take many different approaches when you want
to annoy your Web site's visitors. You can fill the pages
with slow-loading graphics, or introduce an incomprehensible
navigation system, or force users to sit through irrelevant
Flash movies before they can enter—all of which require a lot
of work on your part.

When you want to make users shudder and turn their heads
in disgust, however, sometimes the simplest approach is the
best—and nothing is simpler than a Web page background.
Choose the right (that is, the wrong) background color or
wallpaper, and you can make users shield their eyes, toss
their lunch, and develop painful migraine headaches. And
when you pair your garish background with clashing-colored
text—as discussed in Chapter 2, "Tedious Text"—users
won't be able to read a single word on your page!

The great thing about a bad page background is that you can
achieve a very powerful result with comparatively little work.
In this chapter, I show you more than a dozen tricks for
annoying your users with bothersome backgrounds—so open
up your HTML editor and let's get down to business!

Trick #1: Pick an Eye-Popping Background Color

You're used to seeing most Web pages designed with black
text on a white background, just like the design for this book.
There's a reason for that—black-on-white is a high-contrast
combination and makes for great readability. The white background doesn't detract from the importance of the text, doesn't
draw attention to itself, and doesn't make your eyes hurt if you
stare at it for too long.

In other words, traditional black-on-white design is highly functional — and extremely boring.

Because so many Web pages use a white background, you can have a tremendous impact by choosing any background color other than white. Look, a tan background — how shocking! Or how about white text on a dark blue background — scandalous, simply scandalous!

Well, okay, maybe not all nonwhite background colors have the proper power to annoy. To be sufficiently annoying, a background color has to be eye-poppingly bright, garish, and loud. Think fluorescent colors. Think neon. Think bright purple, shocking pink, lime green, fire-engine red, and sunrise orange — colors that make you squint if you look directly at them.

When you choose one of these colors as the background for your Web page, you're sure to get a lot of comments. They won't be nice comments, but your efforts will definitely be noticed.

Note   It's impossible to illustrate a bright color in a black-and-white book, so I won't bother trying. You can get a feel for the effect, however, by going to my *Building Really Annoying Web Sites* Web site (www.annoyingwebsites.com) and look- ing at the examples in the Bothersome Backgrounds section.

How to do it

Changing the background color for a Web page involves a single HTML attribute, placed within the <body> tag. The attribute is called bgcolor, and it's used like this:

```
<body bgcolor=#xxxxxx>
```

The color is represented by a six-digit hexadecimal code. (That's the *xxxxxx* in the code above.) Virtually every color you can imagine has its own hex value. All you have to know is which value corresponds to which color, and you're ready to code.

Note   Go to my www.annoyingwebsites.com Web site for an online color picker — just pick the color and it will generate the hex code for you.

To get you started, Table 1-1 shows the HTML codes for a somewhat "vanilla" palette of non-annoying colors. If you're trying to annoy the readers of your Web page, these are the background colors to *avoid*.

Table 1-1
Hex Values for Basic (Non-Annoying) Colors

Color	Value
White	#FFFFFF
Black	#000000
Light Weak Green	#99CC99
Pale Weak Blue	#CCCCFF
Pale Weak Cyan	#CCFFFF
Pale Dull Orange	#FFCC99
Pale Dull Yellow	#FFFF99
Pale Gray	#CCCCCC

 Note   Most Web browsers will recognize words (instead of hexadecimal codes) for a basic palette of colors. Unfortunately, HTML allows for only a handful of basic color words. (Blue is okay; mauve isn't.) Because the most annoying colors are too annoying for words, always enter their color values in hexadecimal code.

Instead, you'll want to choose from the dazzling color values listed in Table 1-2. When used as page backgrounds, these colors are guaranteed to blind any user not equipped with proper eye protection. In fact, some of these colors just plain *hurt* if you stare at them for too long. With great power comes great responsibility; use these colors wisely.

Table 1-2
Hex Values for Annoying Colors

Color	Value
Yellow	#FFFF00
Yellow-Yellow-Spring	#CCFF00
Light Hard Spring	#99FF33
Light Hard Green	#33FF33
Light Hard Blue	#3333FF
Cyan-Cyan-Azure	#00CCFF
Light Hard Pink	#FF3399
Deep Hard Pink	#CC0066

Continued

Table 1-2 *(continued)*	
Color	*Value*
Red	#FF0000
Red-Red-Pink	#FF0033
Pink-Pink-Magenta	#FF0099
Red-Red-Orange	#FF3300
Orange-Orange-Yellow	#FF9900
Orange-Orange-Red	#FF6600
Light Hard Pink	#FF3399
Magenta	#FF00FF
Light Red-Pink	#FF3366

Note that you may not have to set your background color manually. Most advanced HTML editors, such as FrontPage, enable you to set the page background color through a toolbar or menu command, thus sparing you the extremely time-consuming task of entering a single line of HTML code. The color choosers used in some of these programs however, may not include the most annoying colors, which means you still might need to code the background manually.

Practical uses for this technique

Sometimes an annoying color really isn't annoying; sometimes it's *fashionable*. When you think of annoying colors, think the swinging Sixties, think *Austin Powers*, think pop art. (For that matter, think *Wired* magazine — the ultimate home of annoying design.) What is often annoying to the establishment is sometimes quite acceptable and stylish to the trendsetters outside traditional culture — which means that there might be a design award in the cards for that shocking-fuchsia Web page!

Another, quite legitimate reason to use hot colors is to draw attention to your Web page. In an online world where all the major Web sites look pretty much the same (think Yahoo!), a hot-pink page will really stand out from the crowd. There's a reason why retail packaging and sale tags are often bright yellow and orange and red — bright colors attract attention.

So, annoying or not, a bright color will definitely draw attention to your page. The question you have to ask is, is it the right (meaning wrong) type of attention?

How not to be annoying

If you want a background color that isn't annoying, you can't go wrong with plain white. It may not be attention-getting, but just about every other color works well with white — so you can use colorful elements against the white background to grab the user's attention.

If you want to draw attention to your page and still maintain some semblance of readability, think about using a pale yellow, light blue, or light green background. All of these colors are bright and colorful enough to draw attention, yet subdued enough to work well with traditional black text.

Trick #2: Use a Multiple-Colored Background

If one background color, carefully chosen, can be annoying, then two background colors — side by side, or placed on top of each other — must be doubly annoying, right?

The answer, of course, is yes.

Not only are multiple colors annoying, they can also make it next to impossible to find a readable text color to put on top of those colors. If you choose your background colors carefully, you can achieve a high contrast between the two colors. The best example of this is a simple black/white split, as shown in Figure 1-1. You can put light text on the black background, but then you don't have enough contrast between the text and the white background. You can go with a dark text color to work with the white background, but then it gets lost on the black background. There's really no good compromise, which is really annoying.

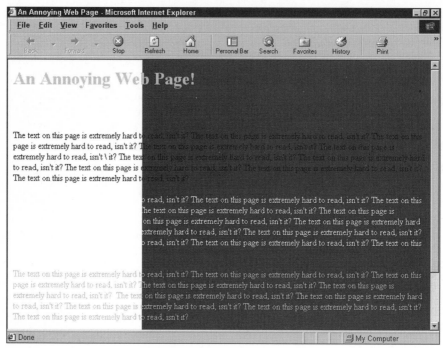

Figure 1-1: When your background is split between a light and a dark color, it's impossible to find a text color that works with both background colors.

Even better is a background that includes a grid of colors, as shown in Figure 1-2. Not only do you have text color considerations, you also introduce the issue of color clash, where all those (presumably bright) colors fight with one another for the user's attention. The user's mind is thinking, subconsciously, "Do I look at the red — or the green — or the orange — or the pink — or the yellow — or the . . .?" The result is that the user's eyes flit from one part of the page to another, trying to find a calming, central point.

Pointlessly, of course.

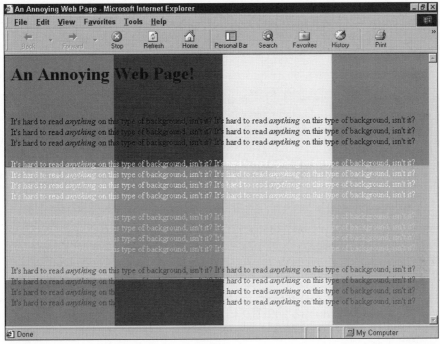

Figure 1-2: For ultimate optical confusion, use a multicolored grid as your Web page background.

How to do it

The easiest way to do this is to create a short, horizontal, multicolored image that you can tile down the entire length of your page. To produce a simple light/dark vertical split (like the one in Figure 1-1), for example, you can create a simple graphic — white on one half, black on the other. The graphic should be one pixel tall, the white side should be 400 pixels wide, and the black side should be 900 pixels wide. (This optimizes the graphic for an 800×600 resolution display but allows for extra black in larger windows; otherwise, the graphic would start to repeat on larger displays.)

> **Tip** The most efficient file format for graphic files is JPG, although GIF files work almost as well — and even better when you're doing flat, single-color backgrounds. As with most graphics discussed in this book, you can use any graphics editing program to create your files. I happen to be a fan of Jasc Software's Paint Shop Pro (available at `www.jasc.com`), although if you have the bucks, Adobe Photoshop (available at `www.adobe.com`) offers a lot of cool features, too.

To effect a checkerboard background, you'll need to create a taller graphic, like the one in Figure 1-3, which has at least two rows of colored blocks. This stripe will then repeat down your page, to produce a background similar to the one in Figure 1-2.

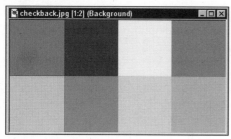

Figure 1-3: To produce a checkerboard of background color, create a taller, multi-row graphic to tile down your page.

After you create your graphic, all you have to do is code it into the background of your Web page. You do this with the `background` attribute, used within the `<body>` tag. The code should look something like this:

```
<body background="filename.jpg">
```

Obviously, *filename.jpg* is the placeholder for the name of your graphics file; it needs to be enclosed in quotation marks, and include the complete URL or directory path, if located separately from the page you're coding.

Practical uses for this technique

A multiple-colored background doesn't have to be annoying — there are some very practical uses for this technique. Many Web pages create a frame or sidebar effect by using one color for the sidebar background, and another for the background of the main part of the page. You may also *want* to split your page in half, in which case a dark/light background split is easier to code than separate frames or a table.

How not to be annoying

Breaking up a static background isn't always an annoying idea; sometimes it makes actual design sense. In this context, however, you want to use two colors that don't sharply contrast with each other, such as tan and light green, or light yellow and light orange. Choose light colors from the same tonal range, and you'll have an interesting — and not at all annoying — background for your page.

Trick #3: Use Different Backgrounds for Each Frame on the Page

I talk more about frames in Chapter 4, "Senseless Scrolling and Frustrating Frames," but for now just remember that frames are a way to break your Web page into several component parts, each of which can be navigated separately. You typically use frames when you have disparate content to present on the same page; the frames keep the different content separate, yet still tied together.

In and of themselves, frames can be terribly annoying. (Again, turn to Chapter 4 to learn more.) Frames get even more annoying when they disrupt the visual composition of the page — and the easiest way to achieve this result is to code a different background color for each frame.

How to do it

Because each frame within a frameset is a separate HTML page, all you have to do is assign a different background color within each page's `<body>` tag. (See Trick #1 for the basic background code.)

Practical uses for this technique

Sometimes you want your subsidiary frames to stand out from the main frame on your page. In this instance, using different background colors for each frame serves to draw attention to the subsidiary content, and definitely to separate the smaller frames from the main part of the page.

How not to be annoying

The greater the contrast between each frame's background color, the higher the annoyance factor. If you lessen the contrast, you can achieve the same results without greatly annoying your visitors. So if your main frame has a white background, think about a tan or light yellow or light blue background for each subsidiary frame. If you have only two frames (a main and a subsidiary), you can even consider using white for the main and black (or dark blue) for the subsidiary — even though the contrast is high, the black/white combination is a visually acceptable one.

Trick #4: Make the Background Flash On and Off

You're accustomed to loading a Web page and having the background just sit there. You don't expect the page's background to start flashing on and off, like bolts of lightning in a midsummer thunderstorm. In fact, you'd probably find it pretty annoying if a Web page kept flashing at you. If it kept at it, you wouldn't even be able to read the page.

Because of its high annoyance factor, the flashing background is a highly valued design technique. Read on to learn how to flash your pages.

Note   In this instance, flashing Web pages have nothing to do with Flash animation, which is discussed in Chapter 9, "Aggravating Animations and Purposeless Plug-ins."

How to do it

To make your Web page flash, you have to insert a brief bit of JavaScript into your HTML code. In essence, you instruct the page to change the background color from black to white to black to white, over and over again, based on a set timing.

All you have to do is insert the code from Listing 1-1 after the last text on your HTML page. (This allows your text to load first, so it can be visible in between "lightning flashes.")

Listing 1-1: **JavaScript code for a flashing background**

```
<script language="JavaScript">
<!--

var switchcolor=0

function flash()
{switchcolor=switchcolor+1;
if(switchcolor==1){document.bgColor="#FFFFFF";
setTimeout("flash()",100);}
if(switchcolor==2){document.bgColor="#000000";
setTimeout("flash()",100);}
if(switchcolor==3){switchcolor=0; setTimeout("flash()",100);}}

setTimeout("flash()",100);

//-->
</script>
```

This code is actually pretty simple; all it does is switch back and forth between two different background colors (white and black, in this example) after a period of time specified with the setTimeout function. You can change the colors that flash by inserting new color values after the document.bgColor properties. You can also change the length of the flashes by selecting new values for the setTimeout functions.

Practical uses for this technique

The only practical use for a flashing background is to grab the user's attention (unless you call initiating epileptic seizures a practical thing). If you have an important warning page, you may want to flash the page several times to make sure that the user is paying attention. But you want to limit the number of flashes, or else the content on the page will never be readable.

How not to be annoying

You can reduce the annoyance of a flashing page by limiting the number of flashes and then returning the page to its normal state. You can also grab the user's attention without flashing the whole page — a bit of Flash animation (or an animated GIF) at the top of a page can serve as a blinking warning without making the entire page unreadable.

But then, where's the fun in that?

Trick #5: Make the Background Colors Cycle

If a background flashing between black and white is annoying, how about a background that changes colors randomly every few seconds? This effect doesn't give the user time to adjust to any one color before the background changes again. In fact, if you wait long enough, the background is bound to change to the same color as the text, thus rendering all your content effectively invisible!

How to do it

Changing background colors is a relatively easy thing to do in JavaScript, thanks to the `document.bgColor` property. Throw in a few lines of script to randomize the background color, and you have everything you need to drive users insane. Just insert the script in Listing 1-2 after the `<body>` tag in your HTML document.

> **Listing 1-2: JavaScript code for cycling background colors**
>
> ```
> <script language="JavaScript">
> <!--
>
> function ChangeColor()
> {color = "#";
> for (i = 0; i < 6; i++)
> {hex = Math.round(Math.random() * 15);
> if (hex == 10) hex = "a";
> ```
>
> *Continued*

Listing 1-2 *(continued)*

```
if (hex == 11) hex = "b";
if (hex == 12) hex = "c";
if (hex == 13) hex = "d";
if (hex == 14) hex = "e";
if (hex == 15) hex = "f";
color += hex;}
document.bgColor = color;
setTimeout("ChangeColor();",2000);}

ChangeColor();

//-->
</script>
```

You can change the cycling time between colors by changing the `setTimeout` value. The default value (2000) is about two seconds.

Practical uses for this technique

As with a flashing background, a background that constantly changes colors does an effective job of catching the user's attention. It's rotten for actually reading any text on the page, but it is attention-getting.

How not to be annoying

Although rational Web designers probably won't want to change the color of an entire browser window, you could use this effect in a smaller frame within a larger window. The cycling colors in the smaller frame—perhaps along with a large, brief text message—would catch the user's attention, while the larger main frame could feature a more traditional (and more readable) static design. Likewise, you could utilize the color-cycling effect in a small pop-up window to draw attention to special information outside the main browser window.

Trick #6: Use a Text Background Behind the Text

If you're following along, you can see that one of the goals of these background tricks is to make the text on your page unreadable. Another way to accomplish this annoying result is to layer text on text, so that the main text is practically indistinguishable from the background text.

How to do it

To confuse users with multiple layers of text, you need to create a background image that contains nothing but text. Use the text tool in your graphics editor to add random words and phrases to a new graphic; then save the file and insert it in your HTML document by using the `background` attribute in the `<body>` tag, as described in Trick #2. You can use smaller text or larger text; a tightly packed image of small text is especially annoying, as shown in Figure 1-4.

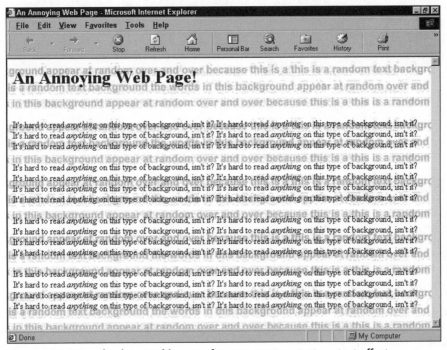

Figure 1-4: Use a background image of text to create a text-on-text effect.

Practical uses for this technique

The practical uses of "hiding" your real text in this fashion are few and far between. If you come up with one, let me know!

How not to be annoying

This particular trick doesn't have to be annoying—it could be a design statement. For this to work, however, the background text has to be a different, lighter color than the real text. You can even use the same basic color for the background text, but with a lighter color value—light gray background text against black foreground text, for example.

Another interesting design is to use this same basic effect, but with the text in the background image displayed at a much larger size than the foreground text. If the foreground text is displayed at 12 points, for example, you might create the background image with the text at 48 points or larger, and in a lighter or contrasting color. (Light blue, light green, and yellow are all good.) Again, an annoying effect can be turned into a stylish design with minimal effort. (Curses—foiled again!)

Trick #7: Use a Busy Background Graphic

When it comes to making it difficult to read the text on a page, there's nothing like a busy background graphic to do the job. This old standby always works, even if it's a relatively common annoyance thanks to dimwitted Web designers and novices who think that fancy backgrounds are "neat."

Note

One of the most annoying uses of busy backgrounds can be found at the "Bud Ugly Design" site at `wackyadvice.com/bud/bud.html`. This is a parody site, as you'll see, that displays some of the most annoying Web design I've ever seen—it's almost as if they designed their site using all the tricks in this book. I love it!

How to do it

Although you can use your graphics editor to create an overly complex image, the easier thing to do is simply to use a photograph for the background image. As you can see in Figure 1-5, photographs are particularly effective in both drawing your eye away from your text and in providing enough differences in contrast to make it difficult to read an entire line of text all the way through.

To define a photograph as your page background, use the `background` attribute in the `<body>` tag, as described in Trick #2. For extra annoying points, use a smaller picture file that won't fill the entire page, so that the annoying photo is tiled within the browser window.

Practical uses for this technique

If you use the right kind of photo, a picture in the background of your page can help to personalize your Web site or even add a stylish design effect. The key is to make the picture recede into the background and not detract from the text and other foreground objects.

How not to be annoying

There are several ways to have your picture and read your text, too.

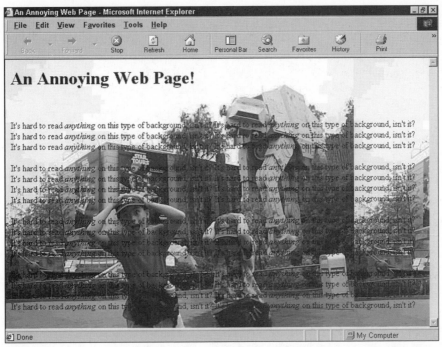

Figure 1-5: Put a photograph in the background to make it difficult to read the text on your page.

The best approach is to edit the photo in a graphics editing program to lighten it up. In Paint Shop Pro, for example, you choose Colors ➪ Adjust ➪ Brightness/Contrast and both increase the brightness and decrease the contrast. When the background image is effectively light, it no longer detracts from the key items in the foreground.

If your goal is to draw attention to your photograph, a better way to display it is as a separate graphic in the foreground of your page — *not* as a background image. See Chapter 7, "Grating Graphics," for more information on placing graphic images on your pages.

Trick #8: Add a Bad Background Gradation

As you saw in Trick #2 and Trick #7, when the background changes contrast, it's virtually impossible for single-colored text to be readable against the entire background. Another way to achieve this result is by using a background blend that gradates from a light color to a dark color. As you can see in Figure 1-6, there's no good text color to use against this type of background, making at least half your page difficult to read.

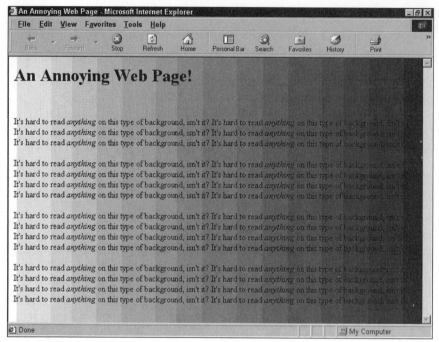

Figure 1-6: Use a gradated background graphic to interfere with the text contrast on your page.

How to do it

You add a gradated background to your page via a background graphic. (You can't specify a gradated background color in HTML, so you have to use a graphic.) For a left-to-right gradation, you can create a short-and-wide image, as described in Trick #2. For a top-to-bottom gradation, you have to create a narrow-and-tall image, as tall as the longest possible scroll length of your page. (If your page is long enough to scroll twice, go with a 2000-pixel height.) Make sure to pick two colors that are in high contrast; black-to-white is good, as is yellow-to-blue or light green–to–dark purple.

Use the `background` attribute in the `<body>` tag, as described in Trick #2, to insert the background image, and you're ready to go.

Practical uses for this technique

Gradated backgrounds are popular among Web designers and add a classy look when used properly. But a bad gradation—one that swings from one end of the color scale to another—is impractical to use behind a block of text. You can, however, effect a horizontal gradation over a smaller area, to the left of the main text, thus creating a kind of colored bar down the side of your page. This will place your body text to the right of the color change and enable you to choose a text color with the proper contrast against the bulk of the background color.

How not to be annoying

If you're trying to be designerly correct (DC), you should employ gradations that stay within the same range of contrast and color saturation. Going from dark blue to dark green, for example, creates a uniformly dark background, upon which you can place light-colored text for the appropriate high contrast. Conversely, gradating from light brown to light orange or yellow creates a light enough background so that you can use traditional black text without running into a background/foreground contrast problem.

Trick #9: Make the Background Image Scroll Automatically

In Trick #7, you saw how annoying a photographic background can be on a Web page. To step up the annoyance factor, imagine that same photograph—but now it's scrolling slowly down your user's browser window!

If you thought a static photograph was bad, one that keeps scrolling down the page, over and over, is really annoying. There is absolutely no way for users to stay focused on your text when the background is constantly moving!

How to do it

A scrolling background is accomplished via the short JavaScript code in Listing 1-3. The effect is achieved by rapidly changing the position of the background graphic and incrementing the vertical position by 1 pixel, over and over.

Just insert the following code after the `<body>` tag in your HTML document. For this script to work, you need to define the background image separately by using the `background` attribute in the `<body>` tag.

> **Listing 1-3: JavaScript code for a scrolling background image**
>
> ```
> <script language="JavaScript">
> <!--
>
> var GraphicPosition = 0;
> var GraphicObject = eval('document.body');
>
> function BackgroundScroll(maxSize)
> {GraphicPosition = GraphicPosition + 1;
> if (GraphicPosition > maxSize) GraphicPosition = 0;
> ```

Continued

Listing 1-3 *(continued)*

```
GraphicObject.style.backgroundPosition = "0 " +
GraphicPosition;}

var ScrollRate = window.setInterval("BackgroundScroll(307)",
10);

//-->
</script>
```

You can change the speed of the scrolling by setting a new value for the last variable in the `window.setInterval` command. The default is 10; set a larger number to scroll slower, or a smaller number to scroll faster.

Note   If you set too slow a scroll rate, your users won't actually see the image scroll; it will look more like an intermittent redraw of the background at a slightly lower position on the page.

Practical uses for this technique

A scrolling background certainly draws attention, which can be good and bad. One possible positive application of this technique is to use a small company logo as your background image, so that your logo is constantly scrolling down the browser window. (It's not-quite-subliminal advertising.)

Another possible application is to embed a text message in the background graphic. If you don't add any text to the foreground of the page, you've created a movie credits–type effect using nothing but a background image.

How not to be annoying

If you like the idea of something constantly scrolling on your page, consider creating a framed page. You can insert the scrolling background in one frame and your main text in a second frame, so the one doesn't interfere with the other.

Trick #10: Force the Background to Remain Stationary

While on the subject of scrolling, how about a background image that *doesn't* scroll at all, even when users scroll down the browser window? This type of static background is called a watermark and can be really confusing to users who are accustomed to everything in the window scrolling when they manipulate the scrollbars.

How to do it

Defining a background image that stays centered in the browser Window is relatively easy. All you have to do is create a style sheet that positions a fixed, untiled, nonscrolling image in the center of the window's background. Listing 1-4 contains the code to insert in the head of your HTML document.

Listing 1-4: Style sheet code for creating a watermarked background

```
<style type="text/css">
<!--
body{background-image:url("filename");
background-attachment:fixed;
background-repeat:no-repeat;
background-position:center;}
-->
</style>
```

You need to replace *filename* with the complete URL and filename of the background image. Unlike the code in Trick #9, for this code to work, you should *not* define a background image in the <body> tag.

Note If you're using FrontPage to design your page, you can accomplish this same effect without any coding. When you choose Format ⇨ Background to insert a background graphic, select the Watermark option; this holds the background image in place when users scroll through your page. Because this code uses Cascading Style Sheets, this technique does not work in Netscape browsers earlier than version 6.

Practical uses for this technique

Using a static background is a good way to impress an image on Web site visitors. You may, for example, want to use a screened-back version of a company logo and have it stay static in the center of the browser window; this technique accomplishes that. For that matter, any dominant image — a picture of a company's headquarters on a corporate page, a picture of a dog on a canine page, and so on — can be watermarked in this fashion.

How not to be annoying

The key to making this effect less annoying is to make the background image look less opaque. Lighten up the brightness and decrease the contrast, or use similar effects to ensure that the background image doesn't detract from any elements that may be scrolling over it.

Trick #11: Use an Animated Background

If you want to add a moving background to your page, you don't have to use JavaScript. You can accomplish a similar effect through the use of an animated GIF file.

As you probably know, an animated GIF is a graphics file format that includes multiple "frames" of animation within a single file. When you open a GIF file in a Web browser, the graphic automatically cycles through the frames, presenting a semblance of animation.

When you use an animated GIF file as the background graphic on a Web page, the animation proceeds the same way it would if the GIF file were a normal foreground element on the page. In fact, if you elect to constantly repeat the image when you create the file, your background image will continue to play, over and over, until your visitors are suitably annoyed.

How to do it

This is a simple one. All you have to do is use a graphics editing program to create an animated GIF file; then specify that file as your page's background graphic, using the `background` attribute in the `<body>` tag, as described in Trick #2.

Note   Not all graphics editors can create animated GIFs. If you need an animated GIF editor, check out GIF Construction Set Professional at `www.mindworkshop.com/alchemy/gifcon.html`.

If you want to make this a *really* annoying effect, use an animated GIF file with relatively small dimensions, so that it repeats several times on your page. The effect of multiple background animations playing simultaneously is almost nauseating in its impact!

Practical uses for this technique

Any animation on a page tends to capture the user's attention. You can use an animated background, then, as a kind of splash page, without obscuring the animation with foreground text. Give your users a "next" button to click when they get bored with the animation, and then direct them to a non-animated page containing your primary information.

How not to be annoying

Trying to read text that is sitting on top of an animation is particularly annoying. If you want to reduce the annoyance factor and still retain the animation, consider putting the animation in the foreground of the page, where you can control its placement—and then flow your text *around* the animation, instead of on top of it.

You can also place the animation in a separate pop-up window or separate frame—anything to distinguish it from the main text on your page.

Trick #12: Make the Background Fade from Black to White

I've discussed a few techniques for fading, flashing, and scrolling backgrounds, all of which are continuing effects—that is, they continue to fade and flash and scroll after the page is done loading. (In fact, there's no way to turn off most of these effects!) I'm now going to turn your attention to an effect that executes while the page is loading and makes users wait for it to complete before the text is revealed on the page.

This effect is easy to describe. When users open the page, the window is completely black. Slowly but surely (with the emphasis on *slowly*), the background fades from all-black to all-white, with the black text becoming visible as the background lightens.

A fading effect like this might be fun to watch (once), but it's definitely a time-waster as far as most users are concerned—which is what makes it annoying.

How to do it

The JavaScript code in Listing 1-5 produces a smooth fade effect, in this example from black to white. Just insert the code in Listing 1-5 at the *end* of your HTML document, after the last line of text. (You want all the text to load before the effect starts.)

> **Listing 1-5: JavaScript code for a black-to-white background fade**

```
<script language="JavaScript">
<!--

var speed = 250

function bfade (n)
{this.length = n;
for (var i =1; i <= n; i++)
{this[i] = ' '}}
fade = new bfade(16)
for(var i = 0; i < 10; i++)
{fade[i] = i}
```

Continued

Listing 1-5 *(continued)*

```
fade[10] = "a"
fade[11] = "b"
fade[12] = "c"
fade[13] = "d"
fade[14] = "e"
fade[15] = "f"
function hexcolor(i)
{return ("" + fade[Math.floor(i/16)] + fade[i%16])}

function fadecolor(r2,g2,b2,r1,g1,b1)
{for(var i = 0; i <= speed; i++)
{var r = hexcolor(Math.floor(r2 * ((speed-i)/speed) + r1 *
(i/speed)))
var g = hexcolor(Math.floor(g2 * ((speed-i)/speed) + g1 *
(i/speed)))
var b = hexcolor(Math.floor(b2 * ((speed-i)/speed) + b1 *
(i/speed)))
document.bgColor = "#" + r + g + b}}

fadecolor(0,0,0,255,255,255);

//-->
</script>
```

You can fade to and from other colors by replacing the numbers after the fadecolor function in the last line of the script. The first three numbers are the starting color; the last three numbers are the ending color. This script uses RGB color values rather than hexadecimal numbers, so remember that 255 in RGB is the same as FF in hex, and 0 in RGB is the same as 00 in hex.

You can also continue the fade from white to a third color (and then a fourth and a fifth and so on) by adding a new fadecolor line at the end of the script that starts with white (255,255,255) and changes to another color. The script will execute each fadecolor line in its turn for as many different fades as you designate. (Which, of course, increases the annoyance factor — when will it stop?)

Practical uses for this technique

You can use a dramatic fade like this to draw attention to the upcoming page. It's a kind of "slow reveal" for the text on your page, which heightens the anticipation for what's there. Used sparingly, this can be a useful effect; if it's overused, you'll definitely raise the ire of visitors to your site.

How not to be annoying

The fade effect as presented in Listing 1-5 is annoying partly because of its slow speed (which might even make some users think that their Internet connection has slowed down!). You can decrease the annoyance factor by speeding up the fade; just use a smaller number for the speed variable in the first line of code. (Replacing 250 with 75 is a good compromise between speed and the smoothness of the transition.)

Trick #13: Force Users to Endure Long Page Transitions

The fade effect in Trick #12 is actually a *transition* effect, as it affects the way a page loads into a browser. Numerous page transitions are possible with normal HTML coding (no JavaScript required) and are typically available as menu options in most advanced HTML editors.

But users really hate page transitions. Where a normal Web page (without transitions) loads almost instantaneously, a Web page using a transition takes several seconds to load. You've been there, watching the seconds tick by as the next page wipes or splits or dissolves into place. Equally annoying is that if you back up from that page, the same annoying page transition is applied to the page you just visited!

You can use a number of different page transitions. You can apply the transitions to page entry or page exit and define how long you want the transition to take. For maximum annoyance, choose a really *long* duration and force visitors to sit through the transition on both arrival and exit.

How to do it

If you're using an HTML editor like FrontPage, you'll find that page transitions are built right in. Using FrontPage as an example, you add a page transition by choosing Format ➪ Page Transition. The Page Transitions dialog box appears; pull down the Event list and choose to apply the transition on Page Enter, Page Exit, Site Enter, or Site Exit. Choose an effect from the Transition Effect list, and then enter a length of time in the Duration box. Click OK to add the effect to your page.

The HTML (actually, Dynamic HTML) code for a page transition uses a meta tag, placed in the head of the document, like this:

```
<meta http-equiv="Page-Enter"
content="RevealTrans(Duration=x,Transition=y)">
```

You set the duration of the transition (replace the x) in seconds, and the type of transition (replace the y) by using the codes in Table 1-3.

Table 1-3
HTML Page Transitions

Transition	Code
Box in	0
Box out	1
Circle in	2
Circle out	3
Wipe up	4
Wipe down	5
Wipe right	6
Wipe left	7
Vertical blinds	8
Horizontal blinds	9
Checkerboard across	10
Checkerboard down	11
Random dissolve	12
Split vertical in	13
Split vertical out	14
Split horizontal in	15
Split horizontal out	16
Strip left down	17
Strip left up	18
Strip right down	19
Strip right up	20
Random bars horizontal	21
Random bars vertical	22
Random	23

To add a transition when a visitor leaves your page, replace `"Page-Enter"` in the code with `"Page-Exit"`.

Note Page transitions work only with Internet Explorer versions 4.0 and later, and not with Netscape browsers.

There's one more transition that uses a slightly different code. This one is called a blend transition and is coded like this:

```
<meta http-equiv="Page-Enter" content="blendTrans(Duration=x)">
```

As with the other transitions, you set the duration length, in seconds. No transition number exists, as only one blend transition is available.

Practical uses for this technique

It's interesting that transitions are good and expected during live slideshows but pretty much disliked and unexpected when used on Web pages. This no doubt has to do with users' expectations about the time it takes a page to load; faster transitions are definitely less annoying than slower ones.

The practical use for this technique, of course, is that it draws attention to what's coming up — and, to some degree, makes your site stand out from all the nontransition pages on the Web. If nothing else, page transitions aren't boring — annoying, perhaps, but not boring.

How not to be annoying

As with the fade effect in Trick #13, you can reduce the annoyance factor of a page transition by decreasing its duration. Use a maximum duration of no more than a second or two, and you won't tick off your users *too* much. Go with a five- or ten-second duration and you'll risk users' clicking away before the page fully loads.

Of course, to avoid any annoyance whatsoever, simply don't employ page transitions, or use them very sparingly. Click, view, click, view, click, view — your pages will be as boring as all the other pages on the Web, but at least you won't be annoying anybody.

Trick #14: Add Falling Objects to the Page

I'll end this chapter with an effect that many people think is cute but becomes really annoying on repeat visits. I'm talking about the ever-popular falling objects effect, typically used to paint falling snowflakes on top of bucolic Web pages full of snowscape-inspired poetry.

The thing with this effect is that the objects keep coming, snowflake after snowflake, each one pretty enough on its own, but as a horde losing their beauty as they overrun your screen. There's no way to stop them, either; clicking the Stop button on your browser doesn't keep them from falling. Once the page is loaded, it starts snowing, and it never stops.

The joy of this particular trick is that you're not limited to falling snowflakes. You can make *any* graphic image fall in this manner; you can have falling logos and falling fish and falling monster trucks. You can even have falling toasters, which creates an effect closely reminiscent of the old After Dark flying toasters screen saver.

How to do it

The code for placing a large number of independently falling images on your screen is somewhat complex, as you can probably tell from the length of Listing 1-6. It's standard JavaScript, though, designed to place 25 copies of a specified image at different places in the browser window and then move them down the screen with a back-and-forth motion.

You can use this script to make any image "fall" on your page; you're not limited to snowflakes. Keeping in mind that there will be 25 of these puppies visible at any one time, you'll want to choose relatively small images. Using a transparent GIF is also a good idea, so that all the text on your underlying page isn't obscured.

To implement this script, start by adding the `onLoad` event handler to your document's `<body>` tag, like this:

```
<body bgcolor="#ffffff" onLoad="fall()">
```

Now, insert the code in Listing 1-6 in the body of your HTML document.

Listing 1-6: **JavaScript code for adding falling objects to a page**

```
<script language="JavaScript">
<!-- Adapted from the Fall script -->
<!-- Original script by Kurt Grigg (kurt.grigg@virgin.net) -->

Amount=20;
Image0=new Image();
Image0.src="file1";
Image1=new Image();
Image1.src="file2";

grphcs=new Array(2)
grphcs[0]="file1"
grphcs[1]="file2"

Ypos=new Array();
Xpos=new Array();
Speed=new Array();
Step=new Array();
Cstep=new Array();
ns=(document.layers)?1:0;
```

```
if (ns)
{for (i = 0; i < Amount; i++)
{var P=Math.floor(Math.random()*grphcs.length);
rndPic=grphcs[P];
document.write("<layer name='sn"+i+"' left=0 top=0><img
src="+rndPic+"></LAYER>");}}

else
{document.write('<div
style="position:absolute;top:0px;left:0px"><div
style="position:relative">');
for (i = 0; i < Amount; i++){
var P=Math.floor(Math.random()*grphcs.length);
rndPic=grphcs[P];
document.write('<img id="si" src="'+rndPic+'"
style="position:absolute;top:0px;left:0px">');}
document.write('</div></div>');}

WinHeight=(document.layers)?window.innerHeight:window.document.
body.clientHeight;
WinWidth=(document.layers)?window.innerWidth:window.document.bo
dy.clientWidth;
for (i=0; i < Amount; i++)
{Ypos[i] = Math.round(Math.random()*WinHeight);
Xpos[i] = Math.round(Math.random()*WinWidth);
Speed[i]= Math.random()*3+2;
Cstep[i]=0;
Step[i]=Math.random()*0.1+0.05;}

function fall()
{var
WinHeight=(document.layers)?window.innerHeight:window.document.
body.clientHeight;
var
WinWidth=(document.layers)?window.innerWidth:window.document.bo
dy.clientWidth;
var
hscrll=(document.layers)?window.pageYOffset:document.body.scrol
lTop;
var
wscrll=(document.layers)?window.pageXOffset:document.body.scrol
lLeft;
for (i=0; i < Amount; i++)
{sy = Speed[i]*Math.sin(90*Math.PI/180);
sx = Speed[i]*Math.cos(Cstep[i]);
Ypos[i]+=sy;
Xpos[i]+=sx;
if (Ypos[i] > WinHeight)
{Ypos[i]=-60;
Xpos[i]=Math.round(Math.random()*WinWidth);
Speed[i]=Math.random()*5+2;}
```

Continued

Listing 1-6 *(continued)*

```
if (ns)
{document.layers['sn'+i].left=Xpos[i];
document.layers['sn'+i].top=Ypos[i]+hscrll;}
else
{si[i].style.pixelLeft=Xpos[i];
si[i].style.pixelTop=Ypos[i]+hscrll;}
Cstep[i]+=Step[i];}
setTimeout('fall()',10);}

//-->
</script>
```

After you enter this code, replace both instances of the *file1* and *file2* placeholders with the URLs and filenames of two graphics files. (You use two different — but similar — graphics so you can have two snowflakes or leaves or whatever falling down your page.) If you need graphics to use with this trick, go to my *Building Really Annoying Web Sites* site (`www.annoyingwebsites.com`) and click on the graphics link; you'll find graphics files there you can download for falling snowflakes, leaves, raindrops, birds, and snot. (Eewww!)

Note   This script, like several others in this book, was written by JavaScript/DHTML master Kurt Grigg. Check out his Kurt's Free Original DHTML site (`website.lineone.net/~kurt.grigg/javascript/`) for more cool scripts and effects.

Practical uses for this technique

You've seen this effect before. Many page designers obviously feel that a practical use of this technique is to create the effect of falling snowflakes on a winter-themed Web page, or falling leaves on an autumnal page. If you're one of those folks, I won't contradict your delusion.

Other designers might see a use for this technique on big-company Web sites, using falling company logos in lieu of snowflakes. If you're in this camp, I won't contradict your delusion, either.

The reality is, no matter why you use it, this trick will irritate just about anyone who visits your site. Get over your delusions and recognize how annoying your page really is.

How not to be annoying

Because there's no practical use for this effect, you have no reason to try to duplicate the annoying results. You can, however, reduce the annoyance factor by using smaller images, as well as lighter, more transparent images — anything to reduce the interference with the other items on your page. You can also reduce the number of images visible; an occasional snowflake is less annoying than a big-time snowstorm.

The Annoying Summary

In this chapter, you learned various ways to use the background of your Web page to annoy visitors. The key to all these effects is to create a background that either interferes with or draws attention from the page's text. Whether that's accomplished by clashing colors or busy designs or some sort of movement is ultimately your personal choice. Just know that when you move the background to the foreground, in terms of visibility, you've created an extremely annoying experience. After all, you wouldn't want to read much more of this book if there were bright red dancing chickens scattered across all the pages, would you?

✦   ✦   ✦

Tedious Text

Most Web pages consist largely of text. All those words and letters provide a tremendous opportunity to annoy people, in a number of different ways. Not only can your content itself be annoying (I can't help you with that, unfortunately), but the way you present your content—which fonts you use, what colors you choose, what types of special effects you employ—can really irritate visitors to your pages.

Like the background annoyances discussed in Chapter 1, the most annoying text effects are relatively easy to accomplish. You really don't have to do anything more than misspell a few words and choose a text color that clashes with your page background and—voilà!—you've created an extremely annoying page. Of course, those of you aiming for the maximum possible annoyance factor can employ some neat JavaScript tricks to make your text blink, glow, jitter, scroll, and move annoyingly on-screen. (And just think: Some Web page designers employ these effects *on purpose*, under the assumption that they'll serve to attract users' attention!)

Trick #15: WRITE IN ALL CAPS!

Simple annoyances are sometimes best.

Or, rather:

SIMPLE ANNOYANCES ARE SOMETIMES BEST!

That's right, the old standby of WRITING IN ALL CAPS—the online equivalent of SHOUTING—is a sure-fire way to annoy your site visitors without the need for any fancy HTML or JavaScript coding. When you enter too many all-uppercase words in a row, not only does the text become extremely difficult to read, but readers become overwhelmed by the unrelenting intensity of word after word receiving undue emphasis.

While you're at it, don't forget to include TOO! MANY! EXCLAMATION POINTS!!!! in your text. And feel free to *** USE ASTERISKS *** and other <<<SPECIAL CHARACTERS>>> to draw attention to specific words and phrases!!! They definitely @@@@DRAW ATTEN-TION@@@@ to specific text on your page and become INCREDIBLY annoying WHEN THEY'RE OVERUSED!!!!

Get the POINT?????

How to do it

Please follow these steps *carefully*:

1. With the little finger of your left hand, press and hold down the Shift key.
2. Using your free fingers, type a message onto your Web page.

Almost as if by magic, the text you type appears in ALL UPPERCASE!

For more advanced Web page developers, I suggest the alternate technique of pressing the Caps Lock key and then using *all* your fingers to enter the uppercase text. But be careful with this approach; it's possible to hit the Caps Lock key *twice* and end up with all *lowercase* text!

Practical uses for this technique

All kidding aside, there is a place for *selected* emphasis within your text. When you need to emphasize a word or phrase, it's okay to use all caps, or boldface, or italics, or even a different text color, to draw attention to selected text. The key in being practical, however, is being *selective*. If you overuse any type of text emphasis, the text you emphasize is no longer special.

How not to be annoying

As stated in the preceding paragraph, one way to emphasize text without being overly annoying is to do so sparingly. Moderation is a virtue, especially when drawing attention to the truly important words and phrases on your Web page.

Another way to reduce the annoyance factor is to use something other than upper-case text to denote emphasis. Boldface is the preferred approach, as it doesn't disrupt the text flow the way that going all-caps does. You can also try other approaches — italics (hard to read on-screen, particularly at small type sizes), different colors (sometimes mistaken for hyperlinked text), underlining (also mistaken for hyperlinked text), and various blinking or glowing effects (too distracting, as you'll learn later in this chapter). All in all, boldfacing is the best way to denote emphasis on-screen.

Trick #16: MiX uPPer- aNd LoWeRCasE tExt

Here's one I picked up from the kiddies.

Ever visit a youth-oriented chat room? These kids get a kick out of employing non-traditional approaches to spelling and grammar (r u 2B my grrl?) and creative methods of capitalization. In particular, they often use a random combination of upper- and lowercase letters, LIkE tHIs. Typically, there's no method to this madness, other than that it gets really annoying, really fast (especially to older users).

So if you want to turn off users not in their teens and make your text almost impossible to comprehend, try randomly mixing your cases. You'LL bE pLEaSed wiTh tHe rESuLTs.

How to do it

I wish there were a more efficient technique, but the way to approach this is no more complex than randomly pressing and depressing the Shift key while typing. You may want to plan your capitalization to some small degree, taking care to avoid capitalizing the first letter of any word and trying not to have more than two consecutive letters of the same case. If you're really into it, you can plan your uppercase letters to spell out some sort of secret message, but that's a lot of work without directly affecting the annoyance factor. No, random capitalization is the way to go, however it works best for you.

Practical uses for this technique

The only practical use for this technique that I can think of is that it lets you pretend that you're a teenager again. If you choose your language well, you may even be mistaken for a hip (or is it phat?) dude. Or not.

Probably not.

Note   If any actual teenagers are reading this section, I apologize for directing the majority of my comments at over-the-hill developers. You certainly don't need to pretend to be young and annoying—you're at the age where it should come naturally.

How not to be annoying

Here's how to mix upper- and lowercase text in a non-annoying fashion—don't do it! There's absolutely no way to do this without irritating the heck out of most of your site visitors. So if you're trying to win friends and influence people, avoid this particular trick completely.

Trick #17: Forget to Check Spelling and Grammer

This next trick is a double-edged sword. Although including misspelled words and questionable grammatical constructions can annoy your Web page visitors (particularly those who were English majors in college), it can also present you, the Web page developer, as a dimwitted doofus just off the bus from somewhere the other side of Mayberry. For that reason, think carefully before you employ this technique; it's entirely possible that your efforts may generate pity and scorn rather than true annoyance.

That said, it *is* annoying to read through a Web page and find blatant and numerous misspelled words — especially proper nouns. It bespeaks a lack of care (and, perhaps, a lack of intelligence) that annoys a certain class of users. Some of these same users will also be annoyed by poor grammar in your text — faulty sentence construction, improper noun–verb agreement, passive sentences, and so on.

Of course, some users won't notice these little annoyances. For those visitors to your site who lack the proper education, come from the wrong social stratum, or speak a language other than English, any efforts you make to intentionally dumb-down your text will be wasted. In fact, they may cut and paste text from your site to use on their own pages or in e-mails and school reports, thus perpetuating the gag.

Which, in and of itself, might make it worth doing.

How to do it

For some developers, using poor spelling and grammar comes naturally. For you near-illiterate souls, the better question is how *not* to write poorly. The answer to this new question, of course, is to get an education — or use the somewhat pervasive electronic language tools at your disposal.

Spell checkers and grammar checkers, however, are the bane of anyone trying to write poorly on purpose. To ensure bad spelling and grammar, the first step is to *not* use any spell checking or grammar checking utilities. Unfortunately, if you were actually a good student back in your high school English classes, this may not be enough; you may have to go through your document manually and *introduce* spelling and grammar errors. Pay particular attention to common names (*President George W. Busch* is one of my favorite misspellings — and one that the spell checkers won't catch), and note that the run-on sentence is one of the easier-to-make grammatical gaffes.

Practical uses for this technique

There's really nothing practical about incorrectly spelled words. Grammar, however, is another subject.

There is correct grammar, and then there is *acceptable* grammar. Adhering to all the grammatical rules often produces text that is stiff and unfriendly, cold and impersonal. It may be in your best interests to loosen up the grammar rules to some small degree, in order to generate at least an appearance of a warm and casual personality for your pages.

And, of course, if you're writing a page for teenagers, all the rules are voided — ya know?

How not to be annoying

Short of going back to school and retaking that basic grammar class, you can minimize poor spelling and writing on your Web pages by using the electronic tools at your disposal. Now if you're writing your HTML code in a text editor like Windows Notepad, you don't have a lot of options. But if you're using an HTML editing program that actually cost you money, such as Microsoft FrontPage, you probably have at least a spell checker available to you. Checking your grammar is a little more difficult, but you can always compose your text in Microsoft Word (which has both a spell checker and a grammar checker). Check your spelling and (particularly) your grammar within Word, and *then* import the text into your HTML editor.

Trick #18: Pick an Unreadable Font

Many Web page designers don't spend a lot of time thinking about fonts. That's too bad; which font you choose for display can directly affect the readability of your text.

You should know a few general font rules — especially if your intent is to break these rules to increase your page's annoyance factor. The first rule is that a serif font, such as Times Roman, is best for long blocks of body text. The second rule is that a sans serif font (such as Arial or Helvetica) is better for very large text, such as headlines.

So if you're trying to make your text less readable, do the opposite of what's recommended. For your body text, go with Arial or another sans serif font. For your headers, go with Times Roman.

Unfortunately, that combination isn't terribly annoying. (It isn't even that hard to read; there's not enough text on even the longest Web pages to make your users' eyes tired if you choose sans serif over serif for the body text font.)

A better approach is to find a font that is less readable than any of the common fonts. (The common fonts are common *because* they're inherently readable!) Just pull down your font list and search for something that looks like it could get annoying after a while, such as the Bauhaus 93, Comic Sans, Brush Script, and (my favorite) Jokerman fonts shown in Figure 2-1. Look especially for thick and complex fonts that get really hard to read at smaller sizes; these are really annoying fonts to use for body text.

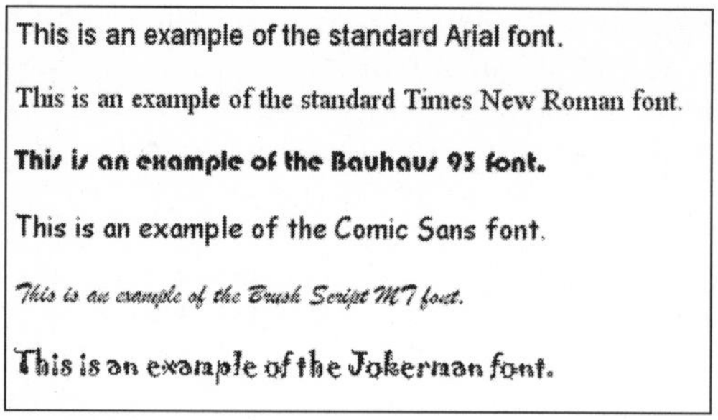

This is an example of the standard Arial font.

This is an example of the standard Times New Roman font.

This is an example of the Bauhaus 93 font.

This is an example of the Comic Sans font.

This is an example of the Brush Script MT font.

This is an example of the Jokerman font.

Figure 2-1: The right (wrong?) font can make your text extremely hard to read.

For extra credit, you can use *multiple* fonts on the same Web page. This technique, first perfected in the early days of desktop publishing, shows readers that you have a lot of fonts installed on your computer and that you know how to use them. (Not in a design sense, of course—just that you know how to insert them all on a page.)

How to do it

If you're using FrontPage or some other fancy-schmancy HTML editor, you change fonts the same way you do in Microsoft Word—just select the text, pull down the Font list, and choose a new font.

If you're hand-coding your text, you change fonts with the `<font>` tag and the `face` attribute, like this:

```
<font face="myfont">text</font>
```

Replace *myfont* with the name of the font you want to use (surrounded by quotation marks) and insert the text to change between the `<font>` and `</font>` tags. To format selected text with the Comic Sans font, for example, you would use the following code:

```
<font face="Comic Sans">text</font>
```

Practical uses for this technique

Selecting a font other than Arial or Times Roman is perfectly acceptable; different fonts can give your page a different style or appearance. Professional designers spend long hours poring over type books to pick just the "right" font for advertisements, catalogs, and other printed materials. Their Web brethren do the same when designing high-profile Web sites. Choosing a nonstandard font for your pages is okay; it gets annoying only when you (deliberately) choose the wrong fonts.

How not to be annoying

If you want to play it safe, go with the default fonts in your HTML editor, or let the user's browser display its default font (typically Times Roman). No one will be annoyed if your page's body text is Times Roman and the headings are either Times Roman, Arial, or Verdana.

But then, if you wanted to play it safe, you wouldn't be reading this book—would you?

Trick #19: Pick a Font That Most Browsers Don't Support

There's another annoying benefit from choosing a nonstandard font—you run the very good chance that some visitors' browsers won't be able to display that font. If you choose something obscure (like the aforementioned Jokerman), it's unlikely that other users will also have that font installed on their computers. And if the font isn't installed, it can't be displayed.

While this might seem like an extremely annoying approach, you might be disappointed in the results—because of what happens when a browser tries to display a font that isn't installed. When a browser accesses your page and finds a `face` attribute that specifies an unknown (to that browser) font, it simply displays its built-in default font (normally Times Roman). The user won't even know that there's a substitution going on, and all your annoying plans will have been for naught.

Unless, that is, you use a foreign-language font.

When you specify a non-English character set (Chinese is always a good choice), the user's browser must have this font installed in order for the page to display properly. If the font isn't installed, the browser displays a bunch of gibberish. In some instances, the user will be prompted to download and install the missing character set, which can take several minutes and eat up several megabytes of valuable bandwidth.

And there are few things more annoying than waiting several minutes to download a font in a language that you can't read anyway.

How to do it

If you want to specify a font that is unlikely to be used by a majority of your visitors, start by looking at the fonts installed in a typical Windows installation. *Avoid them*; everybody has those fonts installed.

Now turn to some of the less-popular programs installed on your computer. It's possible that these programs — which few other users will have — installed some fonts specific to their operation. These are good fonts to choose.

If you want to go to the effort, you can download additional fonts to your system from any number of Web sites specializing in designer or specialty fonts. It is extremely unlikely that other Internet users will have these fonts installed on their machines.

In terms of foreign-language fonts and character sets, the easiest way to write in a foreign language is to change the language defaults in your HTML editor. In FrontPage, for example, select Tools ➪ Web Settings, and then click the Language tab; from here you can change the default page encoding to another language.

In raw HTML, you change the page language via two meta tags:

```
<meta http-equiv="Content-Type" content="text/html;
charset=encoding">
<meta http-equiv="Content-Language" content="language">
```

In the first meta tag, the character set encoding is specified by the `charset` variable; in the second tag, the specific language is specified.

Note   To display foreign-language fonts, you'll probably have to install the language pack for your operating system on your computer. For example, if you are using Windows 95/98/Me, install the Multilanguage Support. (Check the Help files for your particular operating system for specific instructions.)

Practical uses for this technique

Naturally, if you're creating Web pages for an international audience, you may want to create language-specific pages for visitors from outside North America. The sites of some multinational corporations often use an internationalized home page, with links from there to country-specific sites or pages. (Because not all visitors will be able to read English text links, the links to other language/country sites sometimes use images of each country's flag.)

How not to be annoying

The easiest thing to do is to stay with one language — English. If you stick with English, the majority of Web users will be able to read your site, and you won't have to bother with those annoying foreign-language character sets and fonts. If you want to be politically correct (but not inflict a large font download on *all* your visitors), consider referring foreign visitors to AltaVista's Babelfish translation engine (`babelfish.altavista.com`). This site does a decent job of translating English into a variety of other languages, including Chinese, French, German, and Spanish, with no font installation necessary.

Trick #20: Make the Text Too Small — or Too Large — to Read

The first of these two suggestions may sound obvious, but it isn't as widely used as you might expect. If you want to annoy someone trying to read the text on your page, make the text so small that it strains the eyes (particularly of older visitors). Readers will squint and stare for only so long before they get so annoyed and frustrated that they give up completely and move to another page.

What is too small? The "normal" font size is 12 points; going all the way down to 8 points is the fastest route to annoying your page's readers.

As for the second suggestion, it's easy to understand how text can be too small to read, but what about the opposite — is it possible to make text too *large* to read comfortably?

The answer is a resounding yes! Enlarging a block of text so that it doesn't fit comfortably on a single line is simple. Because readers absorb text one line at a time, the less text on a line, the harder it is to scan a block of text.

You can see for yourself in Figure 2-2. The first line of text is displayed at the normal 12-point size and is easy to read. The same text is then repeated at 36 points. Because the lines are so short (relative to the size of the letters), you actually have to slow down to figure out what's written.

Interestingly, some novice Web developers (children, especially) receive great joy from making their on-screen text as large as possible. I'm not sure why.

How to do it

You should be able to change the size of any text selection from within your HTML editor. To do so using raw HTML, use the `size` attribute in the `<font>` tag, like this:

```
<font size="x">text</font>
```

The *x* should be replaced with a number from 1 to 7, as shown in Table 2-1.

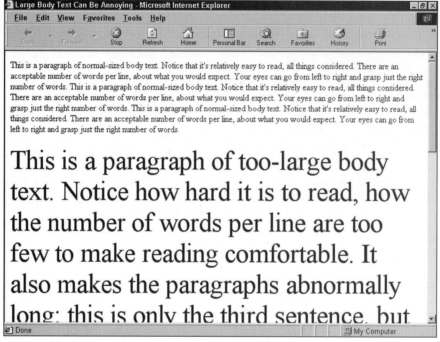

Figure 2-2: Making your body text too large results in its being difficult to read.

Table 2-1	
Codes for Font Sizes	

Code	Size (in points)
1	8
2	10
3	12
4	14
5	18
6	24
7	36

You would use the following code, for example, to format a block of text at 24 points:

```
<font size="6">text</font>
```

Practical uses for this technique

You may have reasons for using a smaller-than-normal font size. You may be presenting less-important background information, such as the types of references and citations typically found in footnotes or endnotes. You may be presenting other "fine print" information that needs to be there, but that you don't expect anyone to read. You may simply have so much information to present that shrinking the text a bit is a viable alternative to letting the page run long or splitting it into multiple pages.

The most common use of large text is for titles and headings — although you're better off using the normal heading codes (<h1>, <h2>, etc.) for these purposes. You can also use large text *sparingly* in your page to draw attention to a phrase or paragraph. (And you should probably think in terms of paragraphs; it's *really* annoying for a word in the middle of a paragraph to be larger than the surrounding text.)

How not to be annoying

If you must present "fine print" information, make sure it's at the very end of your page or range of pages. You may even want to consider putting the fine print in a separate page that users have to deliberately open to read.

If you have to display more valuable information at a smaller type size, try to shrink the text as little as possible. Go down to 10 point, but not all the way to 8 point. And make sure that you use a font that's readable at that small size and place it against a clean, high-contrast background; small text is hard enough to read without having a complex background behind it.

For maximum readability, keep your body text in the 10- to 14-point range, with 12 points typically the best size. Go much larger or smaller than this range and your text becomes hard to read.

Trick #21: Align the Text Awkwardly

There are four different ways to align a paragraph of text on your page: flush left, flush right, centered, and justified (where both the left and right edges line up straight). In HTML, if you don't choose a particular text alignment, the text defaults to being left-aligned (with a ragged right edge).

As readers, we're used to seeing text line up straight along the left edge of a page. Whether the right edge is ragged (left-aligned) or straight (justified) is mostly a matter of style.

What we're *not* used to seeing are long blocks of centered or right-aligned text. While it's common to center titles, headings, and short paragraphs of text, trying to read an entire document with centered text is very tiring. And reading right-aligned text is just *difficult*, period.

So, if you're trying hard to annoy visitors to your Web page, consider centering or right-aligning all the text on your page. Either of these is particularly annoying when you have a very long page with very long paragraphs, thus forcing users to read a *lot* of words in this unusual alignment. You can make things even worse by using a lot of long words. Because HTML does not support hyphenation, this will create awkward line breaks, resulting in lines of varying length, thus exacerbating the effect of the odd alignment.

How to do it

You should be able to apply a new alignment within your HTML editor, typically by formatting paragraph properties. You can also specify paragraph alignment within the raw HTML code, by using the `align` attribute within the `<p>` tag that designates each new paragraph. The code looks like this:

```
<p align="type">text</p>
```

Replace *type* with either `left`, `right`, `center`, or `justify` (within quotation marks, of course), and the entire paragraph between the `<p>` and `</p>` tags will be aligned as specified.

Practical uses for this technique

Centering is an acceptable technique for headings and titles, even when the text that follows is right-aligned or justified. It may also be okay to center short blocks of text, especially if the text doesn't include full sentences; it's an alternate approach to bulleted lists for presenting short chunks of information.

Right-aligned text is less practical, unless you're deliberately trying to free up the left side of the page (for a graphic, perhaps). Again, the effect isn't so annoying if it's used on very short chunks of information, like a short bulleted list.

How not to be annoying

You can avoid annoying people with centered or right-aligned text by using both these effects sparingly — if at all. In no case should you use centered or right-aligned text for information that involves a long read; both these alignments are best suited for information that can be quickly grazed, or absorbed in a single glance.

Trick #22: Make Your Paragraphs Really, Really Long

Speaking of chunks of information, there's something about reading really long paragraphs. The something is that most people don't like to do it — especially when they're reading on their computer screen. When they're reading on-screen text, readers want short paragraphs that can be read in a glance, and they decidedly *don't* want to be forced to scroll down to read a full paragraph.

Which means, of course, that you can really annoy readers by making sure that your text contains some very long paragraphs. Not only does this force you into an inefficient and verbose style of writing (which is quite annoying in itself), it also forces your reader to struggle through a piece of text that, after the first press of the Pg Dn button, seemingly has no beginning and no end. Imagine yourself stuck in the middle of a boring, poorly written paragraph, with no light at the end of the tunnel. Annoying, yes — maybe even a little depressing.

How to do it

The art of writing long, impenetrable paragraphs doesn't always come naturally, especially in this age of sound bites and MTV-style quick-cutting. It's a lost art, really, common to an age of literature that is exceedingly distant from the way information is presented in, say, *People* magazine. Most current writers — especially those writing for Web sites, who typically have little or no formal training in their craft — will find it difficult, if not impossible, to hold a single thought long enough to fill up an entire screen at 800 × 600 resolution. It takes a clarity of vision and a certain dedication, not to mention the ability to inject related information and the occasional stray thought into the narrative stream. It also helps, of course, to possess a degree of verbosity, the ability to drone on and on and on about a single subject in a way that draws as much attention to the style and pacing of the prose as it does to the subject at hand — which, quite frankly, often gets lost by the time the reader valiantly makes his or her way to the very end of the bloated paragraph. (Another useful skill is the ability to embed related thoughts within parentheses, like this.) Oh, you can cheat and simply graft two or more separate paragraphs together, but that isn't the *right* way to do it; no, the best long paragraphs hold a single thought, more or less, from beginning to end, from the top row of menus to the bottom status bar, without a single interruption, creating a dense block of black text without a single line of calming white space, forcing the reader to keep going and going and going to reach the end of whatever it was that the author was writing about in the first place. A great, long paragraph is like a great, long journey, where the trip is every bit as important as the destination, the twists and turns of language like the bends and curves of a snaking strip of blacktop as it meanders from place to place across the landscape, the reader full behind the wheel, aiming that roaring machine toward his final destination, top down and wind roaring in his ears, all the while absorbing the sights and sounds and even the smells of the diners and gas stations and cheap motels that rise up on either side to embrace him on his journey, giving a meaning to the distance between here and there that would be lost on the cartographers who draw the thin lines and the red dots that represent nothing more than ink on paper unless you're there, driving the line, living the dots, mile after mile, until you don't care where or when you arrive, the journey itself reason enough to keep going, not wanting it to end.

Practical uses for this technique

Some types of content and some styles of writing demand the use of longer paragraphs. Think of scientific journals, lawyerly extracts, and anything by James Joyce, for example. You certainly don't want to present an in-depth explanation of the latest killer disease in short *People* magazine–like chunks. (Believe it or not, short paragraphs would be annoying to certain audiences!) No, you want the text on your Web page to reflect its content, as well as the expectations of its readers. If that means overly long paragraphs, so be it.

How not to be annoying

Study after study has shown that the best way to present information on a computer screen is in very short chunks — and on relatively short pages. Readers don't like to scroll, so you're better off creating multiple pages (of short paragraphs) than you are in cramming everything into one super-long scrolling page. Forcing readers to struggle through long paragraphs and long pages increases their annoyance with the material — and makes it less likely that they'll continue to read all the way to the end.

Trick #23: Make Text and Background Colors Clash

Have you ever seen two colors together that clash so much it makes your eyes hurt? What about colors that seem to jump backward and forward right before your eyes, almost as if they were in 3D?

Well, those kinds of color combinations are just the thing to make a Web page extremely annoying. With the right choice of text and background colors, visitors won't be able to look at your page without getting massive migraine headaches — if they can even read the text at all!

How to do it

This is the one time that I wish this were a four-color book, so I could show you some of the most offensive text/background color combinations possible. Because we're printing in black and white, however, there's no way to illustrate this particular technique — except to direct you to the *Building Really Annoying Web Sites* Web site (www.annoyingwebsites.com) for some online examples. (I also have a nice color picker applet on the site, so you can find the right hex codes for the colors you want.)

I can also point out some particularly annoying color combinations. Table 2-2 lists color pairs that sane designers would desperately avoid—and that you can use to create pages that pack a strong annoyance factor. In all cases, it really doesn't matter which color you use for the background and which you use for the text; feel free to experiment on your own.

Table 2-2 Annoying Color Combinations	
Color 1	**Color 2**
Yellow-Orange (#FFCC00)	Cyan (#00FFFF)
Yellow-Orange (#FFCC00)	Lime (#00FF00)
Red (#FF0000)	Fuchsia (#FF00FF)
Red (#FF0000)	Cyan (#00FFFF)
Red (#FF0000)	Blue (#0000FF)
Red (#FF0000)	Green (#009900)
Red (#FF0000)	Teal (#008080)
Red (#FF0000)	Gray (#AAAAAA)
Yellow (#FFFF00)	Cyan (#00FFFF)
Lime (#00FF00)	Silver (#C0C0C0)
Green (#009900)	Teal (#008080)
Green (#009900)	Olive (#808000)
Green (#009900)	Blue (#0000FF)
Green (#009900)	Purple (#800080)
Blue (#0000FF)	Purple (#800080)
Blue (#0000FF)	Teal (#008080)
Blue (#0000FF)	Olive (#808000)
Gray (#AAAAAA)	Fuchsia (#FF00FF)

Note   As an added annoyance, some of these color combinations have similar brightness and saturation and are practically invisible to color-blind users. If you want these visitors to see nothing but a wash of gray when they read your page, try red-on-green and green-on-purple; they'll think they're looking at a blank page!

Practical uses for this technique

One reason to use a particularly annoying combination of text and background color is to stop users in their tracks. You have to admit (once you've seen them), these color combinations are startling and will grab the attention of even the most casual Web surfer. If you want to create a splash page or window to stop users before they surf past, you can't go wrong with these types of text/background combos.

How not to be annoying

In all of these color combinations, you see two colors fighting for the viewer's attention. Neither color will willingly recede into the background; they both crave prominence and clash with the other color in ways that are painful to look at for extended periods.

It's natural that most users will find this sort of thing annoying. When we read text, the best environment brings the important item (the text) clearly to the foreground, while the background recedes almost into invisibility. The best example of this is the black-on-white text of this book; there's no fighting for attention there, just strong black letters supported by an inoffensive plain white background.

If you want to avoid annoying Web site visitors, choose text and background color combinations that have the same high contrast as the black-and-white design of this book. The easiest way to achieve this is with a standard black-on-white Web page design, but you can choose any number of other high-contrast combinations — yellow on dark blue, dark brown on tan, and so on. It's when you have two bright, almost neon colors that you run into trouble; stay away from those combinations to avoid annoying your site visitors.

Trick #24: Use Different Colors Throughout the Text

If you think your users' monitors are configured for 256 or more colors, why not use all of them?

That's the mentality behind this annoying trick, which lets you show off your mastery of the hexadecimal color chart. Don't limit yourself to black text with blue hyperlinks; use as many different text colors as you can find a reason for.

Should this phrase be emphasized? Then color it red! Does that paragraph contain detailed information? Then color it green!

You get the idea. Give yourself the freedom to add color anywhere in your text, as often as you like. It's a particularly colorful way to make your page annoying!

How to do it

The easiest way to format different paragraphs (or words or letters) with different colors is to do so manually, either from within your HTML editor or by using the standard `color` attribute within the `<font>` tag, like this:

```
<font color="#xxxxxx">text</font>
```

Practical uses for this technique

You may have occasions where you want to color-code specific pieces of text on a Web page. Maybe there's a paragraph of fine print that would be less intrusive in a color other than black. Perhaps your page features an interview or a group discussion; it would be helpful to code each person's words in a unique color.

Colorful text is also somewhat acceptable when you're creating Web pages for younger children. Kids like bright colors, so you may want to experiment with multicolored text for this particular audience. You can probably get away with more of this technique if there's less text on the page, and if that text is bigger and bolder—exactly the sort of design you'll find on a lot of children's pages.

How not to be annoying

If you want to draw attention to a specific piece of text, there are better ways than changing the text's color. Boldface, for example, is a more acceptable approach to highlighting. Given that you already have three-color text (the basic text color, plus the color of clicked and unclicked hyperlinks in the text), adding even more colors will get real annoying real fast. (Think about it: Most four-color books still stick with black text on a white background, reserving the color bursts for more graphic elements.)

Trick #25: Cycle the Text Color

Even better than a multicolored textural experience is text that changes colors while you're reading it. It's kind of psychedelic, actually, watching text go from red to orange to yellow to green and back again, cycling through the color spectrum every several seconds. And, unless you're smoking something that you can't buy at a convenience store, it gets quite annoying.

How to do it

The script in Listing 2-1 cycles the color of selected text. Place this code in the body of your document, where you want the colored text to appear. Enter your own text for the *text* in the `ctext` variable, but be careful not to have any quotation marks in any added text—they would break the script.

Listing 2-1: JavaScript for cycling the color of selected text; place in the body of your document

```
<script language="Javascript1.2">
<!--

function colorCycle()
{this.length = colorCycle.arguments.length;
  for (var i = 0; i < this.length; i++)
{this[i] = colorCycle.arguments[i];}}
var selectedText = "text"
var x = 0
var textColor = new colorCycle(
"red",
"orange",
"yellow",
"cyan",
"lime",
"green",
"blue",
"purple",
"fuchsia",
"silver",
"gray",
"black",
"maroon");
if(navigator.appName == "Netscape")
{document.write('<layer id="c">'+selectedText+'</layer><br>');}
if (navigator.appVersion.indexOf("MSIE") != -1)
{document.write('<div id="c">'+selectedText+'</div>');}

function colorChange()
{if(navigator.appName == "Netscape")
{document.c.document.write('<font color="'+textColor[x]+'">'
+selectedText+'</font>');
document.c.document.close();}
else if (navigator.appVersion.indexOf("MSIE") != -1)
{document.all.c.style.color = textColor[x];}
(x < textColor.length-1) ? x++  : x=0;}

setInterval("colorChange()",500)

//-->
</script>
```

You can change the speed of the color cycle by changing the value within the setInterval function. The default speed is 500; a lower number will cycle the colors faster.

Practical uses for this technique

Applying color cycling to selected text may be a viable technique when you're creating ads on your page; the cycling colors (especially on bigger, bolder text) definitely catch users' attention.

How not to be annoying

As with most text effects, the stronger they are, the higher the annoyance factor. You can still draw attention with text that changes colors — but make the effect less annoying — by increasing the cycle time and decreasing the number of colors that are cycled through. A header that flashes from red to blue every few seconds, for example, will catch your users' eyes without necessarily turning them off.

Trick #26: Make Text Blink

Few users would disagree that the most annoying effect possible is that of blinking text. On, off, on, off, on, off — is there anything more annoying?

Interestingly, this effect became widely used (and widely overused) because it was so simple to implement. From the early days of Web development, the Netscape extension to HTML included a `<blink>` tag that made it extremely easy for even the least talented developers to make text blink on and off. The effect was so hated, however, that Microsoft declined to support this tag with its Internet Explorer browser. Today this simple approach to a highly annoying effect works only with Netscape browsers.

How to do it

To make text blink by using the HTML `<blink>` tag, apply the following code:

```
<blink>text</blink>
```

The problem with using the `<blink>` tag is that it works only with Netscape browsers, and you don't necessarily know if your visitors are using them. You *can,* however, add the blink effect to Internet Explorer. You simply have to create a "blink" style sheet and associated blinking effect in JavaScript. With this approach, the `<blink>` "tag" (now a style, actually) in an HTML document will behave the same in IE as it does in Netscape.

Listing 2-2 shows the code to insert in the head of your document. The code has two parts — a style sheet code and a JavaScript code.

Listing 2-2: Style sheet and JavaScript code for blinking text; insert in the head of your document

```
<style>
<!--
blink
-->
</style>

<script language="JavaScript">
<!--

function doBlink()
{var blink = document.all.tags("BLINK")
for (var i=0; i<blink.length; i++)
blink[i].style.visibility = blink[i].style.visibility == "" ?
"hidden" : ""}

function startBlink()
{if (document.all)
setInterval("doBlink()",1000)}

window.onload = startBlink;

//-->
</script>
```

After you insert this script in your HTML code, any text you surround with the `<blink></blink>` tags will blink—even if your visitors are using Internet Explorer!

By the way, when you use this method, you can actually change the blinking speed. Just change the "1000" value for the `setInterval` function; a larger number slows the blink, a smaller number speeds it up.

Practical uses for this technique

Blinking text definitely draws attention to itself. If you have a critical warning on your Web page, or some other piece of extremely important information, preceding the text with a blinking "caution" or "important" header will ensure that the information won't be ignored.

How not to be annoying

The way *not* to be annoying is to not use blinking text—*ever*! Even if you have a caution that you want all your visitors to read, there are better, less annoying ways to highlight that text. You can format the text in bold, or a different color, or even put it in a table with a colored background. Do anything you can to avoid blinking text — unless you deliberately want to annoy users.

Trick #27: Make Text Glow

Any time you draw undue attention to a piece of text, you tend to tick off readers who just want to get from point A to point B without being interrupted. So if you *want* to make it difficult for readers to read, you need a new and unique way to interrupt the standard text.

Thanks to the advanced effects possible with HTML's Cascading Style Sheets (and a little JavaScript magic), you have lots of neat ways to make selected text pop off your page. One particularly effective technique is to put a pulsating glow around your text. Watching a piece of text throb with a bright purple glow is guaranteed to draw your users' eyes away from all the other text on the page.

How to do it

You set up the glowing text effect by defining a style and some functions in the head of your document. You then activate the effect by placing a simple piece of code in the body of your document where you want the effect to appear. (This effect works only with Internet Explorer version 5 and later.)

Listing 2-3 shows the style sheet and JavaScript code to insert in the head of your HTML document. You set the glow color by replacing the *xxxxxx* with a six-digit hex color code.

Listing 2-3: Style sheet and JavaScript code for glowing text; place in the head of your document

```
<style>
<!--
#glowingText{filter:glow(color=#xxxxxx,strength=4);
width:100%}
-->
</style>

<script language="JavaScript1.2">
<!--

function glowEffect(which)
{if (document.all.glowingText[which].filters[0].strength==3)
document.all.glowingText[which].filters[0].strength=2
else
```

Continued

Listing 2-3 *(continued)*

```
document.all.glowingText[which].filters[0].strength=3}
function glowEffect2(which)
{if (document.all.glowingText.filters[0].strength==3)
document.all.glowingText.filters[0].strength=2
else
document.all.glowingText.filters[0].strength=3}

function glowNow()
{if (document.all.glowingText&&glowingText.length)
{for (i=0;i<glowingText.length;i++)
eval('setInterval("glowEffect('+i+')",250)')}
else if (glowingText)
setInterval("glowEffect2(0)",250)}

if (document.all)
window.onload=glowNow

//-->
</script>
```

Then insert the following code in the body of your document where you want to place the glowing text:

```
<p><span id="glowingText">text</span></p>
```

This effect works best on larger text — surround the <span> tag with standard <font>, formatting, and heading tags to change the size and formatting of the selected text. You may also want to change the text color to white (with the <font> tag around the <span> tag) for a more striking effect.

Practical uses for this technique

Glowing text is actually an interesting technique for the headers on a Web page. Make sure that you set the color of the header to white, and use the same glow color for all the headers on your page.

How not to be annoying

Overuse of this effect will quickly increase an existing annoyance factor. Particularly annoying is putting a glow around text in the body of your document; it's difficult to read long blocks of glowing text at a small type size. To avoid annoying your site visitors, use this effect sparingly — if at all.

Trick #28: Make Text Fade In and Out

Text animation annoys users because it's difficult to read text when it's pulsating or jiggling or fading or otherwise not just sitting there quietly, waiting to be read.

When you're looking for a really annoying text animation effect, go no further than a simple fadeout. Watching a piece of text vanish before your eyes is kind of neat—unless someone was trying to read the text. After all, it's impossible to read something that isn't there!

This particular trick plays games with your readers' eyes. First the text fades away, then it fades back in, then it fades away again—over and over and over. What can I say? It's just really annoying.

How to do it

To fade a piece of text in and out (from white to black and back again), you use a two-part script. The first part of the script goes in the head of your HTML document; the second part goes in the body where you want the fading text to appear. (This effect works only with Internet Explorer, by the way.)

Listing 2-4 contains the code to insert in the head of your document.

Listing 2-4: JavaScript code for fading text; place in the head of your document

```
<script language="JavaScript1.2">
<!--

ie4 = ((navigator.appVersion.indexOf("MSIE")>0) &&
(parseInt(navigator.appVersion) >= 4));
var count = 0, count2 = 0, add1 = 3, add2 = 10, timerID;

function textFade()
{if (ie4)
{count += add1;
count2 += add2;
delay = 30;
if(count2 > 100) count2 = 100;
if(count > 100)
{count = 100;
add1 = -10;
add2 = -3;
delay = 350;}
if(count < 0) count = 0;
if(count2 < 0)
```

Continued

Listing 2-4 *(continued)*

```
{count2 = 0;
add1 = 3;
add2 = 10;
delay = 200;}}
fader.style.filter =
"Alpha(Opacity="+count2+",FinishOpacity="+count+",style=2)";
timerID = setTimeout("textFade()", delay);}}

window.onload = textFade;

//-->
</script>
```

Now insert the following code in the body of your document; replace *text* with the text you want to fade.

```
<div id="fader" style="width:480;
Filter:Alpha(Opacity=0,FinishOpacity=0,style=2)">text</div>
```

You can apply any normal HTML formatting to the fading text, by inserting `<font>` or formatting or heading tags around the `<div>` tag.

Practical uses for this technique

This effect has few, if any, practical uses outside of drawing attention to the effect itself. It's not even good for drawing attention to a particular piece of text, because the text itself isn't there half the time. Nope, this is an effect for effect's sake — which is an annoying reason to do something in the first place.

How not to be annoying

If your intent is to show off your effects prowess, don't do it on your main Web page. (Can you imagine a single page filled with all different types of blinking and fading and moving text? Ugh!) Create a link on your main page to each specific effect, so that each effect appears by itself, on its own page. That way various special effects won't interfere with one another, and users can see the full effect of each effect on its own.

Trick #29: Make Text "Type" On-screen, Very Slowly

There's nothing like having to wait for information to make that information seem more important. Of course, if the information *isn't* all that important, you get peeved because you had to wait around for it.

One good way to make your site's visitors wait for information is to make it appear one letter at a time. Think of the way text appears on-screen as you type it; if you had to do all your reading that way, always waiting for the next letter and word to appear, you'd slowly go out of your mind.

Well, now you can make selected text appear on your page as if you were typing it yourself, in real time. This typewriter effect is cute at first, but visitors will quickly find themselves mouthing the next word before it is typed, trying to use all their mental powers to make the typing *speed up*, for gosh sakes!

How to do it

You use JavaScript to create a typewriter effect for selected text on your page. Insert the code in Listing 2-5 in the body of your document where you want the text to appear.

Listing 2-5: **JavaScript code for typewriter text; insert in the body of your document**

```
<script language="JavaScript1.2">
<!--

var speed = 500;
var speed2 = 2000;

function typeText()
{this.length = typeText.arguments.length;
for (var i = 0; i < this.length; i++)
{this[i] = typeText.arguments[i];}}

var messsageScroll = new typeText(
"text-line1",
"text-line2"
);
var messsageScroll2 = messsageScroll;
var x = 0;
var y = 0;
```

Continued

Listing 2-5 *(continued)*

```
if(navigator.appName == "Netscape")
{document.write('<layer id="ticker"></layer><br>');}
if (navigator.appVersion.indexOf("MSIE") != -1){
document.write('<span id="ticker"></span><br>');}

function varScroll()
{if (y > messsageScroll2.length - 1)
{y = 0;
setTimeout("varScroll()",speed);}
else
{if (x > messsageScroll2[y].length)
{messsageScroll = messsageScroll2[y];
x = 0; y++;
setTimeout("varScroll()",speed2);}
else
{messsageScroll = messsageScroll2[y].substring(0,x++);
setTimeout("varScroll()",speed);}
if(navigator.appName == "Netscape")
{document.ticker.document.write(messsageScroll);
document.ticker.document.close();}
if (navigator.appVersion.indexOf("MSIE") != -1)
{ticker.innerHTML = messsageScroll;}}}

setTimeout("varScroll()",speed);

//-->
</script>
```

Enter your text where the code lists *text-line1* and *text-line2*. If you want to go with a single line of text, delete the *text-line2* line and the comma at the end of the preceding line. If you want to use additional lines of text, add them after the *text-line2* line; make sure that there are commas after every line of text *except* the final line.

Like many of these text effects, this one works better with slightly larger text. You can surround the <script> tags with normal HTML formatting tags to change the font size and type. This trick is particularly effective with Courier text — it makes it look just like the text from an old typewriter!

Practical uses for this technique

The typewriter trick is actually a decent way to present breaking news on a Web page. It draws attention to the text and makes readers hang on every word (and letter) as it's typed. If you employ this technique in this manner, just make sure that the information contained in the text is important enough to your visitors to warrant the wait.

How not to be annoying

This effect is less annoying if the text appears faster. To that end, change the speed (*not* the speed2) variable to a lower number. (Going all the way to 50 makes a really big difference.)

Trick #30: Make Text Grow and Shrink

If you're trying to get the user's attention, it's hard to beat this particular effect. From a blank space, a line of text suddenly zooms out, growing larger and larger until it reaches its peak, from which it starts to shrink and zoom back out to nothing again.

How to do it

To put growing/shrinking text on your Web page, insert the JavaScript code in Listing 2-6 into the body of your document where you want the effect to appear.

Listing 2-6: **JavaScript for growing and shrinking text; insert in the body of your document**

```
<script language="JavaScript">
<!--

var speed = 100;
var effectPause = 1000;
var textLarge = 28;
var x = 0;
var y = 0;
var messageText, size;

function initArray()
{this.length = initArray.arguments.length;
for (var i = 0; i < this.length; i++)
{this[i] = initArray.arguments[i];}}

var messageText2 = new initArray(
"text-line1",
"text-line2"
);

if(navigator.appName == "Netscape")
document.write('<layer id="wds"></layer><br>');
if (navigator.appVersion.indexOf("MSIE") != -1)
document.write('<span id="wds"></span><br>');
```

Continued

Listing 2-6 *(continued)*

```
function upwords()
{messageText = messageText2[y];
if (x < textLarge)
{x++;
setTimeout("upwords()",speed);}
else setTimeout("growShrink()",effectPause);
if(navigator.appName == "Netscape")
{size = "<font point-size='"+x+"pt'>";
document.wds.document.write(size+"<center>"+messageText+"</cent
er>"+"</font>");
document.wds.document.close();}
if (navigator.appVersion.indexOf("MSIE") != -1)
{wds.innerHTML = "<center>"+messageText+"</center>";
wds.style.fontSize=x+'px'}}

function growShrink()
{if (x > 1)
{x--;
setTimeout("growShrink()",speed);}
else
{setTimeout("upwords()",effectPause);
y++;
if (y > messageText2.length - 1) y = 0;}
if(navigator.appName == "Netscape")
{size = "<font point-size='"+x+"pt'>";
document.wds.document.write(size+"<center>"+messageText+"</cent
er>"+"</font>");
document.wds.document.close();}
if (navigator.appVersion.indexOf("MSIE") != -1)
{wds.innerHTML = "<center>"+messageText+"</center>";
wds.style.fontSize=x+'px'}}

setTimeout("upwords()",speed);

//-->
</script>
```

Enter your text where the code lists *text-line1* and *text-line2*. If you want to go with a single line of text, delete the *text-line2* line and the comma at the end of the preceding line. If you want to use additional lines of text, add them after the *text-line2* line; make sure that there are commas after every line of text *except* the final line.

Practical uses for this technique

This technique could have a variety of real-world uses. Imagine a Web page advertisement zooming out to grab users' attention, or today's latest headlines rushing out to fill up the page. In fact, just about any short message that you want to draw attention to is appropriate for this technique.

How not to be annoying

The problem with this technique, as with most text animation techniques, is that it's effective at drawing attention the first time you see it, but then it gets annoying on future visits. For that reason, if you employ this technique on your page, you may want to give visitors the option of clicking a link to bypass the animation and go to an alternate page that presents the same information less annoyingly.

Trick #31: Make Text Scroll

One of the most common annoying text animations is that of scrolling text. You can find text scrollers on any number of Web pages, slowly but surely delivering information from side to side across the screen like the news tickers of old.

Why is scrolling text so annoying? It's all about *waiting*. Users have to wait for a particular piece of information to finish scrolling across the screen, and if they missed the information the first time, they have to wait even longer for that particular text to appear again. Whether they're waiting for news headlines, sports scores, weather reports, or stock quotes, the longer and slower the scroller, the more annoyed they'll get.

How to do it

Fortunately for those of us into frustrating other Internet users, it's relatively easy to add scrolling text to any Web page. The infamous `<marquee>` tag exists for just this purpose. You employ this tag in the following fashion, within the body of your document:

```
<marquee>text</marquee>
```

By default, this creates a horizontal marquee that scrolls from right to left across the entire width of the screen. You can make the text between the tags as long as you'd like, as long as you don't try to force a line break (`<br>`) or new paragraph (`<p>`); inserting either of these tags in a marquee will end the marquee text at that point.

You can modify this tag in a number of ways — you can reverse the direction of the scroll, you can make the text scroll vertically, you can change the background color, and so on. Here are some of the more annoying attributes you can apply:

✦ behavior="scroll" (the default mode; text cycles from one side to the other, over and over)

✦ behavior="slide" (text enters from one side of the screen and comes to rest at the opposite side)

✦ behavior="alternate" (text enters from one side and then reverses direction when it reaches the opposite side)

✦ bgcolor="#*xxxxxx*" (replace *xxxxxx* with a hexadecimal color code to change the background color of the marquee)

✦ direction="*xxx*" (specifies the direction of the scroll; acceptable values are left, right, down, and up—the last two resulting in vertically scrolling text)

✦ height=*xxx* (specifies the height of the marquee, in pixels—useful when creating a vertical marquee)

✦ width=*xxx* (specifies the width of the marquee, in pixels; the default is the full width of the window)

To create, for example, a standard horizontal scroller with a red background and white text, you'd use this code:

```
<marquee bgcolor="#FF0000"><font
color="#FFFFFF">text</font></marquee>
```

To create vertically scrolling text in a 200 × 200 pixel gray box, you'd use this code:

```
<marquee direction="down" bgcolor="#C0C0C0" height=200
width=200>text</marquee>
```

One particularly annoying application of this trick is to throw a huge block of text into the marquee and use a downward scroll with the slide effect to cause all the text to stack up on the bottom of the page. Here's the code:

```
<marquee direction="down" behavior="slide"
height=480>text</marquee>
```

Make sure you include plenty of text between the on/off tags; the effect is excruciating!

Note   The only problem with the <marquee> tag is that it's specific to Internet Explorer; it doesn't work at all with Netscape browsers. To create a true cross-browser scroller requires some rather sophisticated JavaScript code. See www.annoying websites.com for links to some of the more popular JavaScript scrolling-text scripts.

Practical uses for this technique

As I stated previously, text scrollers have plenty of legitimate uses. News tickers, stock tickers, sports tickers, weather tickers—all are widely used on the Web, and in the real world, as well. You can even use a vertically scrolling text box to introduce important information, or to display the credits for a particular page or project.

How not to be annoying

Even though scrolling text seems like a good idea, most users hate waiting for that one piece of information they're interested in to scroll back around. You can reduce the annoyance factor by making your ticker messages relatively short, so that the repeat cycle is shortened. You may also want to increase the type size of the scrolling text slightly; the difficulty of reading moving text is mitigated to some degree with larger type.

Trick #32: Make Text Ripple Across the Screen

While we're exploring animated text effects, how about one that creates a kind of wave across a line of text? The text ripple trick forces each letter, one after another, to rise slightly from its standard position. The result is like a group of people at a sporting event doing the wave — and, like that kind of wave, it's fun once or twice but quickly gets old.

How to do it

Like many of the scripts that create text effects, this one has two parts. The first bit of JavaScript sits in the head of your HTML document, and the second part is inserted in the body section, where you want the rippling effect to appear.

Listing 2-7 details the code to insert in the head of your document; replace *text* with the actual text to which you want to apply the effect.

Listing 2-7: **JavaScript code for rippling text; place in the head of your document**

```
<script language="JavaScript1.2">
<!--

rippleText="text"
ns6switch=1
var ns6=document.getElementById&&!document.all
mes=new Array();
mes[0]=-1;
mes[1]=-4;
mes[2]=-7;
mes[3]=-10;
```

Continued

Listing 2-7 *(continued)*

```
mes[4]=-7;
mes[5]=-4;
mes[6]=-1;
num=0;
num2=0;
altText="";

function ripple0()
{if (ns6&&!ns6switch)
{ripple.innerHTML=rippleText
return}
else
{for(i=0; i != rippleText.length;i++)
{altText=altText+"<span style='position:relative;'
id='n"+i+"'>"+rippleText.charAt(i)+"</span>"};
ripple.innerHTML=altText;
altText="";
ripple1a()}}

function ripple1a()
{nfinal=(document.getElementById)?
document.getElementById("n0") : document.all.n0
nfinal.style.left=-num2;
if(num2 != 9)
{num2=num2+3;
setTimeout("ripple1a()",50)}
else{ripple1b()}}
function ripple1b()
{nfinal.style.left=-num2;
if(num2 != 0){num2=num2-3;
setTimeout("ripple1b()",50)}
else{ripple2()}}

function ripple2()
{altText="";
for(i=0;i != rippleText.length;i++)
{if(i+num > -1 && i+num < 7)
{altText=altText+"<span
style='position:relative;top:"+mes[i+num]+"'>"+rippleText.charA
t(i)+"</span>"}
else{altText=altText+"<span>"+rippleText.charAt(i)+"</span>"}}
ripple.innerHTML=altText;
altText="";
if(num != (-rippleText.length))
{num--;
setTimeout("ripple2()",100)}
else{num=0;
setTimeout("ripple0()",100)}}

// -->
</script>
```

Listing 2-8 contains the code to insert in the body of your document where you want the rippling text to appear.

Listing 2-8: **JavaScript code to activate rippling text; place in the body of your document**

```
<div id="ripplex"></div>
<script>
if (document.all||document.getElementById)
{ripple=(document.getElementById)?
document.getElementById("ripplex") : document.all.ripplex
ripple0()}
else
document.write(rippleText)
</script>
```

Practical uses for this technique

This one's like the fading text trick — practically useless. Yes, it draws attention to itself, but that's about it.

How not to be annoying

This technique is pretty much annoying no matter how it's employed.

Trick #33: Make Text Jiggle

We've had fading text, typing text, expanding text, even rippling text. How about jiggling text?

Yes, thanks to Cascading Style Sheets and JavaScript code, it's now possible to make your text jiggle like a bowlful of Jell-O. It's a neat effect if you haven't seen it before, but sure to put off most users in a short period of time.

How to do it

It's actually a three-step affair to create the jiggling text effect. First, you need to insert style sheet and JavaScript code into the head of your document. Second, you need to define an `OnLoad` event handler within your document's `<body>` tag. Third, you have to activate the effect with specific code within the body of your document.

Listing 2-9 shows the JavaScript code to insert in the head of your document.

Listing 2-9: Style sheet and JavaScript code for jiggling text; place in the head of your document

```
<style type="text/css">
<!--
#jiggleText {position: relative;}
-->
</style>

<script language="JavaScript">
<!--
dw=0;
dh=0;

function jiggle()
{w = (Math.round(Math.random()*10)%5)-2; dw+=w;
h = (Math.round(Math.random()*10)%5)-2; dh+=h;
if (dh>10) {h=(0-11);dh=0;}
else if (dh<(0-10)) {h=11;dh=0;}
if (dw>10) {w=(0-11);dw=0;}
else if (dw<(0-10)) {w=11;dw=0;}
vers = parseInt(navigator.appVersion);
if (vers>=4)
{if (navigator.appName=="Netscape")
{document.jiggleText.left+=w;
document.jiggleText.top+=h;}
else if (navigator.appName=="Microsoft Internet Explorer")
{document.all.jiggleText.style.pixelLeft+=w;
document.all.jiggleText.style.pixelTop+=h;}
setTimeout("jiggle()",100);}
else {}}
// -->
</script>
```

This next bit of code needs to be inserted within the `<body>` tag in your document, like this:

```
<body OnLoad="jiggle()">
```

Finally, insert the following line of code into the body of your document, where you want the effect to appear.

```
<div id="jiggleText">text</div>
```

This is definitely an effect that plays better at larger font sizes; just surround the `<div>` tag with the desired `<font>`, formatting, or heading tags.

Practical uses for this technique

What in the world could be a practical use of jiggling text? Maybe if you're trying to convince visitors that they've had too much caffeine. . . . No, not even then. This one is worthless, except for its high annoyance factor.

How not to be annoying

You can't not be annoying with jiggling text. There's just no way. It's an annoying effect that serves no useful purpose — perfect when you want to irritate visitors to your site!

The Annoying Summary

In this chapter, you learned a number of extremely annoying ways to format the text on your page. These techniques revolved around either making the text unreadable, drawing undue attention to specific pieces of text, or slowing the display of the text on the page. Because most people come to a Web page to read what's there, any time you can interfere with that mission, you're being annoying. But in the case of many of these techniques, you also get to display some really neat special effects on your page. Is it your fault that they also happen to make your text less readable?

✦　　✦　　✦

Loathsome Links

In Chapter 2, you learned how to use text to be annoying; this chapter looks at a special type of text — hyperlinked text — and how to employ link-specific effects to tick off visitors to your site.

Links are so integral to the Web page experience that when you change one little thing about how a link behaves, you really throw off your visitors. Make an alert box pop up or a rude noise sound when the user moves over a link, make regular text look like (but not behave like) a link, make a link go nowhere when clicked, or make your links fade away before they can be clicked, and you've not only confused users, you've also started to make steam come out of their ears. When users see links on a page, they want to click those links (almost obsessively, in some cases) to jump to another page; they don't want any weird, unexpected stuff happening.

Which is why it's so annoying when you start messing with the way links look and act.

Trick #34: Ensure Lots of Dead Links

When it comes to links, nothing is more frustrating than clicking on a link and *not* being taken to where you thought you were jumping. When a link links to a page that's no longer active, you have what is called a *dead link*. Users *despise* dead links; it's a sign of poor Web site maintenance and a lack of regard for the site's users. The more dead links on a page, the more likely it is that the page itself hasn't been updated for a while and won't likely be updated anytime soon. Dead links equal carelessness and neglect, and any user would be annoyed to be held in such disrespect.

How to do it

There are two ways to put dead links on your page.

The first method is to deliberately (or carelessly) code the link incorrectly. By now, you probably know the HTML code for adding a link to your page:

```
<a href="url">linktext</a>
```

For the code to work correctly, the *url* has to include the full address of the page being linked to, including the `http://` (as in `"http://www.molehillgroup.com"`). The URL has to be surrounded by quotation marks, as well. Failure to follow this rather unforgiving protocol will result in a link that doesn't link.

 Note   Misspelling the link's URL is also a good way to keep users from jumping to the right page.

The second way to ensure dead links is to code your page once and then never revisit it. Because Web pages and sites fade in and out of existence with some regularity, it's a good bet that if you create a page with ten different links, two or three of those links will either change or go dead within a year. If you don't regularly check all the links on your site, you'll end up with a high percentage of dead links in a relatively short time — with absolutely no effort expended on your part.

Practical uses for this technique

What could be practical about links to dead pages from your site? When users click on a link, they expect to be taken somewhere; jumping to a "page not found" error page is disappointing and — after a few more dead links pop up — extremely annoying. After a user encounters enough dead links on the same site, that user won't come back.

How not to be annoying

To fix the problem of dead links, you have to check all the links on your site — frequently. Click on *each link* to make sure it links to where it's supposed to link, and that the target page is still up and running. You can do this manually (click click click click) or use a link-checking software utility or service. Among the most popular of these are SiteOwner.com (`siteowner.bcentral.com`) and .NetMechanic (`www.netmechanic.com/maintain.htm`).

Trick #35: Underline Text That Isn't a Link

Users have been trained to look for colored (usually blue) underlined text on a Web page. The presence of the blue underline means (so they've been trained) that that particular text is a link and can (or must) be clicked.

This type of Pavlovian response can be observed by using HTML commands to underline a piece of text that isn't a link. Users will read through the page, stumble across the underlined text, and then maneuver the mouse into position and start clicking on the nonexistent link. Click click click they'll go, with absolutely nothing at all happening in response. "It's underlined — it must be a link," they'll think, while you're laughing yourself sick in the background.

It's a particularly annoying trick, which makes it good for more than a few laughs.

How to do it

You can underline normal text by employing the HTML <u> tag, like this:

```
<u>text</u>
```

To amplify the effect, go ahead and change the text color while you're at it, to the blue normally used for real linked text. The full color/underline code looks like this:

```
<font color="0000FF"><u>text</u></font>
```

The resulting text looks just like an actual, bona fide link — but doesn't do anything when clicked.

Practical uses for this technique

In the world of printed documents, it's acceptable to underline pieces of text under various conditions — if you want to emphasize the text, for example, or if you're citing a newspaper or magazine or movie or some other proper item. If you adhere to strict Strunk and White rules of style, you'll want to keep your formatting consistent when composing for the Web.

How not to be annoying

Because underlining is okay in print (although it's seldom used), the temptation is simply to repeat the procedure online. It's also possible that you've copied a print document onto your Web page and kept all the text formatting intact.

The problem, as I've already noted, is that underlined text means something altogether different on a Web page from what it does in print. If you want to emphasize or otherwise single out a specific piece of text, consider using a more Web-acceptable effect, such as italic, bold, or a different color. Do not, under any circumstance, use underlining for anything other than hyperlinks!

Trick #36: Randomly Change Link Colors

Users expect linked text to be underlined, and they expect it to be a certain color (most likely blue). How does it look when your links are a different color — and then start cycling through an entire rainbow of colors?

How to do it

To make your links cycle through a range of colors, about one color per second, insert the JavaScript code from Listing 3-1 into the head of your HTML document.

> **Listing 3-1: JavaScript code for link color cycling; place in the head of your document**

```
<script language="JavaScript">
<!--

function initArray()
{for (var i = 0; i < initArray.arguments.length; i++)
{this[i] = initArray.arguments[i];}
this.length = initArray.arguments.length;}

var colors = new initArray
("red",
"orange",
"yellow",
"cyan",
"lime",
"green",
"blue",
"purple",
"fuchsia",
"silver",
"gray",
"black",
"maroon");

delay = .5;
link = 0;
vlink = 2;

function linkColorCycle()
{link = (link+1)%colors.length;
vlink = (vlink+1)%colors.length;
document.linkColor = colors[link];
document.vlinkColor = colors[vlink];
setTimeout("linkColorCycle()",delay*1000);}
```

```
linkColorCycle();

//-->
</script>
```

Note that this script works only with Internet Explorer.

Practical uses for this technique

If you really want to draw attention to the links on your page, there's no better way than to make them change color like this. Visitors will definitely see the links — even though they may be confused as to what they actually are. (Unclicked links normally don't change color, do they?)

How not to be annoying

This effect is less annoying if you have only a handful of links on your page. The more links, the more annoying the effect. Imagine a situation where you have a lot of text but only one very important link. Cycling the color of that link will definitely draw users directly to where you want them to click; this is less effective if there are a dozen separate pieces of text cycling through the color spectrum at the same time.

Trick #37: Make a Link Disappear

Users expect links to be underlined. They expect links to be a certain color (and a certain color only!). They also expect links to sit there on your page, just waiting to be clicked.

Imagine, then, users' surprise when they go to click a link — and the link disappears! Can you click a link that isn't there? Or is it really there, but just invisible? (Yes, actually.) This effect is so confusing as to be totally vexing; it's tough to beat for pumping up the annoyance factor.

How to do it

While there is a complicated way to fade your links to white (using JavaScript mouseover events), there's also a simple way, using Cascading Style Sheets. Of course, these style sheets work only in Internet Explorer version 4+ and Netscape version 6+ — but that ought to catch *most* of your users, anyway.

This trick assumes that the background color of your page is white and switches the color of any hovered-over link to white. If your background color is a color other than white, change the color in the code.

Speaking of the code, here it is. All you have to do is insert the code in Listing 3-2 into the head of your document.

Listing 3-2: HTML style sheet code for a disappearing link; insert in the head of your document

```
<style>

a:hover {color:#ffffff;}

</style>
```

Practical uses for this technique

What practical use is there to make something you want users to click disappear? This is a purely mischievous effect, guaranteed to annoy click-happy visitors to your site!

How not to be annoying

If you want to *not* be annoying, don't make things disappear. This trick has the effect of grabbing a hot dog out of a diner's mouth just before he chomps down for a bite. There's no way not to be annoyed by that!

Trick #38: Add a Mouseover Message

Another thing you can do with a mouseover event is to cause a message to appear when the cursor hovers over a link. While this isn't necessarily annoying in and of itself, it becomes annoying when you have a lot of links on your page — and thus a lot of unwanted messages.

How to do it

There's a simple way to display a mouseover message, and a complicated way. The simple way puts the message in the browser window's status bar and requires but a simple line of code:

```
<a href="url" onMouseOver=" window.status='message'; return
true" onMouseOut="window.status=' '; return true">linktext</a>
```

Insert the message you want to appear for the *message* text, of course.

The problem with this simple approach is that it really isn't annoying. (It really isn't helpful, either — who ever looks in the browser's status bar?) To be truly annoying, you need your message to pop up onscreen, right in the user's face.

(As an aside, my editor points out that there actually *are* users who studiously monitor the browser's status bar for messages. These are typically hardcore developers, the kind of folks who get annoyed when you replace the standard status bar URL with more user-friendly messages, like "Here's the site you're linking to." Normal folks won't notice one way or another, which is why you have to hit them in the face with whatever annoying message you wish to impart.)

Which leads us, of course, to our second approach. This one activates a mouseover message similar to a Windows Tool Tip, popping up right next to the link that was hovered over.

You start by putting the code from Listing 3-3 in the head of your HTML document.

Listing 3-3: **JavaScript code for a mouseover message; insert in the head of your document**

```
<script language = "JavaScript">
<!--

function initSetup()
{var x = navigator.appVersion;
y = x.substring(0,4);
if (y>=4) setVariables();}

var x,y,a,b;

function setVariables()
{if (navigator.appName == "Netscape")
{h=".left=";
v=".top=";
dS="document.";
sD="";}
else
{h=".pixelLeft=";
v=".pixelTop=";
dS="";
sD=".style";}}

var isNav = (navigator.appName.indexOf("Netscape") !=-1);

function popLayer(messageText)
{desc = "<table cellpadding=0 border=0
bgcolor=#FFFF99><td><font face=Arial size=-1>";
```

Continued

Listing 3-3 *(continued)*

```
desc += messageText;
desc += "</font></td></table>";
if(isNav)
{document.object1.document.write(desc);
document.object1.document.close();
document.object1.left=x+25;
document.object1.top=y;}
else
{object1.innerHTML=desc;
eval(dS+"object1"+sD+h+(x+25));
eval(dS+"object1"+sD+v+y);}}

function hideLayer(a)
{if(isNav)
{eval(document.object1.top=a);}
else object1.innerHTML="";}

function handlerMM(e)
{x = (isNav) ? e.pageX : event.clientX;
y = (isNav) ? e.pageY : event.clientY;}

if (isNav)
{document.captureEvents(Event.MOUSEMOVE);}
document.onmousemove = handlerMM;

//-->
</script>
```

Next, insert the following code within the `<body>` tag, like this:

```
<body OnLoad="initSetup()">
```

Now add the following code directly after the `<body>` tag:

```
<div id="object1" style="position:absolute; visibility:show;
left:25px; top:-50px; z-index:2"></div>
```

Finally, this is the code for the link itself:

```
<a href="url" onMouseOver="popLayer('message')"
onMouseOut="hideLayer(-50)">linktext</a>
```

Enter the pop-up message for the *message* text, and the *url* and *linktext* as you normally would. Now, when users hover their cursor over that link, a Tool Tips–type
message will pop up.

Practical uses for this technique

There's value in providing more information to the user about a link than just the target URL. You can enter the name of the target page, or a description of the page, or whatever you feel is appropriate to display in the mouseover message. (The more information in the message, the more valuable it is.)

How not to be annoying

This trick sounds quite useful on first blush — who wouldn't want to know a little more about the target page before clicking a link? The annoyance derives from the fact that the message appears every time users move the cursor over a link, whether they want to see it or not. (It's the same reason users get annoyed with Windows' Tool Tips — you typically want to read the message only once, if at all.) When you combine this basic annoyance with multiple links on a page, you end up with lots of little pop-ups whenever you nudge the mouse. Ugh!

You can reduce the annoyance factor in two ways. First, keep the message text to a minimum; smaller, shorter pop-ups are less annoying than larger ones with longer messages. Second, don't apply this effect to every link on your page. If only the most important (or most confusing) links have pop-ups, the user's screen won't get littered with these little electronic Post-it notes.

Finally, if you really want to reduce the annoyance factor, use the status bar approach instead of the pop-up message approach. Status bar messages don't clutter the screen, and they can more easily be ignored than big yellow pop-ups.

Trick #39: Display a Mouseover Alert

If you thought users' having to see a yellow pop-up message every time they hover over a link is annoying, imagine their having to deal up with a much bigger dialog box instead. Not only is a dialog box more intrusive, the user has to click it to make it go away.

Use this trick, then, to display an alert message in a dialog box whenever a link is hovered over. Users have to experience this only a few times to start getting extremely irritated!

How to do it

Surprisingly, the script to create a mouseover alert box is extremely simple. Begin by inserting the code in Listing 3-4 into the head of your HTML document.

> **Listing 3-4: JavaScript code for a mouseover alert box; insert in the head of your document**
>
> ```
> <script language="JavaScript">
> <!--
>
> function linkAlert(messageText)
> {newMessage = messageText
> alert (newMessage);}
>
> //-->
> </script>
> ```

Now use the following code within the body of your document to associate an alert box with a specific link; replace *message* with the desired text for your dialog box.

```
<a href="url" onMouseOver="linkAlert('message')">linktext</a>
```

When a user hovers over the link, the dialog box will appear and stay visible until the user clicks the OK button. What's *really* annoying is that the user can't ever click the link—the dialog box keeps popping up and getting in the way! Ha ha!

Practical uses for this technique

This technique is actually a good way to warn users of dead or not-yet-activated links. If you've coded a link to a page that isn't active yet, alert users to this fact by displaying the mouseover alert box. (You could also just leave out the link, if you wanted to be a minimalist about it.)

How not to be annoying

Not only is this trick annoying, it's disruptive—it prevents users from actually clicking on the selected link. If you actually have a link that you don't want users to click, think about removing it completely rather than going through this extremely frustrating procedure.

Trick #40: Link Without Clicking

You've seen several tricks in this chapter that use a mouseover event to do something—display a status message, pop up an alert box, and so on. Now let's get to the most irritating and confusing use of the mouseover event you can think of— to cause a link to activate before it's clicked!

That's right, you can use this trick to send users to another page without their proactively clicking the link. As soon as they move the cursor over a link, it activates, and loads the linked-to page. This is a devious little effect, and many users won't even know what happened. One second they're rolling their mouse around the page, the next second they're viewing some completely different page. What happened? Only you know for sure!

How to do it

This bad boy is one of the simplest tricks to implement. All you have to do is use the following HTML code for the link you want to activate:

```
<a href="" onmouseover="parent.location='url'">linktext</a>
```

That's it. As soon as the user's cursor rolls on top of the link, the link is activated and the browser is redirected to the specified URL.

Practical uses for this technique

You can use this trick just to be annoying, or you can use it to send users unwittingly to a page they probably wouldn't have visited of their own free will. It's a sneaky way to force users to view an advertisement or some other page they weren't otherwise interested in.

How not to be annoying

Forcing users to view an unwanted page is tough to do in a less-than-annoying fashion. You may be able to mitigate irritation by some small degree, however, by providing clear navigation on the linked-to page to get back to the page they were unceremoniously linked from — something like a really big "Click here to return to previous page" button.

Trick #41: Force a Link to Open in a New Window

You've probably been to Web sites where you clicked a link and, instead of the next page opening in the same browser window, the page appeared in a new window that was launched on your desktop. If you're a neat freak, this is irritating because the new window interferes with the undoubtedly orderly appearance of your desktop; even if you're not that neat, you'll soon be overwhelmed by all the new windows that keep opening up every time you click a link. (Plus you'll be using up valuable system resources on your PC. Open up enough windows, and your machine will crash!)

This annoying technique is relatively easy to implement; all you need to do is add a new `target` attribute to the standard HTML link tag.

How to do it

To force a link to open in a new window, put the following code around the selected link:

```
<a href="url" target="_new">linktext</A>
```

That's it; the `"_new"` value for the `target` attribute is what does the trick. When the link is clicked, a new window will open, pointed to the designated URL.

Note   An alternate approach to this effect—one that allows you to more accurately control the look and feel of the window the user sees—is possible with the `OpenWin` function in JavaScript. To learn more about the JavaScript technique, go to Chapter 5, "Pointless Pop-ups and Worthless Windows."

Practical uses for this technique

This effect is useful if you want to keep users on your site yet still enable them to link elsewhere. By opening a new window when they click a link, they still have the original window for your site open, still (at least in theory) collecting visitor eyeballs.

How not to be annoying

This technique gets most annoying when every link on a page opens in a new window—even those linked-to pages that are part of the original site. You can mitigate the annoyance factor by minimizing the number of links to which you apply this effect—and especially by removing this effect from all internal links to other pages on your site.

Trick #42: Add Sounds to Your Links

Our final annoying trick in this chapter will really get on visitors' nerves. Normally, hovering over a link is a nonevent: quiet and without consequence. (Until one clicks the link, of course.) Thanks to our friend the JavaScript mouseover event, however, you can now make hovering a noisy affair. Just associate any WAV-format audio file (the longer and louder, the better) with a specific link and content yourself with the knowledge that when users move their mice, they'll hear music. (Or explosions, or shattering glass, or any other sound you want to use.) Oh, what joyous cacophony!

How to do it

To employ this effect, add the code in Listing 3-5 to the head of your HTML document. (Note that this code works only with Internet Explorer browsers version 5.5 and later.)

Listing 3-5: JavaScript code for audible links; insert in the head of your document

```
<script language="JavaScript">
<!--

document.write('<bgsound src="#" id=mysound loop=1
autostart="true">');

function linkSound(thesound)
{if (document.all)
document.all.mysound.src = thesound;}

//-->
</script>
```

Use the following code when you want to associate a link with the sound; enter the filename for the WAV file as the *file.wav* value. (This code lets you use different sounds for different links; just remember to upload the WAV files to the same directory as your Web page.)

```
<a href="url" onMouseOver="linkSound('file.wav')">linktext</a>
```

Note   An annoying side effect of this annoying sound effect is that it also slows the loading of your Web page. Each WAV file you specify in your code will be loaded when the page is opened; if you include several large WAV files, you can add several seconds to the page's load time!

Practical uses for this technique

You can really liven up an otherwise dead Web page by adding these link-based sound effects. If you're creating a page for younger children, you can imagine the impact of beeps and boops and buzzes as young users mouse around the page. With a little imagination, you can record your own WAV files with verbal instructions for selected links, or add music to aurally identify specific links.

How not to be annoying

Like most sound-based effects, this one is less annoying if used sparingly. Don't add sound to every link, and make the sounds *short*—not only do users not want to sit through unnecessarily long sound files (or any sound files), they also don't want to spend the time waiting for all those files to load with your page.

The Annoying Summary

In this chapter, you learned how to play around with links to make your Web page more annoying. The key point here is that users expect links to be functional, and when that functionality is disturbed or altered, they get irritated. Any time you mess with people's expectations of what is supposed to happen (or what normally happens), you confuse them and annoy them. Remember that truth, and you'll go far.

✦   ✦   ✦

Senseless Scrolling and Frustrating Frames

The best Web pages are short and sweet, single-screen affairs. Everything your users need is visible at a single glance, no scrolling required — and no divvying up the basic window into little subpages of less-relevant information.

So, in your quest to create the most annoying pages possible, anything you can do to diverge from this path is to be applauded. Users like single-screen pages? Then make your pages so long that users have to use the scrollbars several times to get to the bottom! Users like nice, clean, single-topic pages? Then chop up your page into multiple frames, each competing for the reader's attention!

Even better, why not force *other* Web pages into frames — not of their own making? It's quite annoying and relatively easy to frame any page linked to from your page in your own casing, constantly reminding users where they came from. (If they're going to get annoyed, they might as well know who's doing the annoying!)

Trick #43: Make a Web Page Excruciatingly Long

Users do not like to scroll. They prefer to read a Web page as they would a billboard, all in one glance. If the information can't be contained in a single window, then they want the extra content carried to an additional page — anything to keep them from having to click the window's scrollbar or twiddle that little wheelie thingie in the middle of their mouse.

Knowing this, one annoying strategy is to deliberately place long documents on your pages. Don't break them into parts, leave them intact, so that users are forced to scroll down and down and down and down again to read through all the text. Then, to put the icing on the cake, don't put any navigational controls, such as "Click here to return to top," at the bottom of the page; instead, force users to scroll all the way back to the top to navigate through the rest of your site. And never — I mean *never* — let users jump to a specific point on your page with an internal anchor or bookmark. That's just too easy!

How to do it

Making a long Web page is as simple as gathering enough content to stretch over multiple screens. In some instances, you may want to accomplish this result by taking content originally designed for multiple pages and combining it all together on a single page. In any case, make sure you have enough text (and pictures) to make users press Pg Dn several times to reach the bottom.

Practical uses for this technique

Having all your information on a single page is actually useful if users are going to be printing the information. Some Web sites that feature multiple-page articles include a "print this page" link that displays the entire article on a single page; it's easier to print one long page than it is to print several shorter ones.

On the other hand, some documents or articles can't easily be split into parts. If that's the case with your particular content, you have little choice but to let the page run long.

How not to be annoying

If you insist on creating super-long pages, you can at least divide the page into component parts and announce each new part with the appropriate heading. You can then insert a table of contents for that page at the top of the page, with each heading listed. You can even link the headings in the TOC to the headings in the document, via anchor links (or what FrontPage calls "bookmarks"), so that readers can click a link in the TOC and automatically jump to the proper section on the page.

You format a piece of text as an anchor with the following HTML code preceding its appearance in your document:

```
<a name="bookmarkname">bookmarktext</a>
```

You reference an anchor on your page with this code:

```
<a href="#bookmarkname">linktext</a>
```

If the page is excruciatingly long, you may even want to provide the occasional link back to the top of the page. (You accomplish this by setting a bookmark at the top of the page and then linking back to it at appropriate places in the text.) You should also repeat any top-of-page navigational elements at the bottom of the page, so that users won't have to repeat their scrolling to get back to the top of the page.

Trick #44: Force Users to Scroll Horizontally

If scrolling down a page is bad, being forced to scroll from right to left to read a page is even worse. With normal vertical scrolling, users are at least mimicking the conventional reading down the page of a book or newspaper; there is no comparable precedent for horizontal scrolling in the real world.

Not only is horizontal scrolling unusual, it is also unusually irritating. Users want to see a complete sentence in one glance, even if they have to move their eyes (or their heads, if they're reading something really big) from left to right when reading. Not being able to see the end of a line—because the line's too long to fit in the browser window—is disconcerting, at the very least.

How to do it

There are a number of ways to force horizontal scrolling on a page. They all involve putting an object on your page that is wider than the standard browser window.

Note
Forced horizontal scrolling is dependent on the screen resolution of a particular computer system. For users with older systems configured at 640 × 480, you can force horizontal scrolling with an object 640 pixels wide. Users running at 800 × 600 (probably the most common resolution) require an object at least 800 pixels wide to extend past the edge of the window. Users running at 1024 × 768 or above present a special challenge, requiring even larger objects to force the scroll.

A simple way to induce horizontal scrolling is to insert a large graphic on your page. Make sure the width is 1200 pixels or more, just to be safe, and that annoying horizontal scrollbar will automatically appear in your users' browsers when the page is loaded.

The simple approach may not force text to run off the side of the screen, however. To create really long lines of text, you need to insert a table onto your page and insert your text into the table. The table doesn't have to be fancy (one row by one column is sufficient); it merely has to be wider than the standard browser width.

Use the code in Listing 4-1 to create a single-cell table (with no visible borders) 1200 pixels wide; the `width` attribute is what forces the table to extend a fixed number of pixels.

Note You can also specify the width as a percent, and make it more than 100 — as in `width="150%"`.

Listing 4-1: HTML code for an extra-wide single-cell table

```
<table border="0" width="1200" cellpadding="0" cellspacing="0">
  <tr>
    <td>text</td>
  </tr>
</table>
```

Insert all your text between the `<td>` and `</td>` tags — and be sure to create enough text to make it all the way across the screen!

Practical uses for this technique

Extra-wide Web pages aren't very practical for anyone concerned. The only possible reason to make pages this wide is if you're presenting long formulae or programming code that needs to be kept on a single line. By creating a wide table and putting the long formula inside, you ensure that the formula isn't inadvertently split in two.

How not to be annoying

Sometimes you can't avoid horizontal scrolling — especially when users have smaller monitors that force them to use the 640 × 480 setting, or insist on sizing their window to some fraction of the available screen space. You don't have to employ a wide table to cause problems on a smaller screen; large pictures will also do the trick.

You can mitigate this problem by making sure that all your pictures are sized at a maximum of 600 pixels wide. You can do the same with your tables, or use the optional percentage value (rather than a fixed pixel value) for the table's width. (In Listing 4-1, replace `width="1200"` with `width="90%"` — or some similar value of 100% or less.)

Trick #45: Change the Scrollbars' Color

Here's a neat trick for users with Internet Explorer version 5.5 or later. You can change the colors of the scrollbars in the user's browser window — at least while they're viewing your Web page!

For people used to Windows' standard gray scrollbars, going to your page and seeing their scrollbars change to bright yellow or sea green can be a bit of a shock. Inexperienced visitors might even think that there is something wrong with their PCs, not suspecting that code on a Web page can actually reconfigure the browsers on their computers.

How to do it

This trick doesn't work with Netscape, nor with versions of Internet Explorer before version 5.5. It uses an HTML style sheet to change the attributes of the various objects that make up the scrollbar.

Listing 4-2 contains the HTML code to insert in the head of your document.

Listing 4-2: HTML style sheet code to change the browser's scrollbar color; place in the head of your document

```
<STYLE type="text/css">
BODY
{scrollbar-base-color: #xxxxxx}
</STYLE>
```

Replace the *xxxxxx* with the appropriate hexadecimal color code, or just insert the common name for a color.

Note If you want to be *really* annoying, you'll make the scrollbars the same color as the background of your page — which makes the scrollbars *extremely* hard to find and grab! (This works really well with colored backgrounds, by the way.)

Users with older versions of IE or Netscape won't notice any change because of this code; it's harmless unless viewed with IE 5.5 or later. The user's scrollbars return to their original color as soon as another Web page is loaded.

Practical uses for this technique

You may want to employ colored scrollbars if you're trying to present the user with a unified design experience on your pages. For example, if your pages are all various shades of blue, going with dark blue scrollbars fits in with the overall color scheme. (Okay, so this isn't really practical per se, but it can be aesthetically pleasing.)

How not to be annoying

The best uses of this technique are subtle. Go with darker colors, and colors that blend in with the overall color of your pages. If you want to avoid irritating users, do not change the scrollbar color to a bright, eye-popping color (yellow, for example), nor to one that clashes with the underlying page color (red scrollbars on a blue page would do it).

Trick #46: Break a Page into Unnecessary Frames

Even though people are used to seeing information presented in visually separate chunks (think of the different stories in a newspaper, or the overlays of scores, stats, and other data during the broadcast of a sporting event), for some reason that same visual separation of data doesn't go over as well when viewing information on a computer screen. Maybe it's because of the size of the screen; it's hard to tell, but computer users prefer to see one thing at a time—two, maybe, if you count some sort of navigational menu.

Although users don't like it, there is a long-established and widely used mechanism to present multiple sources of information on a single Web page. This mechanism is the frame, and you can easily split a Web page into any number of horizontal or vertical frames, each containing its own separate information.

One reason that users don't necessarily like frames is that they can be confusing. If you're using your computer keyboard to scroll through a page, what element does the scrolling affect? The entire page or a specific frame? And then, *which* specific frame? If you want to print a page, do you print the entire page or do you print a specific frame? And how do you print a frame that contains a long, scrolling document? And what happens when you want to bookmark a page—will the bookmark point at the entire page, or just at one of the framed pages? Besides all that, just how do you use your keyboard to jump from one frame to another, anyway? Good questions, all.

To make things even more irritating, some older browsers (including the WebTV browser) don't display frames properly, or at all. And, of course, many Web page developers don't always code frames properly, resulting in all sorts of visual complications—not the least of which is the very aggravating frame-within-a-frame effect.

How to do it

In reality, each frame on a page contains a separate Web page. The page that holds all the frames is called the *frame document*, and each combination of frames is called a *frameset*.

The easiest way to create a frame document is to let your HTML editor do it. Most editing programs contain special commands that automate the frame creation process; some even let you draw the frames on a page, in WYSIWYG fashion, and then generate the underlying code automatically.

If you want to code your frames in raw HTML, keep a few things in mind. First, instead of the normal `<body>` tag, use the `<frameset>` tag. Second, you have to choose whether you want frames to split your page like rows or like columns, and then specify the size of each frame. Finally, you have to enter the URL for the page you want to display in each frame. It's complicated.

Just to give you a feel for the complexity involved, Listing 4-3 includes the complete code for a frame document with just two frames, as shown in Figure 4-1. The left frame is set for 30% of the page width, with the right column set for 70% of the width.

Listing 4-3: **HTML code for a frame document with two side-by-side frames**

```
<html>

<head>
<title>document-title</title>
</head>

<frameset cols="30%,70%">
  <frame src="url-1">
  <frame src="url-2">
</frameset>

</html>
```

If you want to combine row frames and column frames on the same page, it gets more complex. To accomplish this effect, you need to master *nested frames*, where a frame is split into additional subframes. As an example, Listing 4-4 starts with the same two-frame column layout as in Listing 4-3 and Figure 4-1 but splits the left column into two row frames, as shown in Figure 4-2. Note that the code adds a second frameset *within* the first frameset.

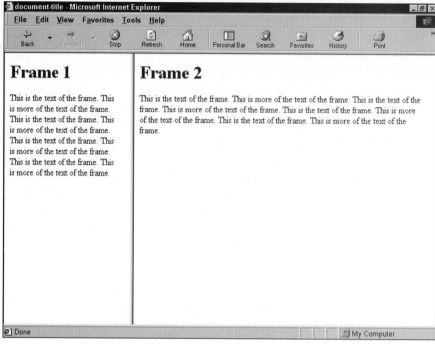

Figure 4-1: A page with two frames in a column layout

Listing 4-4: **HTML code for a page with nested frames**

```
<html>

<head>
<title>document-title</title>
</head>

<frameset cols="30%,70%">

  <frameset rows="50%,50%">
    <frame name="name1" src="url-1">
    <frame name= "name2" src="url-2">
  </frameset>

  <frame src="url-3">

</frameset>

</html>
```

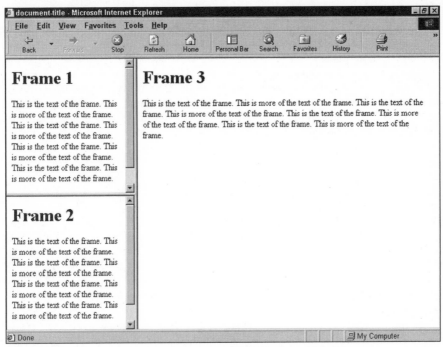

Figure 4-2: A three-frame document containing frames within frames

Practical uses for this technique

Frames are widely used because they're a good way to present different types of content on the same page. You might have your main content in a big frame, and then subsidiary information in one or more smaller frames. You can also dedicate a frame to navigational elements, such as a table of contents of the pages on your Web site. You can even use a frame (typically a short row frame) to contain branding information for your Web site — your site's name, logo, and so on. In short, anything subsidiary to your main content can be placed within its own unique frame.

How not to be annoying

All that said, users still don't like frames — and there are alternative approaches you can employ. Chief of these is the table, through which you can place a variety of different information, using different cells for each item. The advantage of a table is that it's a single Web page, it doesn't result in multiple scrolling elements, and it prints all at once with a single command. You can even code each cell with a different color background, to maintain the same sort of independent element nature of a framed page — but without the resultant user confusion.

Note It's also easier to keep a similar design theme within a table than it is with separate pages joined together in a frame document where each page can have its own unique look and feel that may or may not work together with the other pages in the other frames.

Whether you use frames or tables, you'll reduce the annoyance factor if you keep the number of separate elements to a minimum. Using one frame or cell for your main content and a second frame or cell for a navigational menu is probably okay, but adding a third or fourth frame or cell for other content is pushing your luck.

Trick #47: Make a Frame So Small That It *Has* to Scroll

Frames get really annoying when they're too small for the information they contain. Think about it—each frame contains a full HTML page. If you design a page for a normal 800×600 window and then cram that same page into a 200×200 frame, you're going to have a bit of a display problem—and the user is the one who'll have to deal with it.

If you think having a scrolling frame isn't that terribly annoying, think about having *multiple* scrolling frames on the same page. As you can see in Figure 4-3, you can see only the start of each piece of information; you're forced to click a scrollbar to completely view any one of the frames. In addition, all those scrollbars look ugly and start to take up a fair amount of screen real estate. It's an approach guaranteed to induce all manner of muttering and cursing among your site's visitors.

How to do it

The key to forcing a frame to scroll is to make sure the framed page is longer than the height of the frame. This may be difficult if you have only column frames in your frame document; fortunately, you can induce horizontal scrolling of those frames by including objects (graphics, tables, and the like) of sufficient width.

You can exacerbate the scrolling frame effect by turning off scrollbars within a frame. Imagine the frustration when a user sees that there's more information farther down in the framed document, but there aren't any scrollbars to click to get down there!

You can turn scrollbars on or off with the scrolling attribute in the <frame> tag. This trick defeats any type of scrolling—including with the PgDn button or your wheelie mouse.

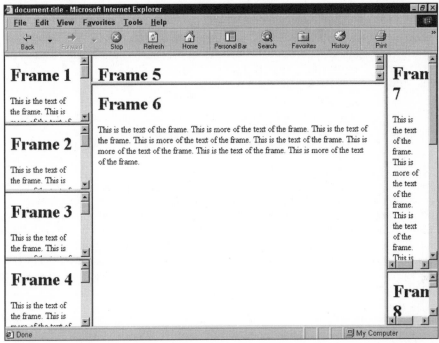

Figure 4-3: Multiple scrolling frames on the same page — which do you scroll first?

To make the contents of a frame completely nonscrolling, use this code:

```
<frame src="url" scrolling="no">
```

The default, obviously, is for this attribute to be set to `yes` or `auto`.

Practical uses for this technique

Scrolling frames may be necessary if you absolutely, positively have to put a large document in a small space. That doesn't make it practical, of course — just necessary.

There is a combination of techniques that you can employ to make scrolling frames somewhat useful. If you have news headlines or similar information you want to present, you can force that content into a small frame, turn off the frame's scroll-bars, and then use the technique presented in Trick #31 (Chapter 2) to make the text scroll up or down the frame. It's the way a lot of news and sports sites present up-to-the-minute headlines and scores, and it's actually more useful than annoying.

How not to be annoying

Almost any type of scrolling frame is annoying. If you have a lot of auxiliary information to present, consider putting it on a separate page and linking to that page from your main page, instead of forcing that content into a too-small frame. Not everything needs to be on your default page, after all.

Trick #48: Force Your Frame Around All Linked-To Pages

You've no doubt seen this trick in action. You're at a particular site, such as About.com (`www.about.com`) or Ask Jeeves (`www.askjeeves.com`), and you click a link to jump to another page. Instead of jumping cleanly to that other page, however, the new page opens in a frame in your browser window, with some sort of branding or other information related to the original site displayed in a separate smaller frame. Even when you click a link on the new page, the original site's frame remains in place, constantly reminding you of where you've been.

This is hugely irritating, for a number of reasons. First, you don't get a full-window view of the other sites, because the branded frame takes up part of the available screen real estate. Second, you never get to see the URL of the linked-to pages, because the URL in the address bar reflects the complete frame document that contains both the pages. Third, you're forced to look at that stupid branding frame; it's always there, no matter where you want to go.

For all these reasons, you may want to add a forced frame to all the links on your Web pages. It's relatively easy to do and will ensure that visitors will remember you (with decidedly mixed feelings) long after they've left your site.

How to do it

To force your own frame around any linked-to pages, you first have to create the document that will be displayed in that frame. The code in Listing 4-5 creates a row frame across the top of the screen that is 100 pixels high (and displays across the full width of the window), so you'll want the content in your document to be the same height. You can include anything you want in your forced frame; most sites include a logo, some explanatory text, and a link back to the original page.

Once you've created this new HTML document, you have to code your original page for the forced-frame effect. Begin by entering the code in Listing 4-5 into the head of the document.

> ## Listing 4-5: JavaScript code to create a forced frame around linked-to pages; insert in the head of your document
>
> ```
> <SCRIPT LANGUAGE="JavaScript">
> <!--
>
> frameSize = "100";
>
> function forceFrame(pageurl, frameurl, frametype)
> {var framewin = window.open("","annoyingFrame");
> with (framewin.document)
> {write("<html><frameset " + frametype + "=" + frameSize +
> ",*>");
> write("<frame src=" + frameurl + ">");
> write(" <frame src=" + pageurl + ">");
> write("</frameset></html>");}
> return false;}
>
> //-->
> </script>
> ```

Now, for each link you want to open in a forced frame, add the following HTML code:

```
<a target="_new" href="url" onClick="return forceFrame('url',
'frame-url', 'rows');">text</a>
```

Enter the URL of the linked-to page for both the *url* values, and the URL of your forced-frame document for *frame-url*. When users click on the link, a new window will open with your content in the top frame, and the linked-to page on the bottom. You can adjust the size of the forced frame by changing the value of the `frameSize` variable in the JavaScript code.

Practical uses for this technique

Obviously, commercial Web sites see branding value in creating a persistent presence for their sites — which forcing you to look at their frame (even after you "leave" their site!) supposedly does. If you want to remind visitors that they got to where they are by going through your site first, by all means employ the forced-frame effect.

You can also employ this technique within your own site. Create a forced frame that contains navigational elements for your site (links to other pages, or even just a big link for your home page), so that any visitors who get lost can use the links in the forced frame to get back to where they want to be.

How not to be annoying

If you insist on using the forced-frame trick and want to try to be as nonirritating as possible, make the size of your carryover frame as small as possible, resist the urge to include annoying graphics (especially animated GIFs) in your frame, and make sure to include a link back to your home page.

Trick #49: Ensure That Users Can't Bypass Your Frames

With all this force-framing going on, users are learning how to break pages out of frames. Internet Explorer users can right-click in any frame on a page and select Open Frame in New Window, which defeats the forced-frame effect. There are even a ton of JavaScripts available that you can place in your own page's HTML to counter any attempts to frame your page.

With all these (and more) counter-measures available, how do you ensure that the frames you create will always surround your pages?

The last trick in this chapter is simple to execute and ensures that any attempts to load a page directly will instead load the page within a frameset, as you originally intended. In other words, this trick keeps users from breaking a framed page out of the frame; when a reload of the page is attempted, the framed document will always appear.

For users who go to all the trouble to open a framed page without the frame, being thwarted in this manner is most assuredly maddening!

How to do it

This trick keeps users from unframing a framed page on your site, meaning that if they enter the URL of a normally framed page (to display that page only, without your normal frameset), you'll still force your frameset page around the other page.

All you have to do is insert the code in Listing 4-6 into the head of the page you want always contained within the frameset. (The frameset page should reference the subsidiary page as well, of course.)

> **Listing 4-6: JavaScript code to force a frame around the current page; insert into the head of your document**
>
> ```
> <script>
>
> if (parent.location.href == self.location.href)
> {window.location.href = 'frameset-url'}
>
> </script>
> ```

Substitute the URL for your frameset page for *frameset-url*. Users who try to load the URL of this page directly will find their browsers redirected to your frameset page, as you originally intended.

Note   By the way, if you accidentally enter the URL of the current (to-be-framed) page instead of the frameset page, you create an infinite loop that will eventually crash the user's system. You probably wouldn't want to do this. Right?

Practical uses for this technique

This trick defeats those scoundrels who would try to avoid the persistent branding message of your forced frames. (Woe to those who interfere in the ways of the Web!) In addition, there may be some pages on your site that really don't stand alone — if they were meant to be displayed on a frame page, they may not contain any navigational elements, for example. If a page wasn't meant to be displayed on its own, then use this technique to force it into the appropriate frames.

How not to be annoying

Rather than forcing a frame around a page, you can offer the framing as an option. Include a link on all your pages with a message that states something like "Click here to view this page within the necessary frames" and have the link call the URL of your frame page. This way, users can choose to view the page al fresco, or as it was originally designed.

The Annoying Summary

In this chapter, you learned why frames annoy people; and you learned techniques to go beyond this basic annoyance into more advanced levels of irritation. (As if frames weren't annoying enough on their own.) After all, any time you can make users work harder to obtain the information they came for — or force them to view things they don't want to view — you stand a much better chance of ticking them off and making sure they never visit your site again.

(Which begs the question — at least partially answered by the forced-frames trick — of how will you continue to annoy visitors after you drive them away?)

✦   ✦   ✦

Pointless Pop-ups and Worthless Windows

This is the chapter you've been waiting for — the one where you learn how to create those immensely irritating pop-up windows. You know what I'm talking about: a new browser window that pops up when you enter or leave a site and often spawns additional pop-ups when you try to close it. All Internet users *hate* these things — which makes the lowly pop-up window the number-one annoyance on the Web.

The unwanted pop-up isn't the only way to use browser windows and dialog boxes to annoy visitors to your site, however. Thanks to Cascading Style Sheets and JavaScript, you can customize the look and feel of almost any browser window that displays your pages, even to the point of forcing a window to display full-screen without any navigational elements. (That particular trick really frosts me — how do you close a window without a close button?)

In addition, you can elaborate on the basic annoying pop-up window to create pop-ups that "hide" themselves behind other windows, that fill up users' entire screens (and hide their taskbars!), and — here's the holy grail of annoying effects — that users simply can't close, no matter how hard they try. After you learn these tricks, how much more annoying can you get?

Trick #50: Display an Alert or Confirm Dialog Box

Before going into pop-up browser windows, there's something almost equally annoying that you wouldn't want to miss — pop-up alert dialog boxes. Most of these dialog boxes pop up to alert you that you've done something wrong (and who wants to be reminded that they did something wrong?) or to ask you to confirm an action you've just made (and who wants to be nagged about whether they did or didn't really want to do something?). In short, any time you see an alert or a confirmation dialog box, you're going to get ticked off.

Which means, of course, that the more dialog boxes you can make pop up on your Web site, the more annoying your site will be.

How to do it

There are two types of dialog boxes you can make appear on your Web page — *alert* boxes and *confirm alert* boxes. The difference between the two is the number of buttons; an alert box has one, and a confirm alert box has two.

Of these two types of dialog boxes, the alert box is the easier to implement. A basic alert box, such as the one shown in Figure 5-1, has a single button; when that button is clicked, the box closes. That's it, no other action is taken.

Figure 5-1: A typical single-button alert box

To add an alert box to your page, use this simple bit of code:

```
alert("message-text")
```

Add your own text in place of *message-text*, such as "Click OK to close this dialog box" or something similar.

You have to make the dialog box appear when a particular event happens. You could associate it with a mouseover event, or clicking a button, or clicking a link, or something as simple as the Web page's opening or closing. As an example, here's the code for generating an alert box when users hover their cursors over a link:

```
<a href="url" onMouseOver='alert("message-text")'>link-text</a>
```

A confirm alert box, such as the one shown in Figure 5-2, differs from a normal alert box in that it has two buttons, OK and Cancel. Pressing the OK button causes some event to happen, typically by calling another JavaScript function. Clicking the Cancel button causes the dialog box to close with no additional action taking place.

Figure 5-2: A typical two-button confirm alert box

The generic code to add a confirm alert box to your page is shown in Listing 5-1. Add this code to the head of your HTML document.

Listing 5-1: **JavaScript for confirm alert box; insert in the head of your document**

```
<script language="JavaScript">
<!--

function genericConfirmAlert()
{if (confirm("message-text"))
{new-event;}}

// -->
</script>
```

Replace *message-text* with the text message you want to appear above the two buttons. Replace *new-event* with the code or function for what you want to happen when the user clicks OK.

For example, to make users jump to a new Web page when they click the OK button, you'd use the code in Listing 5-2.

Listing 5-2: **JavaScript for a confirm alert box that loads another Web page; insert in the head of your document**

```
<script language="JavaScript">
<!--

function genericConfirmAlert()
{if (confirm("message-text"))
```

Continued

> **Listing 5-2:** *(continued)*

```
{location.href = "url";}}

// -->
</script>
```

Replace *message-text* with the text message you want to appear in the alert, and *url* with the Web address of the site or page you'd like to redirect visitors to. Then use the following code to surround the link that will generate the confirm alert box:

```
<a href="JavaScript:genericConfirmAlert()">link-text</a>
```

Practical uses for this technique

Alert boxes are often used to inform users that they've done something wrong. You can also cause an alert box to load when the page loads to give users a welcome greeting or instructions; they have to read the message in the box and click OK before the page will fully load.

The confirm alert dialog box is more useful in that it actually gives users a choice. They can click OK to proceed or initiate something happening, or they can click Cancel to go back to what they were doing. As an example, you can use a confirm alert box to warn users that a particular link leads to adult material; they can click OK to continue to the naughty new page, or click Cancel to opt out.

In short, any time you want to give the user a chance to back out of a decision to go forward is an opportunity to use a confirm alert box.

How not to be annoying

Use alert and confirm alert boxes sparingly; overuse is highly irritating. Calling one of these boxes should be done only when an alert or a decision is absolutely necessary; you shouldn't nag users about every little thing they might do on your site. In many cases, an in-text warning is sufficient; you don't always have to pop up a dialog box that requires additional user action.

Trick #51: Create Annoying Pop-up Windows

You know 'em, you hate 'em, you can't get rid of 'em. I'm talking about unwanted pop-up windows — the ones that appear without warning when you load a new page, exit a page, or hover near a link. Some of these puppies are so annoying that they never go away; every one you try to close just spawns another one (or two) until your desktop is filled with these miniature browser windows, producing more clutter (and using more system resources) than you could ever have imagined.

Pop-up windows are, without a doubt, the single most annoying effect you can put on your Web pages. (They're also the most asked-about special effect; everybody hates them but wants to know how to make their own!)

There's a reason you see so many of these pop-up windows on the Web. They're easy to make, so everybody makes them. Thanks to JavaScript, adding a pop-up window to your page is as easy as writing a few standard lines of code. You even get the bonus of being able to almost completely customize the look and feel of the pop-up window, from where it sits onscreen to what navigational controls are displayed—if any.

Read on to learn how to create your own annoying pop-ups — and then continue through the chapter for specialized applications of this hated special effect.

How to do it

Pop-up windows are activated by the `window.open` method. You call this method in a piece of JavaScript code and define a series of variables to control the look and placement of the window.

To create your own pop-up window, start with the code in Listing 5-3. Insert this code in the head of your HTML document, and then call the function with a specific event code, discussed later in this section.

Listing 5-3: **Generic JavaScript code for an annoying pop-up window; insert in the head of your document**

```
<script language="JavaScript">
<!--

function genericPopup(popupAddress)
{new_window =
window.open(popupAddress,'windowName','variable1=x,variable2=x,
variable3=x')}

// -->
</script>
```

This is actually pretty simple code once you figure out all the variables. First, know that the variables are all separated by commas *without* spaces; throwing in a space will muck up the code. Second, each variable has to be accompanied by a corresponding value. For example, to display a status bar in your pop-up window, the variable looks like this:

```
status=1
```

Finally, you have to know which variables to choose from—which is where Table 5-1 comes in. The default value for each variable is in boldface; if you don't include a particular variable in the statement, the default value will be used.

Table 5-1 Variables for the window.open Event	
Variable	**Description and Values**
windowName	The name you assign to the pop-up window (You *must* assign a name for the windows.open event to work.)
toolbar	1 (displays a toolbar in the pop-up window) **0** (displays window without the toolbar)
menubar	1 (displays a menu bar in the pop-up window) **0** (displays window without the menu bar)
status	1 (displays a status bar in the pop-up window) **0** (displays window without the status bar)
directories	1 (displays directory buttons in the pop-up window) **0** (displays window without directory buttons
location	1 (displays the location address entry box in the pop-up window) **0** (displays the window without the location box)
width	Width of the pop-up window in *xxx* pixels
height	Height of the pop-up window in *xxx* pixels
left	Position of the pop-up window from the left edge of the screen, in *xxx* pixels
top	Position of the pop-up window from the top edge of the screen, in *xxx* pixels
resizable	1 (enables user to resize the pop-up window) **0** (disables resizing of the pop-up window)
fullscreen	1 (displays pop-up window in full-screen window) **0** (displays pop-up window in normal browser window)

Note The fullscreen variable works only with Internet Explorer browsers. There are other variables that are Netscape-specific, but that limitation makes them unsuitable for widespread use.

Note that the only variable you have to include in the statement is windowName. For all unstated variables, the default value is assumed. If the size and position of the pop-up are not stated, the new window will assume the same size and position as the last opened browser window.

Note   The `windowName` variable cannot contain any spaces or dashes; it must be a single string of contiguous alphanumeric characters.

The typical pop-up is void of all menus and scrollbars — just a window, containing whatever Web page you designate. Figure 5-3 shows a typical pop-up, sized at 300 (wide) by 200 (high) pixels. The code to generate this pop-up is in Listing 5-4. (Obviously, this listing doesn't include the code for the page within the pop-up window.)

Figure 5-3: Typical annoying pop-up window with no scrollbars or menus

Listing 5-4: **JavaScript code for the 200 × 300 pop-up window in Figure 5-3; place in the head of your document**

```
<script language="JavaScript">
<!--
function genericPopup(popupAddress)
{new_window =
window.open(popupAddress,'AnnoyingWindow','width=300,height=200
')}

// -->
</script>
```

Once you've added the code for the pop-up window to the head of the document, you have to instruct the browser to open the window, using one of a number of methods. You can cause the pop-up to open when the page is first opened, when the page is closed, when a link is clicked, or when a link is just hovered over. Table 5-2 shows the codes for each of these events. In each case, replace *popup-url* with the URL of the page to be loaded into the pop-up window.

To generate a pop-up window when your page is first opened, add the `onLoad` event to the `<body>` tag, as shown in Table 5-2.

Table 5-2
Ways to Launch a Pop-Up Window

Launch Method	HTML Code
When your main page is loaded (insert this code within the `<body>` tag)	`<body onLoad="genericPopup ('popup-url')">`
When users leave your main page (insert this code within the `<body>` tag)	`<body onUnload="genericPopup ('popup-url')">`
When a link is clicked	`<a href="javascript:genericPopup ('popup-url');">link-text</a>`
When a link is hovered over	`<a href="url" onMouseOver= genericPopup('popup-url');> link-text</a>`

We'll visit specific applications of these various techniques throughout the rest of this chapter — although you should feel free to experiment with creating your own uniquely annoying pop-up windows right now if you want to!

Practical uses for this technique

Web site developers can talk themselves into assembling a long list of real-world uses for the pop-up window. Among the uses they can probably rationalize are the following:

✦ **Splash window:** Launches when your main page loads (using the `onLoad` event), displaying some sort of welcome screen or pre–home page advertisement or instructions.

✦ **Subsidiary content window:** Launches when a user clicks a link to obtain more information about a particular item on your page.

✦ **Thank you window:** Launches when a user exits your site (using the `onUnload` event), displaying some sort of thank you or come back soon message.

✦ **Ad window:** The most common type of pop-up, containing advertising content or links to advertiser-supported sites; it's typically generated via either the `onLoad` or `onUnload` events.

This last application really doesn't benefit your site's visitors, but it might benefit you if you get compensated for the users you drive to an advertiser's site.

How not to be annoying

Given the proliferation of pop-up windows on the Web, it's hard not to be annoying if you choose to join in on the fun. Still, there are things you can do to mitigate the irritation caused by your pop-up windows. Here are a few:

✦ Keep your pop-up windows small, preferably in the 200×200 range, but definitely no more than 600 (wide) $\times$ 300 (high).

✦ Keep the pop-up window uncluttered by removing most (if not all) of the menus and navigational controls.

✦ Provide a prominent way for users to close the window, such as a "close this window" button. Listing 5-5 shows the HTML code for one of these window-closing buttons; insert this code in the page contained within the pop-up, and users will be able to close the pop-up with a single click.

Listing 5-5: **HTML code for a "close this window" button; insert in the body of your pop-up window document**

```
<form name="closer">
<input type=button value="Click here to close this window"
onClick="self.close()">
</form>
```

✦ Don't hide your pop-ups; use the code in Trick #52 to make your pop-up pop to the front of the pile.

✦ Keep the contents of your pop-up window to a minimum; don't force users to sit through long loading times for an already-annoying pop-up. (For example, don't put big graphics inside the pop-up!)

✦ If you think users might want to print the pop-up page, leave the menu bar visible (via the `menubar=1` variable) so they can access their browser's Print command.

Trick #52: Force a Pop-up to the Top — or the Bottom

Controlling the positioning of the pop-up window — whether it appears on top of or below the parent window — is important. Either position can be annoying; a useless pop-up that obscures more important information in the main window is highly irritating, as is a pop-up that a user can't dismiss because it keeps itself hidden.

How to do it

When you want your pop-up to appear on top of all the other windows on your users' screens, use the `onBlur` command. Just insert this command in the `<body>` tag of the pop-up window's document, like this:

```
<body onBlur="window.focus();">
```

This is a very effective technique, as it will always raise the pop-up to the top — even when users try to change the focus of other onscreen windows.

When you want to send a pop-up window to the bottom of the pile, you're creating what developers call a *pop-under* or a *pop-behind*. To do this, you use the `blur` method, which is similar to the `onBlur` command — except that it sends the popped-up window to the bottom position on your users' desktops. All you have to do is use the code in Listing 5-6 to create your pop-under.

Listing 5-6: JavaScript code to send a pop-up window to the bottom; insert in the head of the parent document

```
<script language="JavaScript">
<!--

function popUnder(popupAddress)
{new_window =
window.open(popupAddress,'windowName','variable1=x,variable2=x,
variable3=x')
new_window.blur()}

// -->
</script>
```

Then you call the `popUnder` function from within the main document's `<body>` tag, but with an added attribute, like this:

```
<body onLoad="popUnder('popunder-url'); window.focus();">
```

(This particular technique is most effective if you set the size of the pop-under so that it's relatively small — smaller than the parent window.)

Practical uses for this technique

Forcing a pop-up window on top of your main window may be necessary if it contains information that needs to be read before users read the balance of the parent page. It's also necessary if you're displaying any type of caution or warning pertinent to the contents of the parent page.

Using a pop-under window is more subversive and is typically employed when you don't want the user to know that a window has opened. Perhaps the pop-under contains some sort of tracking or information-gathering code, or automatically loads an advertiser's site (for which you get paid for each visitor you send the advertiser's way). In any case, using the forced-bottom trick when hiding the pop-up window is important.

How not to be annoying

If you force a pop-up on top of the parent window, be sure to display a very visible means of closing the pop-up window so that users can clear the desktop and get back to reading the main page. Also go with as small a pop-up as you can, so as not to obscure too much of the original page.

Trick #53: Make a Window Fill the Entire Screen

Have you ever been the victim of a full-screen pop-up window? As you can see in Figure 5-4, this puppy fills your entire screen, with no navigation controls visible, so that you can't even close it! It is one of the most annoying variants of an annoying effect and will totally overwhelm less-experienced users who don't know that they can toggle away from that huge window by using Alt+Tab.

Note   Because no navigational controls are visible, the only way to close a full-screen pop-up is to press Ctrl+W.

How to do it

Creating a full-screen pop-up is as easy as inserting the `fullscreen=1` variable in the standard pop-up-generating code, as shown in Listing 5-7.

> **Listing 5-7: JavaScript code for a full-screen pop-up window; insert in the head of the parent document**

```
<script language="JavaScript">
<!--

function genericPopup(popupAddress)
{new_window =
window.open(popupAddress,'windowName','fullscreen=1')}

// -->
</script>
```

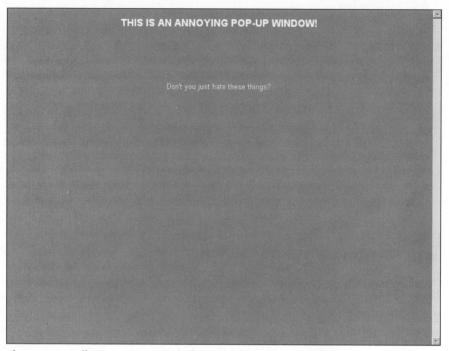

THIS IS AN ANNOYING POP-UP WINDOW!

Don't you just hate these things?

Figure 5-4: Full-screen pop-up window — look, Ma, no controls!

(Remember to call this code with one of the event methods listed in Table 5-2.)

Because all the navigational controls for the pop-up are off by default, you don't have to specify any other variables in this code. I love this trick because it's so easy — and so vexing, even to moderately experienced users! (After all, how many users know the Ctrl+W command?)

Practical uses for this technique

This trick is practical only if you want to take total control of the user's screen. Naturally, you find many advertisers using this trick, especially those advertising adult-oriented sites. (A full-screen porn ad that you can't close is not only exasperating, it's potentially embarrassing!)

How not to be annoying

You can minimize the frustration this effect induces by including a very visible "close this window" button, as described in Listing 5-5. Without a clear way to close the window, many users will resort to rebooting their entire system just to get rid of your page — an extreme reaction to a very simple trick!

Trick #54: Create a Delayed Pop-up

Pop-up windows are annoying enough on their own. But what about a pop-up that pops up when it's least expected—a good twenty seconds after the original page has loaded?

A delayed pop-up is a great way to set your site visitors at ease and then spring that nasty pop-up on them seemingly out of the blue. It's all done with timers, of course. (No mirrors involved.)

How to do it

The code for this one involves a `setTimeout` command that you place within the `onLoad` event handler in the `<body>` tag of the parent document. You use this code along with the `genericPopup` function introduced in Trick #51.

Here's the new `<body>` tag code:

```
<body onLoad="setTimeout('genericPopup(\'popup-url\')',20000)">
```

As usual, replace *popup-url* with the URL for the pop-up window. The 20000 controls the delay before the pop-up appears; choose a bigger number for a longer delay, or a smaller one for a shorter one.

Practical uses for this technique

Perhaps you have some information you want to impart, but not immediately when visitors first open your page. Maybe it's an advertising offer, or a notice of site policy changes, or . . . well, whatever. Yeah, maybe that's it. You have something you don't want to spring on users right away. Whatever it is, this is the way to do it.

How not to be annoying

I'm not sure about this one. Is it less annoying to pop up quicker, or less annoying to pop up slower? Well, whichever it is, that's the one you should do—if you want to annoy your users less, that is.

Trick #55: Create a Pop-up Window That Won't Stay Closed

There are so many ways to use pop-up windows to annoy people. Here's one of my favorites. Users do something (they're never sure quite what) to open a pop-up window on their screen. Annoyed (of course), they click the close button to dismiss the pop-up. As soon as the pop-up closes, a new pop-up window appears. They close that one, and another one appears. They close this last one, and yet another one appears. They keep clicking until their finger cramps, yet the pop-ups keep coming; for each one they close, a new one pops back up. They can't get rid of them!

Ever wonder how *you* can annoy people in this fashion? It's really easy — read on and I'll tell you how it's done!

How to do it

The key to the constant pop-up is to create a constant series of onUnload events. All you have to do is insert the code in Listing 5-8 into the head of your pop-up window document.

> ### Listing 5-8: JavaScript code for an uncloseable pop-up; insert in the head of your pop-up window document

```
<script language="JavaScript">
<!--

repeatNum = 1
function openAgain()
{if (repeatNum == 1)
{repeatWindow=window.open('popup-url','')}}

//-->
</script>
```

Next, insert the following onUnload event code into the body of your pop-up window document:

```
<body onUnload="openAgain()">
```

Voilà! Let's see your visitors try to close the pop-up window now!

Practical uses for this technique

Let's see . . . other than annoying people, this technique apparently has appeal for site owners who get paid for each click-through to an advertiser's site. Each new pop-up that opens is another click-through!

How not to be annoying

If you want to give your users an out from this pop-up window-from-hell, insert the following code into the body of the pop-up document; this will let them close the pop-up without rebooting their computer:

```
<a href="javascript:self.close()">Click here to close this
window</a>
```

Trick #56: Create a Pop-up Bomb

If you thought that last trick was nasty, you ain't seen nothin' yet.

This next trick is so nasty that I can't in good conscience recommend that you ever, *ever* use it on one of your Web pages.

You see, here's what happens.

This trick opens up a pop-up window. Then another one. Then another one. Then another. Then another. Then another then another then another then another, faster than your users can close them.

Yup, this trick bombs the user's computer with an infinite number of pop-up windows.

So many windows, in fact, that your computer will crash. (If you don't turn the computer off first, that is.)

Trust me, this trick really works. So don't test it on your own computer. You won't like what happens!

How to do it

All you have to do is insert the code in Listing 5-9 into the head of your parent document.

> Listing 5-9: **JavaScript code to launch an infinite number of pop-up windows; insert in the head of your parent document**

```
<script language="JavaScript">
<!--

function popBomb()
```

Continued

> **Listing 5-9:** *(continued)*
>
> ```
> {while(true) window.open("popup-url");}
>
> //-->
> </script>
> ```

Then, of course, you call the function popBomb with one of the event methods listed in Table 5-2. For example, if you want to start the bombing as soon as your parent page loads, include the following onLoad event in the <body> tag:

```
<body onLoad="popBomb()">
```

Note   Do *not* test this code on your computer—you'll be bombarded with an infinite number of unwanted pop-ups!

Practical uses for this technique

The only possible use for this trick is to intentionally crash someone's computer. If that seems practical to you, so be it.

How not to be annoying

I don't know of any way to crash someone's computer without their being at least a little annoyed. Sorry.

Trick #57: Launch Two or More Pop-ups at Once

If the pop-up bomb is too cruel, how about just launching a few pop-ups at the same time? Using this little trick, you can launch as many simultaneous pop-up windows as you like—each with its own dimensions and placement.

How to do it

This one is just too easy. All you have to do is take the standard genericPopup code from Trick #51 and add more window.open events! Add as many as you want, and feel free to vary the size and placement of each window.

If you're unsure of how to do this, use the code in Listing 5-10.

Listing 5-10: **JavaScript code to launch multiple pop-up windows; insert in the head of your parent document**

```
<script language="JavaScript">
<!--

function multiplePopup()
{
new_window1 = window.open('url-
1','windowName','variable1=x,variable2=x,variable3=x')}
new_window2 = window.open('url-
2','windowName','variable1=x,variable2=x,variable3=x')}
new_window3 = window.open('url-
3','windowName','variable1=x,variable2=x,variable3=x')}

// -->
</script>
```

The big difference between this and the previous code is that you identify the URLs for the pop-up windows within the code itself — *url-1*, *url-2*, and so on. Add as many lines as you like, as long as you keep the sequential numbering for each new window. Then call the entire function like this:

```
<body onLoad="multiplePopup()">
```

You can use any of the launch methods in Table 5-2 (Trick #51), of course.

Practical uses for this technique

If you have multiple messages (or advertisements) to communicate to your users, you might as well get them all out of the way at once. Right?

How not to be annoying

It would be most annoying if all the windows were the same size and stacked directly on top of one another. As annoying as all these windows are, it isn't quite as bad if you can see all of them. That means varying the X/Y positioning and the window dimensions.

Trick #58: Make a Pop-up Look Like an Alert Box

Here's a neat way to trick users into clicking through to a site of your choosing. All you have to do is launch a pop-up window that looks, acts, and feels like a system alert dialog box and include a message that convinces users to click the button in the box. When they click the button, they're transferred to another Web page in a normal browser window.

I particularly like the "You have two messages waiting" approach shown in Figure 5-5; it makes users think that there's some sort of weird e-mail thing going on. Alternately, you scare the user into clicking the button with a message like "Windows has detected that a virus has been downloaded onto your system. Click here to delete the infected file."

In any case, use your imagination, and see how well you can fool your site's visitors!

Figure 5-5: Trick your users into clicking the button — and linking to a page of your choice.

How to do it

You start this trick by somehow launching a pop-up window from your parent document, as described in Trick #51. You'll want this pop-up to be relatively small and wider than it is tall; 250 × 100 is a good size.

Next, load the code in Listing 5-11 into the head of your pop-up document (the one you want to look like an alert box).

Listing 5-11: JavaScript code to launch another window from your pop-up; insert in the head of your pop-up document

```
<script language="JavaScript">
<!--

function popupLink(popupAddress)
{new_window =
window.open(popupAddress,'newWindow','width=640,height=480,resi
```

```
zable=1,status=1,toolbar=1,menubar=1,location=1,directories=1')
}

//-->
</script>
```

Next, insert the following background color code in the pop-up document's `<body>` tag:

```
<body bgcolor="#C0C0C0">
```

Finally, insert the code in Listing 5-12 (and *only* this code!) into the body of your pop-up document.

Listing 5-12: JavaScript code to simulate an alert box in a pop-up window; insert in the body of your pop-up document

```
<form>
<p align="center"><font face="Tahoma" size=3><b>message-
text</b></font></p>
<p align="center">
<input type=button value="button-text"
onClick="popupLink('url')">
</p>
</form>
```

Naturally, you should replace *message-text* with the alert message to appear above the button, *button-text* with the text to appear on the button itself, and *url* with the full URL of the page you want to link to.

The result will be a pop-up window that looks like an alert box (gray background and all) and that opens a new page (in a new browser window) when its button is clicked.

Practical uses for this technique

This technique is quite devious, which makes it perfect for sending users to pages that they wouldn't access of their own volition. If you get a commission for each click-through to a particular site, this is a great way to up your click-throughs; users click to that site without knowing it. And, chances are that they'll get annoyed at the next site, not yours; it's likely that they'll think the trick was played by the other site!

How not to be annoying

You can reduce the annoyance factor by being honest in the message you display in the phony alert box. Say something like "Click here to visit such-and-such's site," and no one will accuse you of misleading your users. Of course, you don't supply a cancel button, so they don't have much of a choice (other than closing the pop-up window manually), but it's still an honest approach.

Trick #59: Create a Frameless Pop-up

One neat effect for your pop-up windows is removing the frame that typically surrounds a window. This effectively displays the pop-up page only—no borders, no controls, no other elements. Web designers call this a *containerless window*; you can see what this looks like in Figure 5-6.

Figure 5-6: A frameless pop-up window—no borders, no controls, no nothing

How to do it

This effect requires more than a simple `window.open` code. In essence, you have to load an empty window, and then stuff it with the proper code to do away with the borders, and then load your pop-up page into the window. That requires a bit of code, but the results are worth it.

To generate your frameless pop-up, insert the code from Listing 5-13 into the head of the parent HTML document. Replace both instances of *popup-url* with the actual URL of the pop-up page and fill in your own values (in pixels) for `windowW` (window width), `windowH` (window height), `windowX` (distance from left edge of screen), and `windowY` (distance from top of screen).

Listing 5-13: JavaScript code for a frameless pop-up window; insert in the head of the parent document

```
<script>
<!--
var windowW=xxx
var windowH=xxx
var windowX = xxx
var windowY = xxx

winVars = "width="+windowW+",height="+windowH;
var beIE = document.all?true:false

function framelessPopup()
{if (beIE)
{noframeWindow =
window.open("","popFrameless","fullscreen,"+winVars)
noframeWindow.blur()
window.focus()
noframeWindow.resizeTo(windowW,windowH)
noframeWindow.moveTo(windowX,windowY)
var frameString=""+
"<html>"+
"<head>"+
"<title>title</title>"+
"</head>"+
"<frameset rows='*,0' framespacing=0 border=0 frameborder=0>"+
"<frame name='top' src='popup-url' scrolling=no>"+
"<frame name='bottom' src='about:blank' scrolling='no'>"+
"</frameset>"+
"</html>"
noframeWindow.document.open();
noframeWindow.document.write(frameString)
noframeWindow.document.close()}
else
{noframeWindow=window.open(popup-
url,"popFrameless","scrollbars,"+winVars)
noframeWindow.blur()
window.focus()
noframeWindow.resizeTo(windowW,windowH)
noframeWindow.moveTo(windowX,windowY)}
noframeWindow.focus()}

//-->
</script>
```

Note   For best effect, make sure that the pop-up window is sized larger than any graphics or scrolling text on the pop-up page, otherwise scrollbars will appear in the pop-up.

You can launch the frameless pop-up via any of the methods listed in Table 5-2. Just replace `genericPopup(popupaddress)` with `framelessPopup()` in the code. For example, the code to launch this pop-up from a link looks like this:

```
<a href="javascript:framelessPopup();">link-text</a>
```

Note The containerless window effect works only with Windows versions of Internet Explorer, version 4.0 or later. Where the effect doesn't work, a normal bordered window is displayed.

Practical uses for this technique

A frameless pop-up is quite striking; it's the one thing on your visitor's desktop that doesn't look like a normal desktop object. There are no frames or borders, just a flat page hanging out there all by itself.

Because of this unique appearance, a frameless pop-up is a great way to draw attention to an advertising message. Of course, you can use it where you'd use any normal pop-up — as long as you don't need the window to scroll. (You can turn on scrolling by changing `scrolling=no` to `scrolling=auto` in the "`<frame name='top' src='popup-url' scrolling=no>`" line.)

How not to be annoying

One thing about a frameless pop-up window — there's no way to close it! With this particular type of window, you can't even use the `self.close` approach to close the window. Instead, you have to use this code:

```
<a href="javascript:top.window.close()">Click here to close</a>
```

Trick #60: Launch a Peeker Pop-up

This next trick builds on the script in Trick #58 to launch a frameless pop-up window that slowly rises into view from the bottom of the screen. Some ad industry types like to call this pop-up a *peeker*. In any case, it's one of those effects that are pretty neat on first viewing but grow annoying over time.

How to do it

This particular script creates a peeker that pokes up from the bottom right of the screen with no scrollbars, frames, or other control elements. The script is written so that the peeker loads when the page is loaded and disappears when the user goes to another page.

Begin by putting the script in Listing 5-14 in the head of the parent HTML document. Replace both instances of *popup-url* with the actual URL of the pop-up page and fill in your own values (in pixels) for `windowW` (window width) and `windowH` (window height). You can also change where the peeker appears by changing the `Xmode` value from `right` to `left` or `center`.

Listing 5-14: JavaScript code for a peeker pop-up; insert in the head of the parent document

```
<script language="javascript">
<!--

var windowW=xxx
var windowH=xxx

var Yoffset=0
var windowStep=2
var moveSpeed=10
var autoclose = true

Xmode="right";
Xoffset=35;

var windowX = (screen.width/2)-(windowW/2);
if (Xmode=="left") windowX=0+Xoffset;
if (Xmode=="right") windowX=screen.availWidth-Xoffset-windowW;
var windowY = (screen.availHeight);
var windowYstop = windowY-windowH-Yoffset;
var windowYnow = windowY;

winVars = "width="+windowW+",height="+windowH;
var beIE = document.all?true:false

function slideitup()
{if (beIE)
{peekerPopup =
window.open("","popFrameless","fullscreen,"+winVars)
peekerPopup.blur()
window.focus()
peekerPopup.resizeTo(windowW,windowH)
```

Continued

Listing 5-14: *(continued)*

```
peekerPopup.moveTo(windowX,windowY)
var frameString=""+
"<html>"+
"<head>"+
"<title>title</title>"+
"</head>"+
"<frameset rows='*,0' framespacing=0 border=0 frameborder=0>"+
"<frame name='top' src='popup-url' scrolling=auto>"+
"<frame name='bottom' src='about:blank' scrolling='no'>"+
"</frameset>"+
"</html>"
peekerPopup.document.open();
peekerPopup.document.write(frameString)
peekerPopup.document.close()}
else
{peekerPopup=window.open(popup-url,"popFrameless",winVars)
peekerPopup.blur()
window.focus()
peekerPopup.resizeTo(windowW,windowH)
peekerPopup.moveTo(windowX,windowY)}
peekerPopup.focus()
window.onunload = function(){peekerPopup.close()}
movepeekerPopup();}

function movepeekerPopup()
{if (document.all)
{if (windowYnow>=windowYstop)
{peekerPopup.moveTo(windowX,windowYnow);
peekerPopup.focus();
windowYnow=windowYnow-windowStep;
timer=setTimeout("movepeekerPopup()",moveSpeed);}
else
{clearTimeout(timer);
peekerPopup.moveTo(windowX,windowYstop);
peekerPopup.focus();}}
else
{peekerPopup.moveTo(windowX,windowYstop);}}

//-->
</script>
```

To have the peeker pop when the parent window is launched, insert the `onLoad` event handler into the parent document's `<body>` tag, like this:

```
<body onLoad="slideitup()">
```

Note that the peeker window will not poke up until the main page from which it is launched has fully loaded.

Practical uses for this technique

This type of peeker pop-up is a nice way to present welcome or introductory information on the main page of a Web site. You can also use it to display the latest news or announcements.

How not to be annoying

Even though this peeker is designed to close automatically when the user changes pages, you still might want to put a "close this window" link on the pop-up page, for those users who want to put away the peeker sooner.

Trick #61: Shake a Window

The remaining tricks in this chapter can be applied to any window, pop-up or otherwise. These tricks use the JavaScript moveBy method to make the window jump, shake, or slide across the screen — which, if one is trying to read the contents of the window, can be slightly irritating, to say the least.

This first trick makes a window shake — actually, to shudder (briefly), as if it had a chill. It's just enough of an effect to worry users who aren't expecting it. (Was that an earthquake, or what?)

How to do it

To shake a window, insert the code in Listing 5-15 into the head of your HTML document.

> Listing 5-15: **JavaScript code for a shaky window; insert in the head of your document**

```
<script language="JavaScript1.2">
<!--

function windowShake(n)
{if (parent.moveBy)
{for (i = 10; i > 0; i--)
{for (j = n; j > 0; j--)
{parent.moveBy(0,i);
parent.moveBy(i,0);
parent.moveBy(0,-i);
parent.moveBy(-i,0);}}}}

//-->
</script>
```

To activate the shake when the page is loaded, add the `onLoad` event handler to the `<body>` tag, like this:

```
<body onLoad="windowShake(2)">
```

You can extend the length of the shake by increasing the `windowShake` variable (`default=2`) in the `onLoad` event.

Practical uses for this technique

While it's true that a shuddering window might grab the user's attention, it's not the sort of thing that lends confidence to the page currently being displayed — which means it might not be the best effect for drawing attention to an advertisement or other important message. This is probably one of those effects for effect's sake, with nothing too practical about it.

How not to be annoying

A shaking window is going to be annoying, no matter what you do. Avoid being more annoying than you have to, however, by *not* increasing the `windowShake` variable.

Trick #62: Make a Window Jump Around the Screen

The second of these JavaScript `moveBy` tricks is a little more violent than the shaking window effect. In this one, the window starts to shake, then to bounce, and then to jump all around the screen. Once this puppy gets going, don't be surprised to see the window jump completely off the screen — you may need to press Ctrl+W to shut down the sucker!

Not only is this effect annoying, it can scare the hell out of inexperienced users, who'll think that there is something wrong with their computers. Crafty, eh?

How to do it

This effect is fairly easy to implement. Just insert the code in Listing 5-16 into the head of your HTML document.

> **Listing 5-16: JavaScript code for a jumping window; insert in the head of your document**
>
> ```
> <script language="JavaScript">
> <!--
>
> if(document.layers || document.all)
> {a = 1;
> setInterval("windowJumper()", 50);}
>
> function windowJumper()
> {a = a + 1;
> self.moveBy((Math.random() * a * 2 - a), (Math.random() * a *
> 2) - a);}
>
> //-->
> </script>
> ```

Practical uses for this technique

Well, actually, you see, it's like this . . .

Okay, there are no practical uses for this one. None at all. Zip. Nada. Zilch.

Sorry.

How not to be annoying

There's nothing you can do to mitigate the effect of this little prank. It's going to annoy people, and there's nothing you can do about it.

Trick #63: Make a Window Expand and Contract Automatically

Windows are supposed to be steady, sturdy things. They're not supposed to jump and slide and boing all around the screen.

Which is why this particular trick is so irritating.

When you implement this trick, you display a pop-up window on the user's screen. (So far, so good.) But this particular window—well, it kind of wheezes.

It gets bigger. Then it gets smaller.

It expands and contracts.

It *boings*.

How to do it

All you have to do is insert the code in Listing 5-17 in the head of the document that you want to expand and contract.

Listing 5-17: JavaScript code to launch an expanding and contracting window; insert in the head of your document

```
<script language="JavaScript">
<!--

var littleWidth = 400;
var littleHeight = 400;
var littleX = 100;
var littleY = 100;
var bigWidth = 500;
var bigHeight = 500;
var bigX = 100;
var bigY = 100;
var whichSize = "Little";
var speed = 250;
var bob = parseInt(navigator.appVersion)
var t = null;

function expandContract()
{if (bob >= 4)
{if (whichSize == "Little")
{self.resizeTo(bigWidth,bigHeight);
self.moveTo(bigX,bigY);
whichSize = "Big";}
else
{self.resizeTo(littleWidth,littleHeight);
self.moveTo(littleX,littleY);
whichSize = "Little";}
t=setTimeout('expandContract()', speed);}}

expandContract();

//-->
</script>
```

You can alter the size of the window by changing the `bigWidth`, `bigHeight`, `littleWidth`, and `littleHeight` variables. You can also vary the speed of the contractions by changing the `speed` variable.

Practical uses for this technique

Uh, it attracts attention?

How not to be annoying

Don't make your window expand and contract!

(Sorry. Some of these tricks have no reason to exist *except* to be annoying!)

Trick #64: Make a Window Expand When Moused Over

The magic expanding and contracting window is definitely annoying, but how about a manual version of this trick? The way this one works is that when the users moves his or her mouse over the window, the window expands. When the mouse is moved away, it contracts back to its original size.

How to do it

The code for this is actually simpler than that for the previous trick. Just insert the code in Listing 5-18 into the head of your document. (This is pretty much an Internet Explorer–only trick, by the way.)

Listing 5-18: JavaScript code to create a manually expanding window; insert in the head of your document

```
<script language="JavaScript">
<!--

document.onmouseover=expandWindow;
document.onmouseout=contractWindow;

function expandWindow()
{window.resizeTo(800,600);}

function contractWindow()
{window.resizeTo(400,300)}

//-->
</script>
```

You can change the dimensions of both the large window (in the `expandWindow` function) and the small window (in the `contractWindow`) function. The default size of the large window is 800×600 pixels; the default size of the small window is exactly a quarter of that size (400×300).

Practical uses for this technique

One could envision, if one really tried, a window that contained information that would stay relatively hidden (in a smaller window) until needed. Then the user could mouse over the window, expanding it so that the information inside could be read.

It's a stretch, though.

How not to be annoying

I suppose if the small window were really small (think 100×100), then at least it wouldn't get in the way. (And the user would have less chance of accidentally mousing over it and expanding it.)

Trick #65: Slide a Window Off the Screen

This last trick is both a window trick and a link trick, in that clicking a link causes the current browser window to slide off the screen—to be replaced by a new browser window containing the linked-to page. It looks neat but is slow enough to get annoying on continued use.

How to do it

Like several of the previous tricks, this one relies on the JavaScript `moveBy` method. Just insert the code in Listing 5-19 into the head of your HTML document.

Listing 5-19: JavaScript code to slide a window off-screen; insert into the head of your document

```
<script language="JavaScript">
<!--

function windowSlider()
{for (var i = 1; i < 1001; i++)
window.moveBy(1, 0);
window.moveBy(-1000, 0);}

//-->
</script>
```

Now insert the following code around the linked text in the body of your document:

```
<a href="url"; onClick="windowSlider()">link-text</a>
```

This particular script slides the window off the right side of the screen; it's particularly effective with full-screen windows.

Practical uses for this technique

This `moveBy` trick can function as a kind of full-window page transition effect. It certainly catches the user's attention—where's that window going, anyway?

How not to be annoying

The best way to not annoy people with this trick is not to use it—or to use it very sparingly.

The Annoying Summary

In this chapter, you learned about some of the most annoying effects of all—those associated with pop-up windows. Now you know how to create your own annoying pop-ups, and how to make them pop up in different ways, and with different looks. If you use your code correctly, you can even make your pop-ups shake and slide and shimmy, which are pretty annoying effects in and of themselves.

Now quit reading for a while and go make some pop-ups. You know you want to!

✦   ✦   ✦

Crazy Cursors

The onscreen cursor is an ever-present part of everyone's computer experience. Change the cursor and you upset the way things work. And, of course, anytime you fiddle with people's expectations, you start to annoy them.

This chapter shows you how to annoy users by tampering with the shape and behavior of their cursors. These tricks might sound cute, but live with an animated cursor for awhile and you'll see just how irritating it can be.

(Note that because most of these are animation effects that require the placement of multiple images on the screen and that are dependent on some other event, the JavaScript code is sometimes long and somewhat complex. That can't be avoided; make sure you enter the code *exactly* as printed, and pay special attention to spaces and commas and quotation marks and such.)

Trick #66: Change the Shape of the Cursor

You're used to your cursor looking like a little arrow. It always looks like a little arrow. You use your operating system, it looks like a little arrow. You browse the Web, it looks like a little arrow. You do anything, it looks like a little arrow.

Unless it doesn't.

Ever go to a Web site and find that something on that page has changed the shape of your cursor? Maybe it looks like a cross instead of an arrow. Maybe it looks like a little cartoon figure. Whatever it looks like, it doesn't look like a little arrow, and you're cheesed off about it.

This first cursor trick shows you how you can cheese off visitors to your site by changing their cursor without their consent. It's a small thing, but mighty annoying.

How to do it

There are a few different ways to change the shape of visitors' cursors, all of which are mostly specific to Internet Explorer, and mostly specific to Windows.

The easiest way to change a cursor is to use Comet Cursor. Comet Cursor is a Web service that supplies JavaScript code that enables you to pick from hundreds of different types of cursors to force upon visitors to your Web pages. (They also provide software to change the cursor on your own computer, as well as services for *active cursors* — cursors that activate searching, shopping, encyclopedias, and so on.)

The basic Comet Cursor service is free. All you have to do is go to their Web site (`www.cometzone.com`), select a cursor, and then click the Get Cursor Code link to generate the appropriate JavaScript code. You then copy that code into your HTML document, just above the `</body>` off tag. Then, whenever someone visits your Web page, their cursor is replaced by the Comet Cursor you selected. (When they leave your page, their cursor returns to normal.)

The Comet Cursor site will generate the code for you, but it's really quite simple. Listing 6-1 shows the typical code; replace *filename* with the name of the specific cursor at the Comet Cursor site. (If you want to test this code, use bullwinkle3d01 for the *filename* shown in Figure 6-1; it's a fun cursor of Bullwinkle the Moose.)

Figure 6-1: A Bullwinkle cursor from Comet Cursor

Listing 6-1: JavaScript code for a Comet Cursor cursor; insert just above the </body> tag in your document

```
<script language="javascript">
var Loaded=false;
var Flag=false;
</script>

<script
src='http://files.cometsystems.com/javascript/lc2000.js'
language="javascript">
</script>

<script language="javascript">
if(Loaded&&Flag)TheCometCursor('filename',0,0);
</script>
```

Note

There's a bonus annoyance when you use a Comet Cursor. Because the user is downloading the cursor graphic from Comet's Web site, that causes a (slight) additional delay for the entire page to load. (Something to remember whenever you reference a graphic on another site.)

With Internet Explorer 4 or later (and Netscape 6), you can also use JavaScript to call a style sheet that changes the cursor style. In this instance, you're limited to the built-in cursors in your visitors' systems, but it's still a shock to users when the expected arrow is a hand or an hourglass instead.

Listing 6-2 contains the code to insert in your document, just after the <body> tag.

Listing 6-2: **JavaScript code to change the system cursor; insert in the body of your document**

```
<script language="javascript">
<!--
document.body.style.cursor = 'cursor';
//-->
</script>
```

Replace *cursor* with one of the system cursor names shown in Table 6-1.

Table 6-1
System Cursors

Cursor	Name
+	crosshair
🖑	hand
✛	move
I	Text
⧖	Wait
⦾?	Help
↔	e-resize

Continued

Cursor	Name
↗	ne-resize
↖	nw-resize
↕	n-resize
↖	se-resize
↙	sw-resize
↔	w-resize

Table 6-1 *(continued)*

Practical uses for this technique

Forcing a change to users' cursors helps to provide a distinctive look and feel for your site. If you choose wisely, users will start referring to your site as "the one with the Bullwinkle cursor." Or, more likely, "the one with the @#$%! Bullwinkle cursor."

How not to be annoying

If you've used a strong design theme throughout your site and your cursor ties in with that theme, some users might not be too irritated that you've changed their cursors without asking. For example, if your site is all about snow, and you have a snow background on your pages, and use the falling snow special effect (Trick #14, in Chapter 1), users might not mind if you choose a tasteful snowflake cursor to go along with the overall theme.

If, on the other hand, the cursor is big and distracting and doesn't have anything to do with anything, users are sure to be annoyed.

Trick #67: Make the Cursor Arrow Point in Another Direction

If changing the cursor once is irritating, what about changing it whenever your users move the mouse? This next trick changes the direction of the cursor arrow to follow the direction of mouse movement, so that the cursor is always pointing in the direction in which your users are mousing.

How to do it

This bit of JavaScript code uses the same technique detailed in Listing 6-2 but changes the cursor interactively depending on which direction the mouse is moving. If the mouse is moving up, for example, the cursor is changed to n-resize (an arrow pointing up). If the mouse is moving right, the cursor is changed to e-resize (an arrow pointing right). It's all very simple, when you think about it.

All you have to do is add the code in Listing 6-3 into the head of your HTML document.

Listing 6-3: JavaScript code for changing the cursor arrow direction; insert in the head of your document

```
<script language="JavaScript">
<!--

var x, y, xold, yold, xdiff, ydiff;
var point = Array();
point[0] = "n-resize";
point[1]="ne-resize";
point[2]="e-resize";
point[3]="se-resize";
point[4] = "s-resize";
point[5]="sw-resize";
point[6]="w-resize";
point[7]="nw-resize";
document.onmousemove = XYpoint;

function pointArrow(thisWay)
{document.body.style.cursor = point[thisWay];}

function XYpoint(loc) {
x = (document.layers) ? loc.pageX : event.clientX;
y = (document.layers) ? loc.pageY : event.clientY;
xdiff = x - xold;
ydiff = y - yold
if ((xdiff <  2) && (ydiff < -2)) pointArrow(0);
if ((xdiff <  2) && (ydiff >  2)) pointArrow(4);
if ((xdiff >  2) && (ydiff <  2)) pointArrow(2);
if ((xdiff < -2) && (ydiff <  2)) pointArrow(6);
if ((xdiff >  2) && (ydiff >  2)) pointArrow(3);
if ((xdiff >  2) && (ydiff < -2)) pointArrow(1);
if ((xdiff < -2) && (ydiff >  2)) pointArrow(5);
if ((xdiff < -2) && (ydiff < -2)) pointArrow(7);
xold = x;
yold = y;}

//-->
</script>
```

Practical uses for this technique

There's really nothing practical about this one. The arrow keeps changing direction whenever users move the mouse. Interesting? Yes. Moderately annoying? Yes. Practical? Not really.

How not to be annoying

This effect is what it is. You can't make it any less annoying—although you can make it *more* annoying by switching the cursors assigned to each direction of movement. (Move right, point left—*extremely* irritating!)

Trick #68: Add Trailing Stars to the Cursor

Now it's time to get into the really sophisticated cursor effects, the kind that really honk off most users. This first animated effect, shown in Figure 6-2, is that of a group of multicolored stars that swirl around the cursor and follow it as it moves around your page. It's really neat looking (and looks better on a black background than a white one), but like most of these animated effects, it wears thin really fast.

Figure 6-2: A half-dozen or so colored stars follow the cursor around your Web page—colorful and dynamic, but ultimately irritating.

How to do it

This effect uses a whole lot of JavaScript and HTML magic, from layers to captured events to specific onscreen positioning. You probably don't care how it works, however—you just want to get down to it. So get started by inserting the code in Listing 6-4 into the body of your HTML document.

Listing 6-4: **JavaScript code for adding trailing stars to the cursor; insert in the body of your document**

```
<script language="JavaScript">
<!-- Mouse Stars by Kurt Grigg (kurt.grigg@virgin.net) -->
<!--
colors=new
Array('ff0000','00ff00','3366ff','ff00ff','ffa500','ffffff','ff
f000')

amount=colors.length;
ns=(document.layers)?1:0,step=0.2,currStep=0,my=0,mx=0;
if (ns)
{for (i=0; i < amount; i++)
document.write('<layer name="nsstars'+i+'"
bgcolor='+colors[i]+' CLIP="0,0,2,2"></layer>');}
else
{document.write('<div id="ie
style="position:absolute;top:0;left:0;"><div
style="position:relative">');
for (i=0; i < amount; i++)
document.write('<span id="iestars"
style="position:absolute;top:0;left:0;width:2px;height:2px;back
ground:'+colors[i]+';font-size:2px"></span>');
document.write('</div></div>');}
(document.layers)?window.captureEvents(Event.mousemove):0;

function Mouse(evnt)
{my = (document.layers)?evnt.pageY:event.y;
mx = (document.layers)?evnt.pageX:event.x;}

(document.layers)?window.onMouseMove=Mouse:document.onmousemove
=Mouse;

function stars()
{if (!ns)ie.style.top=document.body.scrollTop;
for (i=0; i < amount; i++)
{var
layer=(document.layers)?document.layers["nsstars"+i]:iestars[i]
.style;
layer.top=
my+Math.cos((20*Math.sin(currStep/20))+i*70)*100*(Math.sin(10+c
urrStep/10)+0.2)*Math.cos((currStep + i*25)/10);
layer.left=mx+Math.sin((20*Math.sin(currStep/20))+i*70)*180*(Ma
th.sin(10+currStep/10)+0.2)*Math.cos((currStep + i*25)/10);}
currStep+=step;
setTimeout('stars()',10);}

window.onload=stars;

//-->
</script>
```

To add more stars to the trail, simply add more colors in the `colors=new Array` line.

Practical uses for this technique

Like most of these cursor effects, there really isn't any practical use—other than showing off your "mastery" of JavaScript.

How not to be annoying

To decrease the annoyance factor, reduce the number of trailing stars and make them all the same color. Or, better still, don't use this effect at all.

Trick #69: Make Any Image Follow the Cursor

If a bunch of little stars following the cursor was annoying, what about something larger? With this trick, you can make any graphic trail your cursor across the screen; all you have to do is provide the image file, and the JavaScript code does the rest.

One particular application of this trick, shown in Figure 6-3, is the "trailing cursor" effect. Use an image file of a cursor, and the result is a bunch of shadow cursors trailing behind the main cursor, trying to play catch-up.

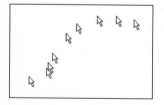

Figure 6-3: Select a graphic of a cursor to create a trailing cursor effect.

How to do it

To make this trick work, enter the code in Listing 6-5 into the body of your document. Replace *filename* with the name and URL of the graphics file you want to follow the cursor. To achieve the trailing cursor effect, use the cursor graphic available for download at my *Building Really Annoying Web Sites* Web site (`www.annoyingwebsites.com`).

Listing 6-5: JavaScript code to make an image follow your cursor; insert in the body of your document

```
<script language="JavaScript1.2">
<!-- Original:  Marcin Wojtowicz (one_spook@hotmail.com) -->
<!--

var trailLength = 8;
var path = "filename";
var isIE = false, isNav = false, range = "all.", style =
".style", i, d = 0;
var topPix = ".pixelTop", leftPix = ".pixelLeft", images,
storage;

if (document.layers)
{isNav = true, range = "layers.", style = "", topPix = ".top",
leftPix = ".left";}
else if (document.all)
{isIE = true;}

function initTrail()
{images = new Array();
for (i = 0; i < parseInt(trailLength); i++)
{images[i] = new Image();
images[i].src = path;}
storage = new Array();
for (i = 0; i < images.length*3; i++)
{storage[i] = 0;}
for (i = 0; i < images.length; i++)
{((isIE) ? document.write('<div id="obj' + i + '"
style="position: absolute; z-Index: 100; height: 0; width:
0"><img src="' + images[i].src + '"></div>') :
document.write('<layer name="obj' + i + '" width="0" height="0"
z-index="100"><img src="' + images[i].src + '"></layer>');}
trail();}

function trail()
{for (i = 0; i < images.length; i++)
{eval("document." + range + "obj" + i + style + topPix + "=" +
storage[d]);
eval("document." + range + "obj" + i + style + leftPix + "=" +
storage[d+1]);
d = d+2;}
for (i = storage.length; i >= 2; i--)
{storage[i] = storage[i-2];}
d = 0;
clearTimeout(timer);
var timer = setTimeout("trail()", 10);}

function processEvent(e)
{if (isIE)
```

Continued

Listing 6-5 *(continued)*

```
{storage[0] = window.event.y+document.body.scrollTop+10;
storage[1] = window.event.x+document.body.scrollLeft+10;}
else
{storage[0] = e.pageY+12;
storage[1] = e.pageX+12;}}
if (isNav)
{document.captureEvents(Event.MOUSEMOVE);}
if (isIE || isNav)
{initTrail();
document.onmousemove = processEvent;}

//-->
</script>
```

The smaller the graphic image, the better this effect works. Really large graphics look extremely dopey — and are particularly annoying.

Practical uses for this technique

Some users claim that trailing cursors help make their pointers more visible on laptop computers and under poor lighting conditions. You could claim to be looking out for these helpless road warriors by outfitting your entire site with trailing cursors. What a good Samaritan you are!

How not to be annoying

The shorter the trail, the less annoying the effect. Change the `trailLength` variable to a lower number (the default is 8) to reduce the length of the trail. (Or, if you're so inclined, *increase* this number to make the effect even more annoying!)

Trick #70: Make a Text Message Follow the Cursor

Why limit yourself to trailing graphics behind your cursor? Why not use a similar technique to trail a text message, instead? (Just think of the advertising possibilities!)

As you can see in Figure 6-4, this trick lets you trail a text message of your choosing behind your cursor. This effect is particularly annoying because one's tendency is to try to read the message — which is nearly impossible to do when the cursor is in motion.

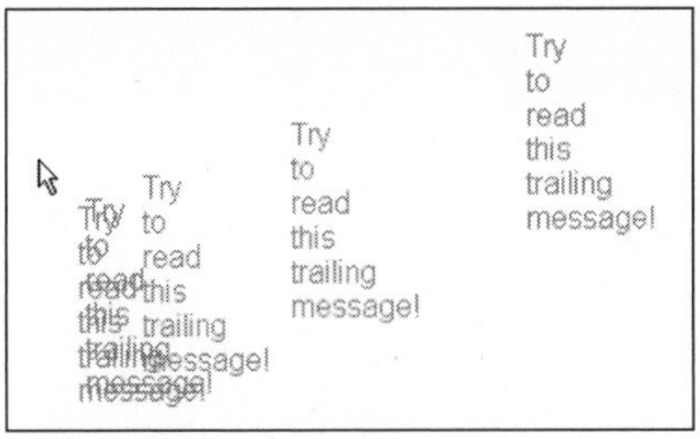

Figure 6-4: An interesting way to get your message across — have it trail the cursor around the screen!

How to do it

To activate this effect, insert the script in Listing 6-6 directly after the `<body>` tag in your HTML document. Replace *message* with your specific message text. (Spaces are allowed.) You can also change the color of the text by inserting a new color value for the `messagecolor` variable.

Listing 6-6: JavaScript code for a trailing text cursor; insert in the body of your document

```
<script language="JavaScript1.2">
<!-- Cursor Trailer II by Kurt Grigg (kurt.grigg@virgin.net) --
>
<!--

var message='message';
var messagecolor='#FF0000'
var dismissafter=0
var
amount=5,ypos=0,xpos=0,Ay=0,Ax=0,By=0,Bx=0,Cy=0,Cx=0,Dy=0,Dx=0,
Ey=0,Ex=0;

if (document.layers)
{for (i = 0; i < amount; i++)
{document.write('<layer name=ns'+i+' top=0 left=0><font
face="Arial" size=3
color='+messagecolor+'>'+message+'</font></layer>')}
window.captureEvents(Event.MOUSEMOVE);
function nsmouse(evnt){xpos = evnt.pageX;ypos =
evnt.pageY;makefollow()}}
else if (document.all)
{document.write("<div id='outer'
style='position:absolute;top:0px;left:0px'>");
```

Continued

Listing 6-6 (continued)

```
document.write("<div id='inner' style='position:relative'>");
for (i = 0; i < amount; i++)
{document.write('<div id="text"'+i+'
style="position:absolute;top:0px;left:0px;font-
family:Arial;font-size:16px;color:'+messagecolor+'">'+message+'
</div>')}
document.write("</div>");
document.write("</div>");
function iemouse(){ypos = document.body.scrollTop +
event.y;xpos = document.body.scrollLeft +
event.x;makefollow()}}

function makefollow()
{if (document.layers)
{document.layers["ns0"].top=ay;document.layers["ns0"].left=ax;
document.layers["ns1"].top=by;document.layers["ns1"].left=bx;
document.layers["ns2"].top=cy;document.layers["ns2"].left=cx;
document.layers["ns3"].top=Dy;document.layers["ns3"].left=Dx;
document.layers["ns4"].top=Ey;document.layers["ns4"].left=Ex;}
else if (document.all)
{outer.all.inner.all[0].style.pixelTop=ay;outer.all.inner.all[0
].style.pixelLeft=ax;
outer.all.inner.all[1].style.pixelTop=by;outer.all.inner.all[1]
.style.pixelLeft=bx;
outer.all.inner.all[2].style.pixelTop=cy;outer.all.inner.all[2]
.style.pixelLeft=cx;
outer.all.inner.all[3].style.pixelTop=Dy;outer.all.inner.all[3]
.style.pixelLeft=Dx;
outer.all.inner.all[4].style.pixelTop=Ey;outer.all.inner.all[4]
.style.pixelLeft=Ex;}}

function move()
{if (dismissafter!=0)
setTimeout("hidetrail()",dismissafter*1000)
if (document.layers){window.onMouseMove = nsmouse}
else if (document.all){window.document.onmousemove = iemouse}
ey = Math.round(Ey+=((ypos+20)-Ey)*2/2);ex =
Math.round(Ex+=((xpos+20)-Ex)*2/2);
dy = Math.round(Dy+=(ey - Dy)*2/4);dx = Math.round(Dx+=(ex -
Dx)*2/4);
cy = Math.round(Cy+=(dy - Cy)*2/6);cx = Math.round(Cx+=(dx -
Cx)*2/6);
by = Math.round(By+=(cy - By)*2/8);bx = Math.round(Bx+=(cx -
Bx)*2/8);
ay = Math.round(Ay+= (by - Ay)*2/10);ax = Math.round(Ax+= (bx -
Ax)*2/10);
makefollow();
jumpstart=setTimeout('move()',10);}

function hidetrail()
{if (document.all)
```

```
{for (i2=0;i2<amount;i2++)
{outer.all.inner.all[i2].style.visibility="hidden"
clearTimeout(jumpstart)}}
else if (document.layers)
{for (i2=0;i2<amount;i2++)
{temp="ns"+i2
document.layers[temp].visibility="hide"
clearTimeout(jumpstart)}}}

window.onload=move;

//-->
</script>
```

Practical uses for this technique

There might be advertising uses for this particular technique. Enter an advertising message ("Eat at Joe's!") and then bombard users with that message whenever they move their mice. They'll hate you for it, but they'll probably remember your message.

How not to be annoying

The shorter the message you trail, the better. Try to limit your message to two to three words, tops — and a single word works best. In addition, the text color can affect the annoyance factor; bright colors, like the red in the default script, are particularly irritating. Consider changing the text color to a light gray or teal.

Trick #71: Add a Roaming Cursor to the Page

This trick is particularly devious — especially if your users are accustomed to various cursor animation effects, such as the "trailing cursor" effect you learned in Trick #69.

In this trick you actually don't do anything to the cursor. Instead, you add an image of a cursor to the top layer of your page and animate it to float around, relatively aimlessly. Less-attentive users will think that it's their cursor that's meandering across the page and start frantically shaking and clicking their mouse. Which, of course, doesn't have any effect on the roaming cursor, which continues its roaming ways.

Ingeniously frustrating!

How to do it

To generate a roaming cursor on your page, insert the code in Listing 6-7 into the body of your HTML document. Replace *filename* with the URL and filename for your cursor graphic. (If you don't have a cursor graphic of your own, feel free to use the one at my *Building Really Annoying Web Sites* Web site (www.annoyingwebsites.com).

> **Listing 6-7: JavaScript code to create a roaming cursor; insert into the body of your document**

```
<script language="JavaScript">
<!-- Roaming Cursor script by Kurt Grigg
(kurt.grigg@virgin.net) -->
<!--

var cursorpath="filename"

if (document.layers)
{document.write("<layer name='PoInTeRs' left=10 top=10><img
src='"+cursorpath+"' width=17 height=22></layer>")}
else if (document.all){document.write("<div id='pOiNtErS'
style='position:absolute;top:10px;left:10px;width:17px;height:2
2px;z-index:50'><img src='"+cursorpath+"' width=17
height=22></div>")}

count=-1;
move=1;

function Curve()
{abc=new Array(0,1,1,1,2,3,4,0,6,-1,-1,-1,-2,-3,-4,0,-6)
for (i=0; i < abc.length; i++)
{var C=Math.round(Math.random()*[i])}
howbend=abc[C];
setTimeout('Curve()',1900);
return howbend;}

ypos=10;
xpos=10;
degree = 60;

function MoveRandom()
{PathBend=degree+=howbend;//ok!
y = 4*Math.sin(PathBend*Math.PI/180);
x = 6*Math.cos(PathBend*Math.PI/180);
if (document.layers){
ypos+=y;
xpos+=x;
document.PoInTeRs.top=ypos+window.pageYOffset;
document.PoInTeRs.left=xpos+window.pageXOffset;}
else if (document.all)
```

```
{ypos+=y;
xpos+=x;
document.all.pOiNtErS.style.top=ypos+document.body.scrollTop;
document.all.pOiNtErS.style.left=xpos+document.body.scrollLeft;
}
T=setTimeout('MoveRandom()',50);}

function edges()
{if (document.layers)
{if (document.PoInTeRs.left >= window.innerWidth-
40+window.pageXOffset)degree=Math.round(Math.random()*45+157.5)
;
if (document.PoInTeRs.top >= window.innerHeight-
30+window.pageYOffset)degree=Math.round(Math.random()*45-112.5)
;
if (document.PoInTeRs.top <= 2+window.pageYOffset) degree =
Math.round(Math.random()*45+67.5);
if (document.PoInTeRs.left <= 2+window.pageXOffset) degree =
Math.round(Math.random()*45-22.5);}
else if (document.all)
{if (document.all.pOiNtErS.style.pixelLeft >=
document.body.offsetWidth-
45+document.body.scrollLeft)degree=Math.round(Math.random()*45+
157.5);
if (document.all.pOiNtErS.style.pixelTop >=
document.body.offsetHeight-
35+document.body.scrollTop)degree=Math.round(Math.random()*45-1
12.5);
if (document.all.pOiNtErS.style.pixelTop <=
2+document.body.scrollTop) degree =
Math.round(Math.random()*45+67.5);
if (document.all.pOiNtErS.style.pixelLeft <=
2+document.body.scrollLeft) degree =
Math.round(Math.random()*45-22.5);}
setTimeout('edges()',100);}

function starteffect()
{Curve();
MoveRandom();// onUnload="opener.gO()"
edges();}

if (document.all||document.layers)
window.onload=starteffect

//-->
</script>
```

As you've no doubt figured out for yourself, you can also use this code to make any picture wander around your page. Just replace *filename* with the URL and filename of the graphic file you want your users to see dancing around in the background.

Practical uses for this technique

This technique isn't really practical at all. You could, I suppose, rig the code so that your company's logo floats around the page, but the annoyance factor probably outweighs any enhanced recognition benefit this might create.

How not to be annoying

If you choose to animate a graphic other than a cursor, keep the graphic small and relatively dull. A big, bright, colorful graphic floating around your page not only is distracting but also obscures a fair amount of your page's content.

Trick #72: Create Fireworks When a Link Is Hovered Over

This final trick is a blend of a cursor trick and a link trick, in that it activates when a user hovers over a link on your page. (In case you're wondering, it uses our old pal, the mouseover event.) Just hover your cursor over a link, and a barrage of colorful fireworks appears. As you can see in Figure 6-5, it's a fun effect — until you apply it to every single link on your page!

Figure 6-5: Just hovering near a link can generate fireworks!

How to do it

To start making fireworks, begin by inserting the code in Listing 6-8 into the head of your HTML document.

Listing 6-8: JavaScript code for mouseover fireworks; insert in the head of your document

```
<script language="JavaScript">
<!--

var debrisnumber=40
var debriscolor=new Array()
debriscolor[0]="FFAAAA"
debriscolor[1]="AA0000"
```

```
debriscolor[2]="770000"
debriscolor[3]="AA4444"
debriscolor[4]="EE4422"
debriscolor[5]="FFFFFF"
var x_debrispos
var y_debrispos
var x,y
var x_random=new Array()
var y_random=new Array()
var max_explsteps=20
var i_explsteps=0
var i_color=0
var pause=10

function checkbrowser()
{i_explsteps=0
x_debrispos=x
y_debrispos=y
for (i=0;i<=debrisnumber;i++)
{x_random[i]=Math.ceil(40*Math.random())-20
y_random[i]=Math.ceil(40*Math.random())-20}
if (document.all)
{for (i=0;i<=debrisnumber;i++)
{var thisspan=eval("document.all.span"+i+".style")
thisspan.visibility="VISIBLE"
thisspan.posLeft=x_debrispos
thisspan.posTop=y_debrispos}
explode_IE()}
if (document.layers)
{for (i=0;i<=debrisnumber;i++)
{var thisspan=eval("document.span"+i)
thisspan.visibility="VISIBLE"
thisspan.left=x_debrispos
thisspan.top=y_debrispos}
explode_NN()}}

function explode_IE()
{if (i_explsteps<=max_explsteps)
{for (i=0;i<=debrisnumber;i++)
{var thisspan=eval("document.all.span"+i+".style")
thisspan.posLeft+=x_random[i]
thisspan.posTop+=y_random[i]}
i_explsteps++
var timer=setTimeout("explode_IE()",pause)}
else
{for (i=0;i<=debrisnumber;i++)
{var thisspan=eval("document.all.span"+i+".style")
thisspan.visibility="hidden"}
clearTimeout(timer)}}

function explode_NN()
{if (i_explsteps<=max_explsteps)
```

Continued

Listing 6-8 *(continued)*

```
{for (i=0;i<=debrisnumber;i++)
{var thisspan=eval("document.span"+i)
thisspan.left+=x_random[i]
thisspan.top+=y_random[i]}
i_explsteps++
var timer=setTimeout("explode_NN()",pause)}
else
{for (i=0;i<=debrisnumber;i++)
{var thisspan=eval("document.span"+i)
thisspan.visibility="hidden"}
clearTimeout(timer)}}

function handlerMM(e)
{x = (document.layers) ? e.pageX :
document.body.scrollLeft+event.clientX
y = (document.layers) ? e.pageY :
document.body.scrollTop+event.clientY}

if (document.layers)
{document.captureEvents(Event.MOUSEMOVE);}
document.onmousemove = handlerMM;

//-->
</script>

<style>
.spanstyle
{
position:absolute;
visibility:hidden;
}
</style>
```

Now insert the code in Listing 6-9 into the body of your document, right after the `<body>` tag.

Listing 6-9: **More JavaScript code for mouseover fireworks; insert in the body of your document**

```
<script language="javascript">
<!--
for (i=0;i<=debrisnumber;i++)
{document.write("<div id='span"+i+"' class='spanstyle'>")
document.write("<table cellpadding=0 cellspacing=0>")
document.write("<tr><td bgcolor="+debriscolor[i_color]+">")
```

```
document.write("<img src='emptypixel236.gif' width=3>")
document.write("</td></tr></table>")
document.write("</div>")
i_color++
if (i_color>=debriscolor.length) {i_color=0}}

//-->
</script>
```

Finally, use the following code to launch fireworks from a specific link; insert around as many links on your page as you want:

```
<a onMouseOver="checkbrowser()" target="_blank" href="url">
>link-text</a>
```

Now your users can sit back and watch the fireworks when they hover over a link! (Lucky them . . .)

Practical uses for this technique

There's no doubt that an explosion will draw attention to a specific link. This is a particularly good effect to use on pages designed for small children, as they get rewarded by finding the links on the page.

How not to be annoying

You can't do much with this one to cut down the annoyance factor, save for using it sparingly. It gets really annoying when your page gets covered in fireworks as your users move from link to link, each generating its own little explosions. Keep the fireworks to a minimum, and they might actually have some impact.

The Annoying Summary

In this chapter, you learned how to use the cursor as an offensive device — to be offensive to your site's visitors, that is. As boring as that little white arrow might be, users will breath a sigh of relief when they leave your pages and their cursors return to normal. All that trailing and swirling and exploding gets really wearing after awhile!

✦   ✦   ✦

Grating Graphics

Even though the Web is at least partially a visual medium, the graphics you find on Web pages are, as often as not, incredibly annoying. Not only do you have the problem of ugly pictures or pictures used where they're really not necessary, but you also have to pay for each picture on a page in terms of download time. Graphics files can be very large (especially in the hands of inexperienced developers); and a large file takes longer to download than a small file. And what could be more irritating than waiting (over a typical 56.6Kbps dial-up connection) for a huge graphic to load, and then realizing that it's an ugly, stupid, totally useless picture of something you don't care about?

Placing big, bad graphics on your Web pages is simple enough for many developers to do inadvertently, but there are many other ways you can use graphics to annoy your users. Read on to learn some of the most maddening tricks, including mouseover-induced graphic fades and the ever-exasperating automated slideshow. Good stuff, here!

Trick #73: Force Users to Load a Really Big Graphic

Even with the emergence of broadband cable and DSL technologies, the vast majority of Internet users still connect via a 56.6Kbps dial-up connection—which typically offers an effective speed somewhere around 40Kbps, give or take a few kilobytes per second. At this speed, it might take several long seconds to download an average graphics file. And those seconds start adding up when a page includes more and bigger pictures.

That's right, there's no easier way to annoy visitors to your site than to force them to sit through interminably long downloads of unnecessarily large graphics files. Just pick a big picture and plop it somewhere on your page, then sit back and watch the irritation build. (You get bonus points if it's a really stupid picture that doesn't need to be displayed anywhere near that big, or at all.)

How to do it

Placing a picture on your Web page is as simple as including the following line of HTML code:

```
<img src="filename">
```

You can supplement this basic code with a variety of formatting attributes, detailed in Table 7-1.

Table 7-1 Attributes for the <img> Tag	
Attribute	**Description and Variables**
width=xxx	Specifies a forced width for the picture; picture will be shrunk or stretched to this precise dimension (in pixels).
height=xxx	Specifies a forced height for the picture; picture will be shrunk or stretched to this precise dimension (in pixels).
border=x	Specifies a border around the picture (in pixels).
alt="text"	Alternate text to be shown if the picture isn't displayed.
lowsrc="filename"	Displays a low-resolution version of the picture while the normal high-resolution picture loads in the background; you must create the low-resolution picture and save it under its own filename. (Netscape-specific.)
align="position"	Aligns the graphic horizontally on the page; choose from left, right, top, texttop, middle, absmiddle, baseline, bottom, absbottom, and center.

For example, if you wanted to insert a picture forced to display at 800×800 pixels, centered on your page with a thin border and a brief line of alternate text, you'd use this code:

```
<img src="filename" width=800 height=800 border=1
alt="alternate-text" align="center">
```

You can increase the annoyance factor by making your picture so big, physically, that it exceeds the borders of the browser. That means making the width 1100 pixels or higher, and the height 900 pixels or more. This can be accomplished by sizing the picture itself to these dimensions from within your graphics editing program, or by using the width and height attributes within the <img> tag. The advantage to making the picture bigger from the start is that you also increase the file size, which increases your page's download time. Using the <img> attributes on a smaller file, on the other hand, stretches the original beyond its optimal resolution, resulting in a pixilated image on your page—yet another way to annoy visitors.

Practical uses for this technique

Obviously, using graphics on a Web page breaks up the tedium of an all-text approach and makes the page more visually interesting to the user. Some things are better shown than said, after all. The problem comes with how large you choose to show it.

Most pictures don't need to fill up an entire browser window — although there are exceptions. If you need to show extremely fine detail, that means using a high-resolution picture displayed fairly large onscreen. Maybe you're showing the effect of makeup on a model's skin, or displaying a satellite map of the mole holes in your backyard. You can't do either one of those things with a 200×200 low-res JPG; in spite of the bandwidth drain, for applications like these you need to go with a large, high-resolution picture.

How not to be annoying

There are many ways to make pictures less annoying, including:

✦ **Don't use 'em.** You probably don't *have* to include pictures on your Web page. Yahoo!, the most trafficked portal on the Web, became popular and remains popular at least in part because of its sleek, fast-loading design — made possible by an almost total lack of graphics.

✦ **Make 'em smaller.** You only *think* that that picture has to be that big. Chances are no one will notice if you size it at 75 percent of the original size — which will speed up the page's loading speed *and* free up more white space on the page.

✦ **Make 'em less detailed.** Most graphics programs enable you to choose among different levels of resolution and color depth. Given that a computer screen is a relatively low-resolution display medium, you probably don't need to choose the highest-resolution settings for your pictures. (See Trick #74 for more on this approach.)

✦ **Thumbnail 'em first.** Instead of forcing users to view every picture at full size and resolution, pop a thumbnail of the picture on your main page and allow users to click on the thumbnail to view the full-size version. (See Trick #75 for more on this approach.)

✦ **Crop 'em tighter.** Maybe you don't need to show the entire picture on your Web page. You may be able to crop less essential parts out of your picture to make the total image — and file size — smaller. (See Trick #76 for more on this approach.)

✦ **Show a low-res version while the high-res version loads.** The `<img>` tag includes a `lowsrc` attribute (Netscape-only, unfortunately) that links to a different picture file and displays that picture while your original picture is still downloading. The thinking behind this attribute is that you're giving users something to look at while the larger, higher-resolution version downloads. To use this attribute, you have to create a low-resolution version of the picture manually (the HTML code doesn't affect the original picture file at all) and then reference it with the following code: `lowsrc="filename"`.

Note You can also use the `lowsrc` attribute to load a totally *different* picture while the main picture loads. You could, for example, load a small and simple "now loading" graphic to display while the bigger picture is eating up valuable bandwidth. (Again, this is a Netscape-only attribute.)

Trick #74: Pick the Least Efficient File Format

Staying on the topic of large graphics files, it helps to know a little bit about all the available graphics file formats. Some formats are less efficient than others, and some formats work better with different types of graphics than others. Choose the right (wrong?) file format and you can force users to spend much more time downloading than is actually necessary.

Table 7-2 lists the most common graphics file formats you can choose from.

Table 7-2 Image File Formats	
File Format	**Description**
BMP	A simple bitmapped graphics format, typically used for Windows desktop backgrounds—but *not* for Web pages. Extremely inefficient with large file sizes, which makes it an extremely annoying choice for Web page graphics. Also, it's not native to the Mac, so your Mac visitors would have to download a QuickTime plug-in just to see the file.
GIF	A popular Web-based graphics format that can include both transparent backgrounds and simple animations. GIF files are relatively efficient, and good for reproducing simple line drawings, illustrations, and cartoon art. (GIF files won't annoy too many people.)
JPG or JPEG	Perhaps the most widely used graphics format on the Web, JPG files are often slightly smaller in size than comparable GIF files and are better at reproducing both black and white and color photographic images. This is the least-annoying format available—although you can still choose various levels of efficiency when creating a JPG file.
PCX	An older, not very efficient graphics format (pronounced "pee-see-ex"), not normally used on Web pages. Use of this format is extremely irritating to most Web users.
PDF	A file type from Adobe (the PDF stands for Portable Document Format) that lets you view pages on your screen exactly as you'd see them on paper. PDF files are typically very large, but reproduce both text and graphics with almost perfect accuracy. If you have a printed document to display online, use the PDF format; it forces users to install the Adobe Acrobat Reader plug-in, which is always annoying.

File Format	Description
PNG	A relatively new graphics format that originally was intended to ultimately replace the GIF format — although that hasn't happened. There's little annoying about this format, as all newer browsers are configured to display these files without the need for additional plug-ins.
TIF	A high-resolution graphics format not widely used on Web pages. TIF files are typically used for printed graphics in magazines and newspapers, create much larger file sizes, and as such are totally unnecessary (and extremely annoying) for Web page use.

Bottom line, if you want to annoy users with an inefficient and nonstandard picture format, go with PCX, BMP, or TIF. All three produce really large files at unnecessarily high resolutions — and may not be viewable by all Web browsers.

How to do it

Not only are different file formats more or less efficient in storing graphics information, you can also create files of varying resolution within the same format. All you have to do is use your graphics editing program, such as Jasc Software's Paint Shop Pro or Adobe Photoshop, to make the appropriate (or inappropriate) choices from the following picture attributes:

✦ **Picture size:** This is the physical size of the picture; as discussed in Trick #73, bigger pictures result in larger files.

✦ **Color depth:** The color depth of an image reflects how many potential colors can be used to reproduce the picture. The more colors, the more realistic the picture — and the larger the file size. For example, 8-bit color reproduces just 256 colors and is acceptable for most Web page viewing. To get 65,336 colors, use 16-bit color; and 24-bit color reproduces 16.7 million colors. While you can typically get by with 8-bit color for most Web pictures, going with 16- or 24-bit color will ensure a more irritating user experience because of the unnecessarily large resulting file size.

✦ **Resolution:** Picture resolution is described in pixels per inch; the more pixels per inch, the higher the resolution, and the more detail that can be seen — and the larger the resulting file size. For most Web use, 72 pixels per inch is sufficient, which means you want to go with 150 or 300 pixels per inch to guarantee the type of resolution overkill that dramatically increases picture download time.

Note

In some graphics programs, you can adjust these three attributes separately; in other programs (especially for specific formats, such as JPG), you adjust an overall "compression" attribute to determine file size and resolution together.

Practical uses for this technique

Why would you ever want to display a picture online at more than 72 pixels per inch and 256 colors? One application would be if you intended for the pictures on your page to be printed on a high-resolution printer. For example, say you created a Web page filled with vacation photos and then directed your friends and family to print those photos for their own use. You'd want those pictures to be configured for optimal printing, *not* for optimal Web page display.

The same holds if you're presenting extremely detailed pictures on your page, pictures that are likely to be displayed and examined on larger, high-resolution monitors. (Think medical photos, or crime scene photos, or something like that.) If visitors need the detail, provide it to them — which you do by increasing color depth and resolution.

How not to be annoying

The plain fact of the matter is that most pictures placed on Web pages do not have to be of super-high resolution. They're not going to be printed (at high resolution, anyway), only displayed on computer monitors that have only moderate resolution (compared with print). There's no point in making the images any more detailed than what can be displayed onscreen.

That said, the ideal resolution for a Web page graphic is 72 pixels per inch. The ideal color depth for illustrations is 8-bit (256 colors), and for photographs 16-bits (65,336 colors).

Your choice of file format depends on what type of graphic you're using:

> ✦ If your graphic is a photograph (either color or black and white), go with the JPG format.
>
> ✦ If your graphic is a line drawing or illustration, go with the GIF format.
>
> ✦ If your graphic (either illustration or photograph) has fine gradations of color, use the JPG format, which is better than GIF in reproducing color blends.
>
> ✦ If your graphic requires several frames of animation, your only choice is an animated GIF file.
>
> ✦ If your graphic has a transparent background (so that it blends in with the colored background of your Web page), your only choice is GIF.

The final consideration is how large to make the image. Keep in mind that many users are still viewing the Web at 640 × 480 resolution — which means that for some visitors, any picture more than 600 or so pixels wide will require horizontal scrolling (which is highly annoying) to see the entire picture. In any case, smaller pictures download faster than larger ones, so size most pictures no larger than 550 × 400.

Trick #75: Never Use Thumbnails

Some conscientious Web developers get around the problem of oversized pictures by displaying thumbnails of their pictures instead of the larger images, as shown in Figure 7-1. (A thumbnail is a smaller version of a larger picture.) For most visitors, viewing the thumbnail is fine; those who want to see the larger, more-detailed picture can click on the thumbnail to display the larger picture (typically on a different page or in a separate window).

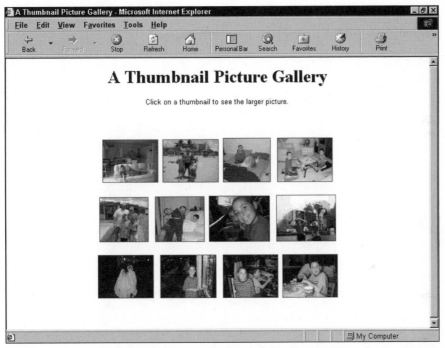

Figure 7-1: How *not* to annoy users — display thumbnails that link to larger pictures.

Note   The topic of thumbnails brings up another way to be annoying — display thumbnails that *don't* link to bigger pictures! Don't you *hate* looking at pictures that are too small to be useful and not having any option of enlarging them for your viewing pleasure? (Well, at least they make for fast page loading. . . .)

If your goal is to annoy visitors to your site, you want to avoid thumbnails like the plague. Thumbnails are convenient and considerate and require very little bandwidth. Even though it's relatively easy to create thumbnail images, you don't want to do it. It's the opposite of annoying; it's much, much more irritating to include multiple large pictures on a single page and force users to download and view everything you have to offer all at once, and at full size.

How to do it

To maximize the annoyance factor, you want to place as many large pictures on your page as possible. Make users wait while picture after picture *after picture* slowly becomes visible on your page—which then has to be scrolled endlessly downward to view them all. Just keep adding <img> tags, one for each picture, one after another. And, while you're at it, try to apply as little design sense as possible; make sure that every picture is sized different, and that they're not ordered or lined up in any way remotely appealing. Just make a page crammed full of different pictures and let the users try to figure them all out.

Practical uses for this technique

What—haven't you ever heard of a photo album?

How not to be annoying

Okay, so maybe you don't want to be *that* annoying. You want to display all your pictures, but in a way that minimizes load time for most users—and presents your pictures in a more organized manner. You want to use thumbnails.

If you're using FrontPage as your HTML editor, it's extremely easy to create thumbnails. All you have to do is insert the full-size picture on your page as you normally would, but then click the Auto Thumbnail button on FrontPage's Pictures toolbar. FrontPage will automatically create a smaller version of your picture, save it under a new filename, and replace the original picture on your page with the new thumbnail. The thumbnail will automatically be linked to the larger original file; when users click on the thumbnail, the original picture will be displayed on a new page.

You can also create your own thumbnails and insert them manually into your HTML documents. Start by using your graphics editing program to create a smaller version of your file; save this smaller picture under a different filename. Then upload both files (the big one and the little one) to your Web server and insert the following code in your document where you want to display the thumbnail:

```
<a href="large-image"><img src="small-image" width=100
height=75 border=x></a>
```

Naturally, replace *large-image* with the filename and URL of the original picture; replace *small-image* with the filename and URL of the smaller thumbnail version.

Trick #76: Don't Crop Dead Space from Your Pictures

Most computer users aren't professional photographers or designers. And even pros make mistakes. So the photos you take might not be framed in the most appealing or efficient manner. In other words, you may have a lot of off-center images with a lot of dead space at the top or around the edges.

You get rid of this dead space (and fix the alignment of the central image) by cropping the edges of the picture. Cropping not only makes better-looking pictures, it also reduces the overall file size by getting rid of the unnecessary bits around the edges. Thinking backward from the result, you can see that *not* cropping your photos can result in amateurish-looking pictures for your Web page — as well as pictures that are unnecessarily large and unnecessarily slow to download.

How to do it

Not cropping a picture is easy — just insert it onto your page exactly as is, without having run it through a graphics editing program first.

Practical uses for this technique

An uncropped, unprocessed picture can have a certain innocent charm, as if it had been taken by a six-year-old with a cheap camera. If you're going for that effect, all power to you.

How not to be annoying

If, on the other hand, you want a more professional, less annoying look, then use a program like Adobe Photoshop or Paint Shop Pro (or even one of the cheap photo editing programs that come with most digital cameras) to crop the dead space out of your photos before you put them online. Figures 7-2 and 7-3 give you a before-and-after look of how cropping can both improve the appearance of a photo and dramatically reduce the image size (and resulting file size).

Note When you're done cropping, feel free to use your software's other image-enhancement features to improve brightness and contrast, and to remove any "red eye" from people in the picture.

Figure 7-2: A typical photograph before cropping . . .

Figure 7-3: . . . and the same photo after cropping; note how your eye is better drawn to the main part of the image, and how the image itself is physically smaller.

Trick #77: Make Pictures Switch When They're Hovered Over

Bad sizing and cropping are easy ways to annoy users with your graphics; you can also employ a handful of graphics-oriented tricks to irritate visitors to your site.

This particular trick is often thought of as a feature by apparently well-intentioned Web page designers. The way it works is that whenever users hover their cursor over an image, that image changes. This may not be the most annoying trick in the book, but it can really get on users' nerves if the two pictures are significantly different.

How to do it

You implement the old picture-change trick by using the now-familiar mouseover JavaScript event. The script itself is fairly simple (although it's pretty much Internet Explorer–specific); just insert the code in Listing 7-1 in the body of your document where you want the picture to appear.

Listing 7-1: JavaScript code for a mouseover picture change; insert in the body of your document

```
<script language="JavaScript">
<!--

function change(picture)
{document.graphic.src = picture}

//-->
</script>

<img src="image1" onMouseOver="change('image2')"
onMouseOut="change('image1')" name="graphic">
```

Naturally, *image1* should be the URL and filename for the image that appears pre-mouseover, while *image2* should be the URL and filename for the image that appears when the first picture is hovered over. Note that you have to insert the first filename *twice* in the <img> tag for this trick to work.

Practical uses for this technique

This technique is actually used a lot on the Web. You see it quite often applied to buttons and other navigational controls; what appears to be a standard button starts to glow or change color when hovered over. That change-on-hovering is actually a second image, scripted to appear during the mouseover event.

You can also employ this trick in some fun ways. For example, if you're presenting some form of game on your page, you can hide the answer to a question within the second image; users can uncover the answer when mousing over the original picture.

How not to be annoying

This effect is most annoying when (1) the two pictures are really big; (2) the two pictures are wildly different in color and brightness; (3) the two pictures are different in size; and (4) the two pictures are so different in subject matter that they don't have anything to do with each other. So, to be less annoying, go with two pictures that are as similar as possible (while still being different—or what's the point?) and that don't fill up the entire page.

Trick #78: Make a Picture Fade In and Out

This next trick takes the old picture-changing trick to a totally different level. What happens here is that your users are presented with a blank spot on your page; when they hover the cursor over this blank spot, the underlying picture slowly fades into view—and fades back out again when they remove the cursor.

It's a neat little trick, and particularly irritating when visitors have to wait a long time to see the picture that should have been visible in the first place.

How to do it

As with most animated effects, the script for this particular trick is a tad lengthy. (It's also Internet Explorer–specific and probably won't work on a Mac.) Take care to get all the syntax right, and insert the code in Listing 7-2 into the body of your document.

Listing 7-2: JavaScript code for a fading picture; insert in the body of your document

```
<script language="JavaScript1.2">
<!--

var startOpacity = 0;
var endOpacity =100;
var currentOpacity = startOpacity;
var fadeSpeed = 2;
var si;
var cleared = true;

function fadeImage(what,doshow)
{if (document.all)
{cleared = false;
(doshow) ? currentOpacity+=fadeSpeed : currentOpacity-
=fadeSpeed;
eval(what+".filters.alpha.opacity="+currentOpacity);
if (currentOpacity <= startOpacity || currentOpacity >=
endOpacity)
{clearInterval(si);
cleared = true;}}
if (document.layers) clearInterval(si);}
```

```
function startFade()
{if (!cleared) clearInterval(si);}

//-->
</script>

<img name="picture1" src="filename" border=0
style="filter:alpha(opacity=0)"
onMouseover="startFade();si=setInterval('fadeImage(\'picture1\'
,true)',10);"
onMouseout="startFade();si=setInterval('fadeImage(\'picture1\',
false)',10);">
```

Replace *filename* with the URL and name of the picture file you want to appear. You can control how fast the image fades in by changing the value of the `fadeSpeed` variable; the higher the number, the faster the change. You can also change the beginning and end opacities by changing the `startOpacity` and `endOpacity` variables; if you do this, make sure that you change the `opacity` value in the `style` attribute (near the end of the code, in the `<img>` tag) to the same value as you set for `startOpacity`.

Practical uses for this technique

As with Trick #77, you can use this technique to reveal hidden information on your page. (Great for mystery or secret agent fans!)

How not to be annoying

This effect is slightly less annoying if you speed up the fade in. In addition, starting with an opacity greater than 0 (20 is good) enables visitors to see a little bit of what's there while they're waiting for the entire effect to complete.

Trick #79: Force Users to Watch an Automated Slideshow

As I hope you've learned by now, one sure-fire way to annoy people is to force them to sit through something they don't want to sit through. When it comes to graphics, the most popular forced-viewing event is the automated slideshow, where users are forced to watch a succession of pictures display on your page, one after another, over and over and over. It's the equivalent of making your neighbors look at your holiday photographs on an old slide projector—maddeningly, mind-numbingly boring!

How to do it

Creating your own automated onscreen slideshow is relatively easy. Start by insert-ing the code in Listing 7-3 into the head of your HTML document. Replace *filename1, filename2*, and so on with the URLs and filenames of the pictures you want to include in your show. You can include as many pictures as you want; just continue the pattern, adding more lines into the array.

(You can also change the speed of the slideshow by specifying a new value for the speed variable; bigger numbers result in a slower show, while smaller numbers make the slides fly by faster.)

Listing 7-3: JavaScript code for an automated slideshow; insert in the head of your document

```
<script language="JavaScript">
<!--

var speed = 4000
var slide = new Array()

slide[0] = 'filename1'
slide[1] = 'filename2'
slide[2] = 'filename3'
slide[3] = 'filename4'
slide[4] = 'filename5'
slide[5] = 'filename6'

var t
var j = 0
var p = slide.length
var loadPics = new Array()

for (i = 0; i < p; i++)
{loadPics[i] = new Image()
loadPics[i].src = slide[i]}

function startShow()
{document.images.SlideShow.src = loadPics[j].src
j = j + 1
if (j > (p-1)) j=0
t = setTimeout('startShow()', speed)}

//-->
</script>
```

You load this program into your visitors' browsers by adding the `onLoad` event into the `<body>` tag of your document, like this:

```
<body onLoad="startShow()">
```

Finally, you position the slideshow on the page by inserting the code in Listing 7-4 in the body of your document, where you want the slideshow images to appear.

Listing 7-4: HTML code to display the slideshow pictures; place in the body of your document

```
<center>
<table border="1" cellpadding="1" cellspacing="0">
<tr>
<td height=250 width=250>
<img src="filename" name='SlideShow' width=250 height=250
border=0></td>
</tr>
</table>
</center>
```

The size of the slideshow image is determined by the `width` and `height` attributes in the `<img>` tag. Set these to the same size as the first image in your slideshow (*filename1*). Also note that you must enter the URL and filename for that first image a second time—first in the `slide[0]` variable in Listing 7-3, and again in this listing's `<img>` tag. You have to use the same filename in both places, or the code won't work.

Practical uses for this technique

A slideshow is an acceptable way to display multiple images within a single physical space. In terms of screen space, a slideshow takes up much less real estate than row after row of multiple pictures or thumbnails. In that regard, a slideshow is a good thing—*if* you have multiple images to present to your visitors.

How not to be annoying

The annoying thing about this particular slideshow is that it's totally automated—there's no way for users to stop it, or to advance manually to the next slide, or to back up to the previous slide. It goes at its own pace, in its own order, whether the viewer likes it or not.

You can make a slideshow less annoying by giving viewers some control over the show. That means adding transport controls, typically in the form of stop, pause, next, and previous buttons. The script to do this is much more complex than for an automated show, and more than I can present here. If you're serious about giving viewers this level of control (which means that they can stop your show, if they want!), go to www.annoyingwebsites.com for links to more full-featured slideshow scripts.

Trick #80: Make a Graphic Wander Around the Screen

Actually, you've seen this one before, in Trick #71 (Chapter 6). In that trick, you created a cursor that wandered around the screen, with the goal of totally confusing users. (Which cursor is the real one? Why is that one moving? What do I do now?) Well, you can use the same code to make *any* graphic meander around your Web page. The effect — depending on what image you choose — can range from mildly amusing to emphatically exasperating.

How to do it

Go back to the code in Listing 6-7 (Trick #71). Replace *filename* (in the cursorpath variable) with the URL and filename for the graphic file you want to animate. Use the rest of the code as is. (And note that this trick — like many of the really cool tricks — works only with Internet Explorer browsers in Windows.)

Here's an annoying tip: The larger the image you animate, the more annoying the effect. Big images floating around the page tend to obscure the text and graphics underneath, which makes it difficult to read and use your page — which makes users *really* annoyed!

Practical uses for this technique

There's not a whole lot practical about this one. A wandering company logo might be viewed as blimp-like advertising, but it ends up being more annoying than effective. Perhaps animating a cartoon character on a Web page for children might be useful, but even kids can get annoyed. (Just wait until a youngster tries to click on the moving image — and nothing happens!)

How not to be annoying

You can reduce the interference caused by this effect by keeping the animated graphic small and relatively dull. A big, bright, colorful graphic floating around your page is not only distracting, but it also obscures a fair amount of your page's content.

Trick #81: Place a Nonscrolling Watermark on the Page

The final trick in this chapter is another one in high demand: the nonscrolling watermark.

You've probably encountered watermarks before. A watermark is like one of those network logo bugs (so-called) you see in the corner of television broadcasts; a Web page watermark, like the one in Figure 7-4, is an ever-present graphic, always in the corner of the screen, even when users scroll down the page.

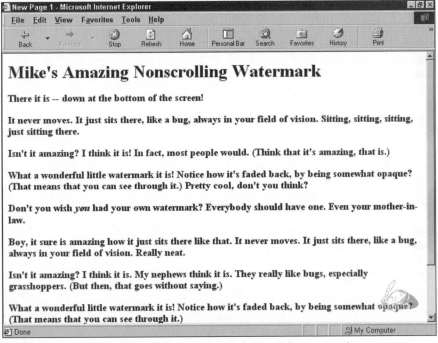

Figure 7-4: Add an opaque watermark to the lower right corner of your page.

It's this refusal to scroll that makes the watermark so effective — and so annoying. Visitors just can't get rid of the sucker, no matter what they do!

How to do it

This script takes a graphic that you specify, makes it somewhat opaque, sticks it in the lower right corner of your page, and forces it not to scroll. Just copy the code in Listing 7-5 into the body of your HTML document.

```
<div class="staticGraphic" ID="staticGraphic"
style="position:absolute;
top:1;
visibility:hide;
filter:alpha(opacity=40);
" zIndex="1000"
align="right">
<img src="filename" border="0">
</div>

<script language="Javascript1.2">
<!--

var graphicW = 40;
var graphicH = 40;
var cornerLeft = 0;
var cornerUp = 0;

var watermarkH = 0;
var watermarkW = 0;
var watermarkX = 0;
var watermarkY = 0;
var left = graphicW + cornerLeft + 15;
var up = graphicH + cornerUp + 15;

if(navigator.appName == "Netscape")
{var watermark = document.staticGraphic;}

if (navigator.appVersion.indexOf("MSIE") != -1)
{var watermark = document.all.staticGraphic;}

function staticImage()
{if(navigator.appName == "Netscape")
{watermarkH = window.innerHeight
watermarkW = window.innerWidth
watermarkX = window.pageXOffset
watermarkY = window.pageYOffset
watermark.visibility = "hide"
watermark.top = (watermarkH+watermarkY-up)
watermark.left = (watermarkW+watermarkX-left)
watermark.visibility= "show"}
if (navigator.appVersion.indexOf("MSIE") != -1)
{if (navigator.appVersion.indexOf("Mac") == -1)
{watermark.style.display = "none";
watermarkH = document.body.clientHeight;
watermarkW = document.body.clientWidth;
watermarkX = document.body.scrollLeft;
watermarkY = document.body.scrollTop;
watermark.style.top = (watermarkH+watermarkY-up);
```

```
watermark.style.left =(watermarkW+watermarkX-left);
watermark.style.display = "";}}}

setInterval("staticImage()",100);

//-->
</script>
```

Replace *filename* with the URL and filename of the image that you want water-marked. You can also include text as a watermark by inserting that text between the `<div>` and `</div>` tags; you can even go text-only (no graphic) by deleting the entire `<img>` tag.

You may need to adjust a few variables to make this script work on your page. The variables `graphicW` and `graphicH` should be set to the actual width and height of the image, text, or whatever you have in the watermark. You can tweak where the watermark appears by adjusting the variables `cornerLeft` (the position left of the vertical scrollbars) and `cornerUp` (the position up from the bottom scrollbars).

Practical uses for this technique

Just like a bug on a television program helps to brand the network, a watermark on your Web page can brand your site. Use your company's logo as the watermark, and your visitors will always know where they're at.

How not to be annoying

The smaller the watermark, the less annoying it will be. You can also change the opacity of the watermark by changing the value of the `filter:alpha(opacity=40)` attribute within the `<div>` tag; a lower number results in more see-through, which is less annoying.

The Annoying Summary

Graphics can be really annoying. They're big, they take up a lot of bandwidth, and they can be made to appear and disappear (and even move around) in really both-ersome ways. For all those reasons, graphics should be a key part of your annoying Web site arsenal. And we haven't even discussed what kinds of images are the most irritating! (I've had some visitors to my site claim that the most annoying page was the one with my personal photo on it — can't say that I'd argue!)

✦　　✦　　✦

Maddening Music and Senseless Streaming

✦ ✦ ✦ ✦

Annoying Things in This Chapter

Force users to listen to music before the page loads

Play a random MIDI file

Play it loud

Pick the least efficient audio format

Add a self-playing movie to your page

Send high-bandwidth media to low-bandwidth users

✦ ✦ ✦ ✦

T he word "multimedia" is often overused. In the pre-PC era, it referred to a type of live presentation that used multiple slide show projectors and maybe a film clip or two. On the personal computer, multimedia has come to signify anything that combines sound and moving pictures. That last definition carries over onto the Web, where multimedia Web pages "enhance" the standard text and pictures with audio and/or video clips.

The interesting thing about multimedia on the Web is how much developers love it (and bank entire business plans on its adoption), compared with how much users hate it. Most users equate browsing the Web with reading a newspaper or magazine, and newspapers and magazines seldom blare music at you or play a movie whenever you turn a page. Adding insult to aversion is the fact that sound and movie files are typically very large, eating up lots of bandwidth and taking forever to download — especially on a dial-up connection. So users are forced to sit through long downloads in order to be subjected to sights and sounds that they don't want to see or hear.

It's a perfect setup for an annoying situation.

Trick #82: Force Users to Listen to Music Before the Page Loads

This one always gets me. I click or jump to a new Web page, and then the page—and my entire computer system—just seems to hang there for several long seconds. By this time, however, I kind of expect what comes next, which is a loud blast of music, a synthesized song being thrust upon me without choice. No doubt the proprietor of that Web page thought the song was nice or cute or added personality to the site (whatever that is); but I couldn't care less about personality, I just want to turn off the blasted music because (1) I didn't ask to hear it, (2) it's interrupting the quiet of my current Internet session, and (3) *I hate that particular song!*

The reason you stumble across so many music-enabled Web sites is that it's really easy to add music to a Web page—too easy.

How to do it

Most Web page background music is in the MIDI format. (See Trick #85 for a more detailed discussion of different audio formats.) MIDI files will play through just about any modern Web browser and can be set to play automatically when your Web page loads, or when a link is clicked.

The most annoying effect, of course, is the file that plays automatically when a page is loaded—and then keeps playing, over and over and over and over, until you press the Stop button on your browser. That is, the music plays in a continuous loop, and there are no transport controls to stop, rewind, or fast-forward the music.

The only complicating factor in adding music to your page is that older versions of Internet Explorer did not recognize the `<embed>` tag, which is used to embed audio and video files in HTML documents. Instead, IE used the `<bgsound>` tag. However, newer versions of IE now recognize `<embed>`, so you can use a single tag—or put together a piece of code, such as the one in Listing 8-1, to make your audio background compatible with all versions of both browsers. Insert this code just after the `<body>` tag in your HTML document, so that the entire audio file has to download before any other elements of your page are displayed.

Listing 8-1: **HTML code to automatically play an audio file when your page is loaded; insert in the body of your document**

```
<embed src="filename" autostart=true loop=true hidden=true>
<noembed>
<bgsound src="filename" loop=infinite>
</noembed>
```

Obviously, you replace *filename* (in both places) with the URL and filename of the audio file you want to play. You can use this code to play MIDI, WAV, MP3, AIFF, AU, and other audio file formats.

Note If you don't care about backward compatibility, you can use just the `<embed>` tag and skip the other three lines of code.

Practical uses for this technique

There are many possibly practical uses for autoplaying sound files. You may want to, for example, record a personal voice greeting to your visitors (in a WAV file) that plays automatically when a visitor hits your home page. You may also have a site *about* music or musicians where background music is more of a necessity than a nicety. (If you have a page dedicated to Faith Hill, it may not be out of line to play a MIDI version of "Breathe" in the background.) Also possible is a site where background sound effects make sense, like a page about NASCAR racing where you play a WAV file of roaring motors and squealing tires.

Then again, maybe you just like to use music to set a mood. Just remember that while you might like the song you pick to play in the background, visitors to your site might not. They also may be visiting your site from work (where listening to music would be inappropriate) or late at night (when your music might wake up everybody else in the house).

Looking for songs to play in the background? Several large MIDI archives on the Web let you download MIDI files for free. The best of these sites include:

✦ Classical MIDI Archives (`www.classicalarchives.com/midi.html`)

✦ Laura's MIDI Heaven (`www.laurasmidiheaven.com`)

✦ MIDI Explorer Search Engine (`www.musicrobot.com`)

✦ MIDI Farm (`www.midifarm.com`)

✦ MIDI Town (`krebs.home.texas.net`)

How not to be annoying

Forcing a user to listen to your favorite song is not only annoying, it's rude. (Extra points!) More polite Web site developers will give users a choice as to whether or not to listen to the music — and not play the music continuously.

The last option is fairly easy. To make the song play just once, change the `loop=true` variable (in the `<embed>` tag) to `loop=false`, and the `loop=infinite` variable (in the `<bgsound>` tag) to `loop=1`.

To give the user a choice of playing or not playing the audio file, don't use the `<embed>` and `<bgsound>` tags. Instead, use the standard `<a href>` tag around a link, like this:

```
<a href="filename">Click here to play background music</a>
```

Replace *filename* with the URL and filename of the audio file.

Finally, if you want to give visitors complete control over audio playback, you can display an embedded media player on your page, such as the one shown in Figure 8-1. The media player (which uses the default media player specified for each user's Web browser) enables users to pause, stop, fast forward, or reverse through your sound file.

Figure 8-1: Let users control audio playback by displaying a media player on your Web page.

Inserting a media player is actually fairly easy to do. Use the code in Listing 8-1, but change the `hidden` attribute (in the `<embed>` tag) from `true` to `false`. Because only the `<embed>` tag supports the media player option, this will display a media player in all versions of Netscape and later versions of Internet Explorer — but *not* in older versions of IE.

Trick #83: Play a Random MIDI File

If you just can't decide which background song to annoy your users with, then assemble a multiple-song playlist and have the songs play randomly whenever visitors access your page.

How to do it

All you have to do is load the code in Listing 8-2 into the body of your HTML document and then fill in a few blanks. In particular, replace *filename1*, *filename2*, and so on with the URLs and filenames of your MIDI files, and the *x* value for the numFiles variable with the number of files in your array. (In this example, there are four MIDI files listed, so you should set numFiles=4.)

You can also add more files to the array (just keep increasing the midiFile number by one for each new file) or even go with a smaller list (delete the extra lines).

Listing 8-2: JavaScript code for a random MIDI playlist; insert in the body of your document

```
<script language="JavaScript">
<!--

var numFiles=x

function Array(number)
{name.length=number
for(var j=1;j<=number;j++)
{name[j]=null}
return name}

function randomMidi()
{var midiFile = new Array(numFiles)

midiFile[1]="filename1"
midiFile[2]="filename2"
midiFile[3]="filename3"
midiFile[4]="filename4"

var numMidi = (Math.random() * numFiles)
numMidi = Math.round(numMidi)
if (navigator.appName=='Microsoft Internet Explorer')
{document.write("<bgsound src="+midiFile[numMidi]+"
loop=infinite>")}
else
```

Continued

Listing 8-2 *(continued)*

```
{document.write("<embed src="+midiFile[numMidi]+" loop=true
hidden=true autostart=true>")}}

window.onLoad=randomMidi()

//-->
</script>
```

Each time someone visits or reloads your page, a different MIDI file will play.

Practical uses for this technique

If you *have* to play background music, and you *must* select from a group of songs, then this trick is the only way to go. If nothing else, users won't get bored with the music if it's different each time they visit!

How not to be annoying

As with Trick #83, you can reduce the irritation by turning off the looping.

Trick #84: Play It Loud

Before we leave the MIDI playlist tricks, there's one last thing. The louder the playback, the more annoying it is. So let's figure out a way to turn up the volume—no matter what level the user has it set at.

How to do it

The `<embed>` tag has a little-known attribute called `volume`. The value of this attribute is expressed as a percent. So if you want to set the volume for your audio playback at 100 percent, use this code:

```
<embed src="filename" autostart=true loop=true hidden=true
volume=100>
```

Practical uses for this technique

If you want to get someone's attention, YOU HAVE TO BE LOUD!

How not to be annoying

Simple. Define a lower volume level for the `volume` attribute — or don't define this attribute at all (in which case your music will play at the user's current volume settings).

Trick #85: Pick the Least Efficient File Format

You can use several different types of audio files on your Web page, although not all are suited for all purposes. Picking the wrong format for the wrong purpose will use unnecessary bandwidth and substantially increase download times — thus increasing the user's annoyance with your page.

Table 8-1 lists the most common audio file formats available on the Web.

Table 8-1 Audio File Formats	
File Format	*Description*
AIFF	File format for Macintosh system sounds, similar to Windows' WAV format; not widely used on the Web, and not always playable on systems running Microsoft Windows. Annoying, but not in a particularly useful way.
AU	A file format (abbreviation for "audio") that originated on the Sun and NeXT computer systems. Not widely used today, and too obscure to be practically annoying.
MID	The MIDI (Musical Instrument Digital Interface) format, an extremely efficient format used to reproduce instrumental music. The most popular format for Web page background music — a particularly annoying use of a format originally designed with the professional musician in mind.
MP3	A widely adopted format that uses data compression to produce high-quality audio in relatively small files; typically requires a separate plug-in or program for playback. MP3 is too widespread and too efficient to be truly annoying.
RA	Developed by Real Networks, a format (abbreviation for RealAudio) designed for real-time streaming audio feeds. Particularly annoying on low-bandwidth connections.
WAV	A widely used file format capable of high-quality sound reproduction, but with correspondingly large file sizes. Using WAV instead of MIDI or MP3 is particularly annoying.
WMA	WMA (Windows Media Audio) is a relatively new file format from Microsoft, promoted as an MP3 alternative with similar audio quality at half the file size. This efficiency makes it less annoying than other formats, although not all browsers (re: Netscape) support the format without the installation of a plug-in.

If you're after the least efficient, largest-sized audio files, you can't go wrong with the WAV format. You can record WAV files at much higher fidelity than the typical computer is capable of reproducing, thus wasting tremendous amounts of bandwidth on data bits that will never be heard.

How to do it

Not only are different file formats more or less efficient in storing audio information, you can also create files of varying fidelity within the same format. This is particularly true of the MP3 format, which lets you vary the bit rate when you're making recordings.

The bit rate is a function of the sampling rate used to record the music, the length of each sample (measured in bits), and the number of channels recorded (for stereo, that's two). The higher the bit rate, the more accurate the sound reproduction—and the larger the file size. When you reduce the bit rate to reduce the size of the resulting files, you quite audibly sacrifice sound quality.

Here's a brief example. Compact discs sample music at a 44.1kHz rate (44,100 times per second), and each sample is 16 bits long. When you multiply the sampling rate by the sample size and the number of channels (two), you end up with a bit rate of 1,400Kbps.

This bit rate is far in excess of what is typical with MP3 files. The most popular bit rate for MP3 files is 128Kbps, which creates a file one-tenth the size of a CD-quality file—but delivers audio quality no better than that of FM radio. Cut the bit rate down to 96Kbps and the audio starts to drop the high end and the sound becomes quite compressed. Go all the way down to the format's 56Kbps bottom limit and it's like listening to a transistor radio in a trash can—quite irritating to any audiophiles visiting your site.

Note   If you need MP3 encoding software, you can't go wrong with MusicMatch Jukebox (www.musicmatch.com). To search for MP3 files on the Web, check out MP3.com (www.mp3.com) and Lycos MP3 Search (music.lycos.com).

Practical uses for this technique

As you saw in Table 8-1, different file types are optimized for different uses. If all you need is background music for your page, use the MIDI format. If you need to reproduce a sound effect or an exact reproduction of a sound, use the WAV format. If you want to play back prerecorded music, use an MP3 file—and fiddle with the bit rate to offer the best possible sound at the smallest possible file size.

How not to be annoying

Playing music over the Web is a constant compromise between file size and fidelity. You can make the music sound better, but doing so creates larger files that take longer to download. You can decrease the file size and download time, but that makes the music less listenable.

When you're recording an MP3 file, you have to take into account where the music will be listened to (and over what type of equipment), as well as the listener's most-likely connection speed. Because most Web music will be listened to on relatively low-fi personal computer systems, which typically connect to the Internet at 56.6Kbps or less, something in the 96Kbps–128Kbps range is probably a good choice. If you think your visitors will be college students with better speakers and faster network connections, then you might want to increase the bit rate to 192Kbps or more. Still, for most applications, 128Kbps is a good choice.

Trick #86: Add a Self-Playing Movie to Your Page

Just as you can have a sound play automatically when a user visits your page, you can also insert a self-playing movie into your page, as shown in Figure 8-2. Not only are movie files *much* larger and slower to download than audio files (we're talking megabytes here), they also take up valuable space on your page—and can contain extremely offensive content, if that's your goal.

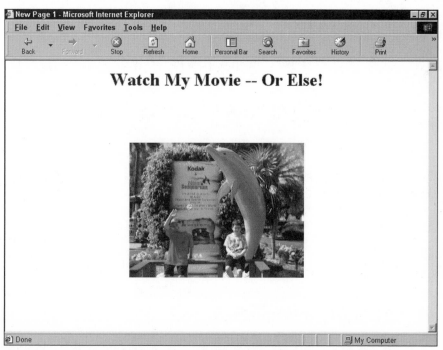

Figure 8-2: Insert a self-playing movie right in the middle of your Web page.

How to do it

To embed a self-playing movie in your page, use the same `<embed>` tag you used for self-playing audio files, but with slightly different attributes. This tag works with MOV, MPEG, AVI, VIVO, and other video file formats.

```
<embed src="filename" autostart=true loop=true
controller=false>
```

By default, the movie window opens at the same dimensions as the original movie file. You can, however, force a specific window size by adding the `width=xxx` and `height=xxx` attributes within the `<embed>` tag.

Practical uses for this technique

There are many reasons why you might want to include a self-playing movie on your Web page. Perhaps you have a new product to introduce and want to subject visitors to a mandatory demonstration. Perhaps you have an animated logo (like a rotating globe) that you want to display in all its active glory. Or maybe you just want to show something fun before the main event, kind of like a cartoon before a feature film.

How not to be annoying

There are several ways to make this type of self-playing movie less annoying. First, by changing the `loop=true` attribute to `loop=1`, you can run the movie only once, instead of over and over. Second, you can add transport functions (so the user can pause, fast-forward, and rewind the movie) by changing the `controller=false` attribute to `controller=true`.

Finally, you can eliminate the autoplay effect by having the movie start with the click of a link. Use this code:

```
<a href="filename">link-text</a>
```

Replace *filename* with the URL and filename of the movie file, and *link-text* with the text for your link (such as "Click here to play movie").

If your movie file is actually a simple animation, you may want to consider using an animated GIF or Flash file — both of which create smaller-sized files — instead of a full-blown movie file. For more information about these animation techniques, turn to Chapter 9, "Aggravating Animations and Purposeless Plug-ins."

Trick #87: Send High-Bandwidth Media to Low-Bandwidth Users

Users connecting to the Internet via a 56.6Kbps (or lower) dial-up connection are seldom thrilled to find Web pages with heavy audio and video content; sound and movie files are just too large to download within a reasonable period of time unless you have some sort of broadband connection. When you encounter a big movie file, for example, you're forced to wait until the entire thing is downloaded (which can take many minutes) before you can begin to view the movie.

One solution to this problem is to stream the delivery of a sound or movie file. With streaming media, playback can start before the entire file is downloaded, thus letting users see and hear what's on the page much quicker than before.

You'd think, then, that streaming media would be a way to *reduce* users' annoyance with multimedia-heavy Web pages — and you'd be partially right. Because streaming media reduces the wait time before a song or movie starts, users' frustration with the site in question is definitely reduced.

However, streaming media is a far from perfect solution to the problem of forcing a big load down a small pipe. (The best solution, of course, is to get a bigger pipe.) First, almost all streaming media formats effect some type of compromise between download speed and playback quality, typically by compressing the content to an even greater extent than it would be otherwise. Second, streaming media is dependent on a relatively clear pipe; if your Internet connection is spotty or overly slow, or if you attempt other online activities while the streaming is going on (like downloading pictures or sending e-mail), the stream itself can get interrupted. Finally, if the stream isn't fast enough, your playback can outpace the download stream, effectively getting ahead of what's available to play and resulting in stuttering or stopped playback.

The most popular streaming technology is Real Networks' RealMedia. RealMedia is versatile enough to stream content at different rates depending on the available bandwidth — which is where you can manually affect the user's annoyance factor. If you choose to stream content at a higher rate than the user can absorb, you'll virtually guarantee the type of jerky, start-and-stop playback that users find most irritating.

> **Note** The audio-only version of RealMedia is called RealAudio — which is what I use for the balance of this technique.

How to do it

Early versions of RealAudio required a special RealAudio server for you to put streaming media on your Web page. Beginning with version 3.0, however, you can use RealAudio on any Web page, without investing in the expensive backend server software.

You start out by creating a RealAudio file with the RealProducer software, available at `www.real.com`. When you save a file with this software, you have several different options on how to encode the files, based on the target bandwidth. You can choose to save content in several different file formats, each corresponding to a specific bandwidth. (More on this later.) All RealAudio files have the .RA extension.

You *could* just link directly to the RA file from your Web page, but that wouldn't provide true streaming audio. This approach actually downloads the entire RA file before playback begins — which definitely isn't streaming!

Instead, you have to create what RealAudio calls a *stub file*. This file, which you can create in your HTML editor or text editor, is a simple text file with an .RAM extension. It should contain a single line of text, containing the full URL and filename of the RA file you wish to play.

Let's say, for example, that your RealAudio file is named myfile.ra and it's located at `www.mywebsite.com/audiofiles/myfile.ra`. The first thing you need to do is create a stub file named myfile.ram, which should contain the following line of code:

```
http://www.mywebsite.com/audiofiles/myfile.ra
```

Then you reference the stub file by adding the following link to your main Web page:

```
<a href="myfile.ram">Click here to play the file</a>
```

Again, note that you call the RAM file, which then calls the RA file. When a user clicks on the link, the RealAudio player is launched and the specified file starts to stream to your visitor's PC — and, when enough of a buffer has been downloaded, the file begins to play.

The really annoying part comes when you save the RA file at a higher bandwidth than most users are likely to have. Just pick any format above the 56Kbps modem level — the higher the better. If the file is optimized for a DSL or cable modem connection and then forced down a standard dial-up pipe, the result will be wholly unsatisfactory for visitors to your site!

Practical uses for this technique

There's plenty of application for streaming media, but little application for mismatched bandwidth. You should consider the use of streaming media if you have a particularly large audio or video file you need to present, so that users can begin listening or watching without the normal wait for the full download.

How not to be annoying

If you want to avoid the potential of overloaded pipes and stuttering playback, offer the user a choice of different versions for different bandwidths. To do this, you have to save several different versions of your RA file and create multiple corresponding RAM files. Then create separate links to the different RAM files, instructing users to click the link corresponding to their current bandwidth. This way, users with a slower modem connection can select the stream that won't overwhelm their connection.

You can provide users with the option of downloading the entire file without streaming. In this case, you'd link directly to the RA file (*not* the RAM file!), which would force the file to download before starting to play.

The Annoying Summary

The inclusion of audio or video on your page may be enough, in and of itself, to annoy a large number of users; anything you do above and beyond this is just icing on the cake. That said, there's nothing like a self-playing MIDI file of a particularly annoying song to do a job on your site visitors. (I particularly like "You Light Up My Life," although I have one friend who swears by the irritating power of polka music.) Just remember—the longer you can keep users waiting for something they really don't want to watch/read/listen to, the more annoyed they'll be.

✦   ✦   ✦

Aggravating Animations and Purposeless Plug-ins

◆　◆　◆　◆

Annoying Things in This Chapter

Force users to watch a boring animation — before they can enter your site

Overuse bleeding-edge technology

Make users upgrade their browsers before they can view your page

◆　◆　◆　◆

In the preceding chapter, I started to get into how you can annoy people with things that move — in particular, self-playing movie files. In this chapter, I extend that concept into other types of animations, in particular those insufferable Flash animations that you have to sit through before you're allowed to enter some Web sites. (I *hate* those things!)

The underlying point here is not just that users hate unnecessary animations or that they dislike any impediments to entering a site — although both those statements are true — but that employing technology for technology's sake is extremely inconsiderate of your site's visitors. When you add the latest and greatest technotrick to your site, you force users to share your momentary obsession and, in many cases, require them to upgrade or update their computer systems in ways they may not want or need to do. If someone did that to you, you'd probably get a tad irritated, if not outright incensed. Which is why, of course, Flash and other new-technology tricks are terrific ways to deliberately annoy users you don't like — or even ones you do!

Trick #88: Force Users to Watch an Annoying Animation — Before They Can Enter Your Site

This has happened to you.

You link to or jump directly to a specific Web page. Instead of seeing the site's home page, however, you're treated to an animated presentation, typically of near-zero interest or value. You have to sit through this annoying animation before you can gain entrance to the page you want (or wanted, by this point in time) to view. When the animation at long last ends and you're finally directed to the site's main page, you've forgotten why you came to this site in the first place and have started to curse Macromedia for ever inventing that cursed Flash technology in the first place.

In other words, you're right peeved.

Make no mistake — people *hate* being forced to sit through these ever-present Flash animations. No, that's not right; hate is too weak a word. People abhor, detest, loathe, and just plain can't stand these animated presentations. They're not impressed with the technology and how easy it is to create sophisticated-looking moving pictures with accompanying sound and music. No, they're merely annoyed that they're forced to watch these things, especially when the animations add little or no value to the site itself.

Which is why, of course, you need to learn how to add Flash animations to your page.

How to do it

There are actually four ways to add pre-entry animations to your Web pages. You can use Flash (of course), you can program a pseudo-animation with JavaScript, you can insert an animated GIF, or you can insert a full-fledged MPEG or AVI movie file. I'll talk a bit about each of these approaches, but know that far and away the most popular way to create annoying animations is with Flash.

Flash method

Flash is a technology — or, more precisely, a development tool — that uses vector graphics to create multiple-frame animations with relatively small file sizes. A Flash animation is much, much smaller than a comparable animated GIF file, which was the previous standard for adding short animations to Web pages. Using vector graphics not only results in small files but also ensures consistent visual quality across all computer platforms, no matter the resolution of the display.

A full discussion of how to develop a Flash animation is beyond the scope of this book (sorry!), but there are lots of resources available to you if you want to learn how to use Flash. First, you can go direct to Macromedia's Web site, at `www.macromedia.com/software/flash/`, where you can purchase a copy of the software and access a variety of tutorials and sample files. Second, there are a lot of Flash books available at your local bookstore, including *Flash 5 Weekend Crash Course*, *Flash 5 For Dummies*, and *Flash 5 Bible*, all from the publisher of the book you're currently reading. Finally, numerous sites on the Web offer Flash how-tos, articles, tricks, and sample animations; the best of these include ExtremeFlash (www.extremeflash.com), Flash Kit (www.flashkit.com), and FlashPlanet (www.flashplanet.com).

Note

Since Macromedia opened up the Flash code, there are now a bunch of free or cheap Flash creation tools available. (Which means you don't have to spend as much money to create annoying animations!) Check out the list of third-party tools at the OpenSWF Web site (www.openswf.org/tools/).

Once you've gotten up to speed and developed the Flash animation you want to use, you need to add that animation to your Web page. Listing 9-1 shows the basic code to embed a Flash SWF file on your page; replace *filename.swf* with the name of your Flash file and fill in the proper values for the width and height variables.

Listing 9-1: **Typical HTML code to embed a Flash animation**

```
<object width="xxx" height="xxx">
<param name="movie" value="filename.swf">
<embed src="filename.swf" width="xxx" HEIGHT="xxx">
</embed>
</object>
```

There's an easier way to embed Flash in your pages, however — let the Flash software do it for you! You do this by selecting File ➪ Publish Settings and then selecting the Formats tab. Make sure that the Flash, HTML, and GIF options are checked, then click the Publish button. Not only will Flash create detailed <object> and <embed> tags for your HTML file, but it can also generate JavaScript code to check if the users' browsers have the Flash plug-in installed — and display a GIF file if a browser can't handle the Flash playback.

JavaScript method

What if you don't want to go to all the time and trouble of learning Flash? Is there a non-Flash way to create annoying pre-entry animations for your Web site?

Fortunately, there is. You can use the JavaScript code in Listing 9-1 to create a Flash-like animation on your main Web page. This is a text-only effect; your welcome message slides down the screen, one word or phrase at a time, taking a maddeningly long time to finish and eventually redirecting users to your main Web page.

Note The scroll effect, because it uses the `<marquee>` tag, will be visible only on Internet Explorer browsers; Netscape users will see each line of text flash onscreen, instead.

To use this script, insert the complete code in Listing 9-2 into a completely blank HTML document. Because this technique uses frames, you won't be including the normal `<body>` tag—just use this code *as is* to create the effect.

Listing 9-2: JavaScript and HTML code to create a pre-entry page animation

```
<html>
<head>

<script language="JavaScript">
<!--

var colorBack = "red"
var colorText = "yellow"
var mainURL = "frametop.htm"
var delay = 6000
var number = 4
var i = 1
var a = " "

function StringArray (n)
{this.length = n;
for (var x = 1; x <= n; x++)
{this[x] = ' '}}

messageScreen = new StringArray(number)
messageScreen[1] = "line1"
messageScreen[2] = "line2"
messageScreen[3] = "line3"
messageScreen[4] = "line4"

function playAnimation()
{hpage='<body bgcolor='+colorBack+'>'
+'<center>'
+'<table border=0 height=100%>'
+'<tr><td valign="top">'
+'<b><font color='+colorText+' size=7>'
+'<marquee behavior="slide" direction="down" width=200
height=300>'
+messageScreen[i]+'</marquee></font></b>'
+'</td></tr></table></center></body>'
if (i == messageScreen.length + 1)
{parent.location = mainURL}
if (i < messageScreen.length + 1)
{parent.ss.location = "javascript:parent.hpage"
```

```
i++
setTimeout("playAnimation()",delay)}}

//-->
</script>

</head>

<frameset border="0" rows="100%" onload="playAnimation()"
frameborder="0">
<frame name="ss" src="javascript:parent.a">
</frameset>
```

Here are the things you can or should change in this script:

- ✦ Change the background color by entering a new value for the `colorBack` variable.

- ✦ Change the text color by entering a new value for the `colorText` variable.

- ✦ Enter the address for your next Web page for *url* in the `mainURL` variable.

- ✦ Put more space between each screen by increasing the value of the `delay` variable.

- ✦ Enter each line of your message for the `messageScreen` variables; enter a longer message by adding more lines (and increasing the count), or make a shorter message by deleting lines. (If your lines get too long, you may need to increase the `width` value in the `<marquee>` tag.)

- ✦ The `number` variable should be equal to the number of message lines you've entered; in the case of this example, there are four lines of text, so `number=4`.

Animated GIF method

If you don't want to mess with either Flash or JavaScript, you can simply insert an animated GIF file into your page. Animated GIFs are typically larger files, and will take longer to download, than a comparable Flash file. (Okay, that's one annoying point in favor of an animated GIF.) Then there's the fact that the rest of the page is accessible while the animated GIF plays (subtract one annoying point); with the Flash or JavaScript approach, the user has to wait for the animation to conclude before proceeding.

To insert an animated GIF, use the following line of HTML:

```
<img src="filename">
```

You can use your animated GIF editing program (such as GIF Construction Set, available at `www.mindworkshop.com/alchemy/gifcon.html`) to determine whether the GIF animation plays just once or loops indefinitely.

Embedded movie method

Finally, you can greet your guests with a simple movie file, as discussed in Trick #86 (Chapter 8). Use this code:

```
<embed src="filename" autostart=true loop=true
controller=false>
```

As with the animated GIF method, users will have access to the rest of your page while the movie file plays. This slight convenience to the user should be offset by the much larger file sizes typical of MPEG or AVI files, which will take a long time to download over a normal dial-up connection.

Practical uses for this technique

I know there has to be a practical use for pre-entry animations. Really, there must be. I just don't know what it is.

I'm *sure* the people behind some of these animation-heavy Web sites think that they're entertaining their visitors, or wowing them with their multimedia prowess, or showing them how much they "get" the Internet by shoving these annoying animations at anyone unfortunate to stumble over their home page. They're wrong, of course, but that must be what they're thinking.

The only other alternative is that they're deliberately trying to tick off their visitors — and who would do that?

How not to be annoying

The best way not to annoy users with your animations is not to use those animations in the first place. A distant second approach is to provide a Skip Intro link on the animation page, so that frustrated users can bypass the animation and go directly to the site's main content.

Trick #89: Overuse Bleeding-Edge Technology

Flash is the big deal du jour for Web page developers across the Internet. Macromedia's neat little tool really does let just about anyone develop attention-getting animations without a whole lot of effort — which, unfortunately, has enabled and encouraged hundreds of thousands of developers to add animations to their pages.

The problem with this, of course, is that most Web pages don't benefit from these animations. Most users just want to get to where they're going, and they don't want to be diverted by lots of bells and whistles on the way there. Unless an animation adds value to the user's experience (which typically means conveying content or delivering a service), then the animation is extraneous and a waste of the user's valuable time.

So why, then, do so many Web sites feature sometimes elaborate Flash animations?

Because it's neat. Because it's fun. Because it's not nearly as boring as entering line after line of HTML or JavaScript code. Because they can.

That's it, really. It's a perfect example of technology for technology's sake. Web page designers and developers have become infatuated with a new toy and have determined to use it as much as possible—whether their users want it or not.

The worst offenders not only force pre-entry animations on their users, they also find lots of other curious places on their sites to throw in another Flash presentation or two. They even use Flash to create text and background animation effects on otherwise-normal pages and to develop online games, audio players, and other applets with Flash.

And it isn't just Flash. New technology always comes available and is then co-opted for Web use. Web designers and developers *love* new toys, not only for what they can do but also because they represent a new challenge. (There's also the thrill of being the first one on the block to have that new toy—which is a fairly important driver.)

The result is a bevy of Web sites with more needless bells and whistles than you can count. Users are inundated with moving and flashing and beeping and beating, to the point where the site's content becomes secondary in importance to its look and feel. Design for design's sake, and use technology for technology's sake, and pretty soon you're driving users away with all the flash and splash.

Now, if you *want* to drive users away, or if you just want to show off all the tricks you've learned, then go ahead and embrace all the bleeding-edge technology you can find. (In a sense, that's what this book is about—right?) Just know that most users prefer a no-frills site over a technology-laden one—especially if they're connecting over a modem (which most users are) or have an older browser. And, as you're well aware, most bleeding-edge Web development technologies are bandwidth hogs, and most aren't backward-compatible with older browsers.

It's no coincidence that the most popular sites on the Web—including Yahoo!, eBay, and Amazon—are primarily text-based and for the most part eschew bandwidth-hogging bleeding-edge technologies. You don't find a lot of big graphics on these sites, nor a lot of JavaScript tricks, and especially not a lot of (if any) Flash animations. Fast, small, and clean is what seems to draw the users in; it may not be flashy or state-of-the-art, but it's what works.

How to do it

If you want to master all the new bleeding-edge technologies, you need to stay on top of Web development trends. The best way to do that is to frequent those Web sites that target state-of-the-art Web development. Here's a short list of sites that should be on your must-browse list:

- ✦ Builder.com (`builder.cnet.com`)
- ✦ Developer's Network Web Development (`webdevelopment.developersnetwork.com/`)
- ✦ EarthWeb Web Development (`webdeveloper.earthweb.com`)
- ✦ Internet.com Web Development Channel (`www.internet.com/sections/webdev.html`)
- ✦ PageResource (`www.pageresource.com`)
- ✦ Webmonkey (`hotwired.lycos.com/webmonkey/`)
- ✦ Webtools (`www.webtools.com`)
- ✦ ZDNet Developer (`www.zdnet.com/developer/`)

Naturally, you should also be up to date on the latest versions of Internet Explorer, Netscape, and other Web browsers, to the point of participating in beta test programs to get a peek at the new software before it's released to the general public. It also helps to set aside a large enough budget to invest in the latest HTML editing and Web development software and to buy a new state-of-the-art PC once a year or so.

Finally, make sure that you always connect to the Internet via some sort of broadband connection — it'll help you forget that most visitors to your site will be connecting via a much slower dial-up connection. If you optimize your site for broadband, you're sure to irritate the great unwashed who try to view your pages over a 56.6Kbps modem.

Practical uses for this technique

Aside from its being neat and all, what good reasons might there be to use bleeding-edge technology on your Web site?

Well, if your site's target audience consists of the high-tech elite, or other Web developers, you need to show them that you're on top of all the latest goings-on. You're not going to impress this crowd with a no-frills text-only site; you need to demonstrate everything you know, even if it results in a bit of overkill for any other visitors.

The same goes if you're selling your Web development services. While one could make a case that clients should be impressed by a clean, fast-loading site design, the reality is that the more bells and whistles you show, the more business you'll get. Your potential clients might not need all that bleeding-edge stuff, but they'll feel better if they hire someone who knows how to use it.

Finally, you may deliberately want to drive less-experienced users (and AOL subscribers!) from your site. Maybe you're an elitist prig, maybe you're just casting your net in a different direction, but whatever the reason, you can easily exclude these folks from your site by building something that they can't use.

How not to be annoying

The less new technology you use — and the more compatible your site is with older browsers and slower connections — the less annoying it will be, especially to non-cutting-edge users. You can also go to the effort of building two sites, a high-tech one and a low-tech one, and redirecting users to the appropriate site either automatically (by sensing browser versions, as discussed in the next trick) or by choice (by forcing users to click a link before entering). This last approach, while time consuming, may be the best way to both show off your bleeding-edge expertise and retain compatibility with less-tech-savvy users.

Trick #90: Make Users Upgrade Their Browsers Before They Can View Your Page

If you're always ahead of the curve, chances are you're going to embrace new technology before most of your site's visitors do. What do you do when you want to inflict some new development tool on your visitors and their browsers aren't yet compatible with that tool?

It's not an uncommon occurrence. Even in this day and age, not every browser is equipped to play Flash or Shockwave animations, or play back MP3 files, or perform some other new-fangled operation. While you could limit your site to a lowest-common-denominator compatibility, that's not very exciting, and it will make your site look somewhat less than state-of-the-art.

A better approach is to include the latest technologies and force ill-equipped users either to upgrade their browsers or download the appropriate plug-ins to fully view your site. There's nothing technophobes like better than seeing an alert box that tells them that they *must* download such and such a file to proceed. They'll suffer from feelings of inferiority, of course, but they'll also experience that sweet fear that comes whenever they try to do something new and unfamiliar with their PCs. You're going to make them upgrade — which is something they've been avoiding for quite some time now. Good for you! Make those technoweenies face their fears by throwing them head-first into the proverbial technological deep end, just so you can subject them to some kind of twirling text or flying monkey effect.

How to do it

First, you have to grab hold of the latest technology and use it prominently on your site — preferably right at the top of your main page. Make sure this technology is not fully supported by most Web browsers currently in use, thus forcing most users to either upgrade their browsers or download the appropriate plug-in for their software.

There are actually two ways you can proceed from here. The first is to include the technology with no warning, so that your page appears to crash or freeze in their browsers. The second approach is to sniff out compatibility with the new technology and then display some sort of warning suggesting how and what they can upgrade or download to view your page.

For example, not all users have Flash-compatible browsers. (This is hard to believe, but it's true.) You can use the code in Listing 9-3 to create a Flash plug-in sniffer, which tests for Flash compatibility and then displays an alert box warning users away (or suggesting that they download the plug-in from Macromedia's Web site).

Listing 9-3: HTML code for a Flash plug-in sniffer; insert in the head of your document

```
<script language="JavaScript">
<!--

if ((navigator.appName == "Microsoft Internet Explorer" &&
navigator.appVersion.indexOf("Mac") == -1 &&
navigator.appVersion.indexOf("3.1") == -1) ||
(navigator.plugins && navigator.plugins["Shockwave Flash"])
|| navigator.plugins["Shockwave Flash 2.0"])
{window.location='flash-url';}

else
{alert("message");
window.location='nonflash-url';}

//-->
</script>
```

Replace *flash-url* with the URL of your Flash-enabled page, *message* with the alert message you want to display to users without Flash installed, and *nonflash-url* with the URL of either a non-Flash version of your main page or the URL of the Flash plug-in download page on the Macromedia Web site. (You can also strand users on your page by eliminating the `window.location` code — that'll show 'em!)

Practical uses for this technique

Look—why should you limit the look or features of your site just because some bozo is still using the version of Internet Explorer that came with the cheap PC he bought back in 1997? You want a state-of-the-art site, and it's not your fault if some users don't follow your lead and upgrade to the latest browser versions every six months or so. If they're that far behind, they don't deserve to see your site anyway!

How not to be annoying

A less annoying approach, however, is to create versions of your pages for both high-tech and lower-tech users. You might have a Flash- and JavaScript-enabled version for users with later-model browsers, and a plain text-and-pictures version for less-equipped users. The challenge, then, becomes one of redirecting users to the right pages.

The most common form of redirect is based on the type and version of browser used, as different browser versions often support different technologies and HTML commands. For example, you can create separate pages for Netscape and Internet Explorer users, and even different pages based on which version of each browser is used.

The simplest approach is to separate version 4 browsers (both Internet Explorer and Netscape) from pre–version 4 browsers. The script in Listing 9-4 redirects pre–version 4 browsers to one page (replace *oldbrowser-url* with the page's URL) and version 4 and later browsers to another page (replace *newbrowser-url* with this page's URL). Just insert this script into the head of your main HTML document.

Listing 9-4: JavaScript code to separate pre– and post–version 4 browsers; insert in the head of your document

```
<script language="JavaScript">
<!--

browserName=navigator.appName;
browserVer=parseInt(navigator.appVersion);

if ((browserName=="Netscape" && browserVer>=4) ||
(browserName=="Microsoft Internet Explorer" && browserVer>=4))
version="ver4";
else
version="other";
```

Continued

Listing 9-4 *(continued)*

```
if (version=="ver4")
  window.location="newbrowser-url";

else
window.location="oldbrowser-url";

//-->
</script>
```

Maybe you just want to separate users based on the type of browser used, without bothering with the specific version number. The script in Listing 9-5 redirects Netscape users to one page (*netscape-url*), Internet Explorer users to another (*msie-url*), and users of other browsers to a third page (*other-url*). Insert this script into the head of your main HTML document.

Listing 9-5: JavaScript code to redirect based on type of browser; insert in the head of your document

```
<script language="JavaScript">
<!-

browserName=navigator.appName;

if ((browserName=="Netscape") ||  (browserName=="Microsoft
Internet Explorer"))

{if (browserName=="Netscape")
version="NS";
else
version="IE";}

else
version="OTHER";

if ((version=="NS") || (version=="IE"))
{if (version=="NS")
window.location="netscape-url";
else
window.location="msie-url";}

else
window.location="other-url";

//-->
</script>
```

Another popular reason to redirect users is based on JavaScript compatibility. The script in Listing 9-6 senses whether JavaScript is enabled in the user's browser and redirects the user accordingly; paste this script into the body of your main HTML document, replacing *javascript-url* with the address of your normal JavaScript-enabled page and *non-javascript-url* with the address of your HTML-only page.

Listing 9-6: **JavaScript code to detect JavaScript compatibility; insert in the body of your document**

```
<script language="JavaScript">
<!-

window.location="javascript-url";

//-->
</script>

<noscript>
window.location="non-javascript-url";
</noscript>
```

You can also redirect users based on their system's screen resolution. The script in Listing 9-7 detects the user's screen resolution and redirects the user to a page specific for that resolution. Insert this script into the body of your main HTML document and replace *640-url*, *800-url*, and *big-url* with the appropriate page addresses.

Listing 9-7: **JavaScript code to redirect based on screen resolution; insert in the body of your document**

```
<script language="Javascript">
<!--

if (screen.width <= 640)
{window.location = "640-url";}

else if (screen.width <= 800)
{window.location = "800-url";}

if (screen.width > 800)
{window.location = "big-url";}

//-->
</script>
```

The Annoying Summary

All this high-tech stuff is great — *if* all your users are on the same level of adoption. If you build your site using all the latest technological doo-dads, you'll alienate a large part of your potential audience. If you don't mind annoying people while you're demonstrating your technological superiority, great. If, on the other hand, you'd prefer to maintain some degree of compatibility, consider either scaling back on the bleeding-edge stuff or providing some way for less state-of-the-art users to access your site. Then, once they're inside, you can subject them to all manner of annoying effects — which they couldn't experience if they'd been turned away at the gate!

✦　　✦　　✦

Nonsensical Navigation

Nobody likes to get lost. Not being able to find your way from point A to point B is frustrating at best and downright dangerous at worst.

Getting lost within a confusing Web site is no less annoying than getting lost in your car — the only difference is that you can't stop your browser and get out and ask directions when you get lost online. True connoisseurs of annoying Web sites will recognize Web site navigation as a time-proven means to frustrate users — and they'll have their favorites among several different possible approaches.

For example, you can choose to confuse with a Byzantine site organization, complete with a nonintuitive directory structure and virtually untypeable URLs for individual pages. You could also choose to confuse by neglecting to include navigation links on your pages, or by ensuring that those links don't always lead to where the user wants to go.

Use this chapter, then, to learn how to be disorganized as well as unhelpful. After all, the more lost visitors get, the more time they'll spend on your site — if only because they can't find a way out!

Trick #91: Create Confusing Buttons and Links

There are many ways to ensure that visitors to your site find themselves somewhere they don't want to be. One interesting approach is to create deliberately misleading navigational elements.

You've no doubt driven enough miles in enough places to have seen your share of confusing road signs. "Did that sign mean to turn left here or *here*?" "Is that arrow pointing right, or up, or what?" "What does it mean when the exit says 'No exit'?"

Well, there's nothing stopping you from adding buttons or links to your pages that introduce a fair amount of uncertainty to the user's experience. What kind of items am I talking about? Here are a few examples you might want to play around with:

✦ Ask the user to cancel an operation by clicking an OK button, not the Cancel button, as shown in Figure 10-1.

✦ Provide multiple links without clear reference within the same piece of text, as shown in Figure 10-2.

✦ Employ extensive use of confusing syntax and double negatives, as shown in Figure 10-3.

You get the idea.

Figure 10-1: The old "Click OK to cancel" trick

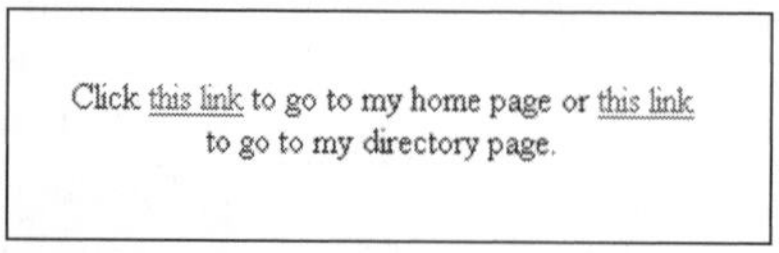

Click this link to go to my home page or this link to go to my directory page.

Figure 10-2: Which "this link" do you click to go where?

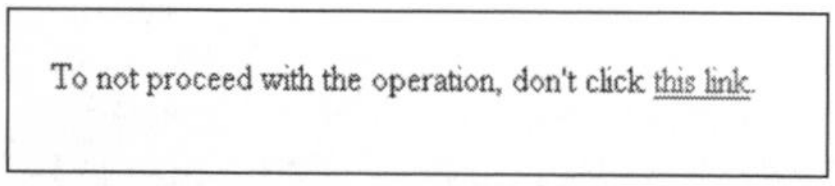

To not proceed with the operation, don't click this link.

Figure 10-3: There's nothing like a double negative not to clarify things.

How to do it

You already know how to add a hyperlink to your Web page. Adding a button is almost as easy; all you have to do is define a form to contain the button, and then define the button. You do this with the code in Listing 10-1.

Listing 10-1: **HTML code to add a button to a Web page**

```
<form>
<input type="button" value="button-text" onClick='operation'>
</form>
```

Replace *button-text* with the text you want to appear on the button, and *operation* with the name of the specific operation you want executed when the button is clicked. For example, to make a button call an alert box or confirm alert box, use this code:

```
<input type="button" value="button-text"
onClick='alert("message")'>
```

To send users to a specific Web page on the click of a button, use the following code:

```
<input type="button" value="button-text"
onClick="window.location.href='url'">
```

Naturally, you should replace *button-text* with the text you want to appear on the button, and *url* with the Web page you'll send your users to.

Practical uses for this technique

Confusing controls help to test the intelligence of your users. If they can figure out what it is that you're trying to say, then they're smart enough to proceed to the next part of your site. If they can't figure it out, they deserve to end up in the wrong place!

How not to be annoying

The less confusing your page, the less annoyed your visitors will be. If you must include a navigational element such as a button or a self-referencing link, make sure that the button/link is clearly labeled and that it actually does what it's supposed to do.

Even better is to use fewer navigational elements. While you want a way for users to return to your home page and back up to the last page viewed, you may want to forgo any additional pointers within your site. Research has found that most users ignore all but the most simple navigational elements, preferring to use their browser's Back button to click back through pages visited, and use a search function to find pages they haven't visited yet.

Given these findings, you may want to add a Site Search box to the bottom of all your Web pages. While you *can* use JavaScript to create your own search engine, that's a very time-consuming and complicated approach. The easier way to add search functionality to your site is to use a third-party search service, such as Atomz (`www.atomz.com`), FreeFind (`www.freefind.com`), or SiteLevel (`sitelevel.whatuseek.com`).

Another navigational feature that many users like is the site map. Create a page that logically organizes the main parts or pages of your site, and then include a link to this site map page on all your other pages. This way, users are one click away from the site map whenever they get lost—and then, theoretically at least, just another click away from the specific page they want to jump to.

Trick #92: Use Extremely Long and Complicated URLs

Users like to type. Really. Most computer users possess extremely advanced typing skills and can think of no better way to spend their time than typing long, convoluted combinations of letters, numbers, and characters. They like the challenge of entering something like `www.mywebsite.com/main-directory/ ~bobbymagill/3569/mypages_42a/465ADP040Ca56@@ge87/revision_12.html` into their browser's Address box.

Well, maybe not.

In reality, most users *despise* typing and at best can hunt-and-peck their way through only the simplest URLs. So if you create a complex and seemingly random naming system for the pages on your site, you stand a good chance of totally frustrating a lot of people.

Note   Of course, some URL naming is out of your control. If you're using a Web hosting service that dumps your pages deep in one of its own directories, you have to live with all the garbage before your actual page name—unless you cough up the spare change for your own domain address.

How to do it

There are several interrelated approaches to creating a convoluted URL. Use all these approaches together for the maximum annoyance factor.

The first place to start is with your Web site's organization. It's a good idea to create as many directories and subdirectories as possible, so that any individual page is buried several levels down from your domain address. The result is a URL with a lot of forward slashes, like this:

`www.mywebsite.com/directory1/directory2/directory3/webpage.html`

Next, make sure you name your directories (and your files) with extremely long names. Don't go for something as simple as `bob`; a name like `thewebpagesofbob-bymagill` creates much more typing for your users.

Now add a bunch of numbers and characters to each name. Hyphens (`-`) and underscores (`_`) are always good, as is the squiggly character (called a *tilde*) at the far upper left of your keyboard (`~`). These characters are difficult to reach on the keyboard and used so infrequently as to be hard to find for many users.

Finally, look over all your directory and filenames to see how self-explanatory they are. If you find something like `www.mywebsite.com/images/vacationpictures.html`, consider renaming the directory and files to something less intuitive, such as `www.mywebsite.com/aaa56@47b/4572a.html`. This way users won't be able to figure out what is where and also will have a harder time remembering the precise URL for any given page on your site.

This particular approach also begs the issue of site organization. The best Web sites (in terms of *not* annoying people) are well organized, using hierarchical directories to store distinct portions of the site, typically arranged by topic or function. (Figure 10-4 shows a typical hierarchical site structure.) Create a less-organized and more complicated structure for your site, and you're bound to foil anyone trying to figure out where a particular page may lie.

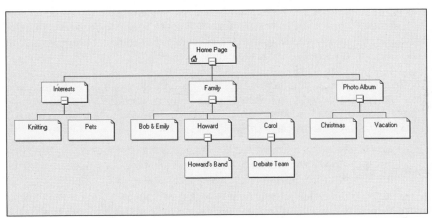

Figure 10-4: A well-organized Web site — guaranteed *not* to annoy your visitors

By the way, you might think that throwing all your pages into a single directory might be another way to annoy users. Unfortunately, this isn't the case — it ensures only that all your files are within one forward slash of the domain address. You're much better off burying files within several layers of subdirectories, thus creating much longer and harder-to-type URLs.

Practical uses for this technique

You might not want casual users to have easy access to all the pages on your site. In that instance, hiding pages underneath layers and layers of subdirectories and obscuring their meaning with totally unrelated filenames helps to keep users from poking around where they don't belong.

How not to be annoying

The least annoying Web sites incorporate a logical (and relatively flat) structure, with few embedded directories and descriptive filenames. If there's a part of your site you don't want the general public to access, use the controls provided by your Web site host to make those pages private. You can even add a bit of JavaScript to a page to keep unauthorized users away; see Trick #103 in Chapter 11, "Rage-Inducing Registrations," to learn how to password-protect a page.

Trick #93: Hide Important Pages Behind Misleading Links

On a related topic, misleading links and page names can engender the same type of confusion as do long and untypeable URLs. A classic example would be to label one of the subsidiary pages on your site (and all links to that page) as "Home." Users will click the Home link thinking that they'll return to your real home page, but instead they get directed to the page called Home.

Along the same lines, if you have a page with a specific purpose, such as a photo album, logic dictates that you title that page "Photo Album." If, instead, you title that page "Sound Files" or "Misc" or "b7789@@g3," then you've totally confused any users trying to navigate by page title.

How to do it

The technique behind this trick is simple—just relabel all the pages in your site to obscure their true meaning. (That means changing the text between the `<title>` and `</title>` tags in the pages' HTML code, as well as renaming the files themselves.) Then check all the internal links to these pages to make sure the link text reflects the obscure titles, and you're all set to hoodwink unsuspecting site visitors.

Practical uses for this technique

Obscuring the titles and filenames of individual pages can serve to disguise or hide specific pages from the general public. You can use this technique when you have a page or two that you don't want casual users (or competitors, if it's a company Web site) to stumble onto accidentally.

How not to be annoying

As discussed in Trick #92 (and detailed in Trick #103 in Chapter 11), a better way to hide sensitive Web pages from prying eyes is to password-protect them—or not to post them in the first place.

Trick #94: Make Sure Your Home Page Isn't Really Home

One advantage of the type of Web site organization shown in Figure 10-4 is that users can type in a simple URL (without a particular page reference) to go to the main page within any given directory. For example, you can enter `www.mywebsite.com/images/` to go directly to the main page within the `images` directory. (That's assuming, of course, that the main page in each directory is named `index.html`; if so, entering just the directory name takes the browser directly to the index page.)

The potential for confusion, then, is created if you name the main page in each directory something other than `index.html`—and don't include any file by the `index.html` name in the directory. If the `index.html` file doesn't exist and the user enters the directory-only URL, then the user either gets a "page not found" error or is presented with a listing of all the files in that directory, either of which is both confusing and annoying.

How to do it

If you're using a fancy-schmancy HTML editing program, chances are that it will automatically assign the filename `index.html` to the main page in each directory on your site. If this is the case, you'll need to override the program's default settings or manually rename the files after they're created. As to what to call the main page, that's up to you—just avoid `index.html` or `index.htm`.

Practical uses for this technique

You may actually want to employ this trick if you're putting a test version of your site online and don't want it to be seen by the general public. By directing testers to the nonindex filename, you'll allow them to view your test home page; casual visitors won't know which filename to jump to if the `index.html` file is not there.

How not to be annoying

If you're trying to hide a site that's under construction by renaming the main page to something other than `index.html`, consider creating a temporary `index.html` page that contains some sort of "under construction" message or graphic. That way users won't be left hanging when they jump to your domain address.

Trick #95: Don't Include Navigation Bars or Menus

If your Web site is overly complex, most experts recommend you be considerate of your visitors and supply some sort of intra-site navigation system—to help them find their way back to your home page, if nothing else. If you deliberately exclude any internal navigation, you'll be thought quite inconsiderate—which is the first step on the path to true annoyingosity.

How to do it

If you're using an HTML editing program, chances are the program will want to insert some sort of navigation bar or menu to every page on your site, by default. You'll need to override this default (or delete any automatically inserted controls) to wipe any navigational links from your pages.

Practical uses for this technique

There may be some pages on a site that you don't want to link back to the site's home page. This might be the case if you're hosting some content independent from your site's main content, or using the same domain address to park pages for multiple users. If this is the case, you'll want to include navigational elements on the site's primary pages but exclude navigational elements from the unrelated pages.

How not to be annoying

If a site without any navigational elements is annoying, the way to reduce the annoyance factor is to include some type of navigational controls. If you're using FrontPage or some similar HTML editor, you should probably use the program's built-in navigational elements. If you're coding by hand, you can create your own navigation bar using JavaScript. The following code will create a menu system like the one shown in Figure 10-5.

Begin by using the following code for your document's `<body>` tag:

```
<body marginheight="30" topmargin="40">
```

Next, enter the code in Listing 10-2 into the body of your document.

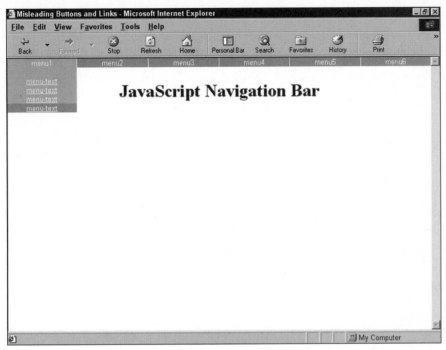

Figure 10-5: To avoid annoying visitors, add a navigation bar to your site.

Listing 10-2: JavaScript code to create a navigation bar; insert in the body of your document

```
<script language="JavaScript">
<!-- Simple Cross Browser NavBar by Kurt Grigg
(kurt.grigg@virgin.net) -->

MenuTitles=new Array()
SubMenuLinks=new Array()

function Rtrn(c)
{if (document.layers) c.bgColor=HighLight;
if (document.all) c.style.background=HighLight;}

function HghLght(c)
{if (document.layers) c.bgColor=MenuBgColor;
if (document.all) c.style.background=MenuBgColor;}

OpenLayer=(document.layers)?"<br><layer width=100%
onMouseOver='HghLght(this)';
onMouseOut='Rtrn(this)'><center>":"<span style='width:100%'
onMouseOver='HghLght(this)'; onMouseOut='Rtrn(this)'>";
```

Continued

Listing 10-2 *(continued)*

```
CloseLayer=(document.layers)?'</center></layer>':'</span>';

/*********** EDIT MENU APPEARANCE HERE **********/

MenuWidth=(document.layers)?131/*NS width*/:129 /*IE width*/;
MenuFont='Arial';
MenuFontSize=2;
MenuFontColor='ffffff';
MenuBgColor='8888ff';
HighLight='aaaaff';
Separater=1;

/***** EDIT, ADD, AND DELETE MENU TITLES HERE ****/

MenuTitles[0]='menu1';
MenuTitles[1]='menu2';
MenuTitles[2]='menu3';
MenuTitles[3]='menu4';
MenuTitles[4]='menu5';
MenuTitles[5]='menu6';

/**** EDIT, ADD, AND DELETE SUBMENU TITLES HERE ****/

SubMenuLinks[0]=""
+OpenLayer+"<a href='url'>menu-text</a>"+CloseLayer
+OpenLayer+"<a href='url'>menu-text</a>"+CloseLayer
+OpenLayer+"<a href='url'>menu-text</a>"+CloseLayer
+OpenLayer+"<a href='url'>menu-text</a>"+CloseLayer

SubMenuLinks[1]=""
+OpenLayer+"<a href='url'>menu-text</a>"+CloseLayer
+OpenLayer+"<a href='url'>menu-text</a>"+CloseLayer
+OpenLayer+"<a href='url'>menu-text</a>"+CloseLayer
+OpenLayer+"<a href='url'>menu-text</a>"+CloseLayer

SubMenuLinks[2]=""
+OpenLayer+"<a href='url'>menu-text</a>"+CloseLayer
+OpenLayer+"<a href='url'>menu-text</a>"+CloseLayer
+OpenLayer+"<a href='url'>menu-text</a>"+CloseLayer
+OpenLayer+"<a href='url'>menu-text</a>"+CloseLayer

SubMenuLinks[3]=""
+OpenLayer+"<a href='url'>menu-text</a>"+CloseLayer
+OpenLayer+"<a href='url'>menu-text</a>"+CloseLayer
+OpenLayer+"<a href='url'>menu-text</a>"+CloseLayer
+OpenLayer+"<a href='url'>menu-text</a>"+CloseLayer

SubMenuLinks[4]=""
+OpenLayer+"<a href='url'>menu-text</a>"+CloseLayer
+OpenLayer+"<a href='url'>menu-text</a>"+CloseLayer
+OpenLayer+"<a href='url'>menu-text</a>"+CloseLayer
```

```
+OpenLayer+"<a href='url'>menu-text</a>"+CloseLayer

SubMenuLinks[5]=""
+OpenLayer+"<a href='url'>menu-text</a>"+CloseLayer
+OpenLayer+"<a href='url'>menu-text</a>"+CloseLayer
+OpenLayer+"<a href='url'>menu-text</a>"+CloseLayer
+OpenLayer+"<a href='url'>menu-text</a>"+CloseLayer

/****  NO MORE EDITING ****/

Spacer=MenuWidth+Separater;
IniPos= -MenuWidth-Separater;
aSpacer=MenuWidth+Separater;
aIniPos= -MenuWidth-Separater;
MenuAmount=MenuTitles.length;

if (document.layers)
{for (i=0; i < MenuAmount; i++)
{document.write("<layer name='submenu"+i+"' top=0
left="+(aIniPos+=aSpacer)+" "
+"height=10 width="+MenuWidth+" bgcolor="+HighLight+"
visibility=hide"
+" onMouseOver='this.visibility=\"show\"; var
cd=this.id.length-1; var ab=this.id.charAt(cd); H(ab)' "
+" onMouseOut='this.visibility=\"hide\"; var ef=this.id.length-
1; var gh=this.id.charAt(ef); B(gh)'>"
+"<center><font face="+MenuFont+" size="+MenuFontSize+"
color="+MenuFontColor+">"
+" <br>"+SubMenuLinks[i]+"<br></font></center></layer>");}
for (i=0; i < MenuAmount; i++)
{document.write("<layer name='nsmenu"+i+"' top=0
left="+(IniPos+=Spacer)+" height=0 "
+"width="+MenuWidth+" bgcolor="+MenuBgColor+" "
+"onMouseOver=\"this.bgColor=HighLight; var e=this.id.length-1;
var d=this.id.charAt(e); On(d)\" "
+"onMouseOut=\"this.bgColor=MenuBgColor; var e=this.id.length-
1; var d=this.id.charAt(e); Off(d)\">"
+"<center><font face="+MenuFont+" size="+MenuFontSize+"
color="+MenuFontColor+">"
+MenuTitles[i]+"</font></center></layer>");}

function On(x)
{for (i=0; i < MenuAmount; i++)
{document.layers['submenu'+x].visibility='show';}}

function Off(x)
{for (i=0; i < MenuAmount; i++)
{document.layers['submenu'+x].visibility='hide';}}

function B(y)
{for (i=0; i < MenuAmount; i++)
{document.layers['nsmenu'+y].bgColor=MenuBgColor;}}

function H(y)
```

```
{for (i=0; i < MenuAmount; i++)
{document.layers['nsmenu'+y].bgColor=HighLight;}}}

if (document.all)
{for (i=0; i < MenuAmount; i++)
{document.write("<div id='sub"+i+"' style='position:absolute;"
+"top:0px;"
+"left:"+(aIniPos+=aSpacer)+";"
+"height:0px;"
+"width:"+MenuWidth+";"
+"background:"+HighLight+";"
+"visibility:hidden'"
+" onMouseOver='this.style.visibility=\"visible\";"
+" document.all[\"headers"+i+"\"].style.background=HighLight';"
+" onMouseOut='this.style.visibility=\"hidden\";"
+"
document.all[\"headers"+i+"\"].style.background=MenuBgColor'>"
+"<center><font face="+MenuFont+" size="+MenuFontSize+"
color="+MenuFontColor+">"
+" <br> <br>"+SubMenuLinks[i]+"</font></center></div>
");}

for (i=0; i < MenuAmount; i++)
{document.write("<div id='headers"+i+"'
style='position:absolute;"
+"top:0px;"
+"left:"+(IniPos+=Spacer)+";"
+"height:0px;"
+"width:"+MenuWidth+";"
+"background:"+MenuBgColor+";"
+"padding:0px'"
+"
onMouseOver='document.all[\"sub"+i+"\"].style.visibility=\"visi
ble\";"
+" this.style.background=HighLight'"
+"
onMouseOut='document.all[\"sub"+i+"\"].style.visibility=\"hidde
n\";"
+" this.style.background=MenuBgColor'>"
+"<center><font face="+MenuFont+" size="+MenuFontSize+"
color="+MenuFontColor+">"
+MenuTitles[i]+"</font></center></div>");}}

//-->
</script>
```

Several sections within this script require your input:

✦ In the EDIT APPEARANCE HERE section, you can opt for the default colors, sizes, and fonts, or change these to reflect your personal tastes.

✦ In the EDIT, ADD, AND DELETE MENU TITLES HERE section, enter as many lines as you want main menus, then replace *menu 1* et al. with specific menu names.

✦ In the EDIT, ADD, AND DELETE SUBMENU TITLES HERE section, enter the information for each item underneath each of the main menus. You can have any number of links in the submenus; replace *menu-text* with the text for each menu item and *url* with the address for each page linked to.

Naturally, you'll need to add this code to each page on your site that you want to display the navigation bar.

Note The code for this trick comes from scriptmeister Kurt Grigg — be sure to visit his Web site at website.lineone.net/~kurt.grigg/javascript/ for more really cool JavaScript code.

Trick #96: Strand Users with No Way Home

As we all learned from *The Wizard of Oz*, there's no place like home — and that's especially true on the Web. No matter how deep users get into a Web site, they'll eventually want to return to the site's home page, which is why most sites include — on every page — a link or a button that users can click to jump back home.

Removing this simple (and expected) navigation element has the effect of stranding visitors in the most remote regions of your site. If they're twenty pages deep with no Home button in sight, they'll have to click their browser's Back button twenty times to get back to where they started from.

Which, of course, is highly irritating.

How to do it

If you're using a decent HTML editing program, you may have to manually instruct the program not to include a Home link on each new page it creates. If worse comes to worst, you can edit the HTML code manually to remove the Home link or button.

Of course, there are even more devious tricks you can play on users who depend on a Home link to take them to the top of your site. For instance, you can include a Home button but have it link to another, non-Home, page on your site — or on another site, just to be doubly confusing. Even better, you can include a Home button that links to a dead link, so that users get a "page not found" error whenever they try to go home. Or, if you're really feeling mean, code the Home button to launch an annoying pop-up window or two (as discussed in Chapter 5, "Pointless Pop-ups and Worthless Windows"). Users will be pulling out their hair when they click your Home button and end up with a screen full of annoying pop-ups!

Practical uses for this technique

What practical reason could you have for stranding users with no direct link home? If your site is a subsite of a larger site—a U.S. branch of a foreign corporation, for example—you might not want your visitors to go all the way back to the parent site's home page. In that instance, you can remove the Home link, or have it link back to *your* home page, rather than to the parent's home page.

How not to be annoying

To be fair, most experienced users can figure out how to get back to your home page by trimming back the page's URL to include only the domain address. Still, if you want to be a good Web citizen (no badges awarded, sorry), you'll include some sort of Home link or button *somewhere* on each and every page of your site.

Trick #97: Redirect Users to Another Page, for No Apparent Reason

While I'm on the subject of navigation, how about actively redirecting users to a page other than the one they intended to visit? Just when they get your page loaded and settle back for a little Web reading, *boom!*—their browsers reload with a completely different page.

It's the online equivalent of pulling your car into San Diego, then looking up and finding out that you're in Cleveland instead.

How to do it

Redirect scripts are relatively easy to implement. This particular example contains a ten-second delay, just long enough to put your visitors at ease before the unexpected redirect.

All you have to do is insert the code in Listing 10-3 into the head of your HTML document.

Listing 10-3: JavaScript code for a time-delayed page redirect; insert in the head of your document

```
<script language="JavaScript">
<!--

var nextPage="new-url"
var timeDelay=10000
```

```
function changePage()
{location=nextPage}

setTimeout("reload()", timeDelay);

//-->
</script>
```

Replace *new-url* with the address of the page you're redirecting to. (Use your imagination here; what page would be the least expected — and least welcome — one to throw in your visitors' faces?) And, if you want to set a shorter or longer delay, feel free to change the value of the timeDelay variable.

Practical uses for this technique

There are many practical reasons to redirect users to another page. For example:

✦ You've moved your page or site to another address; users who go to your old address can be redirected to the new address.

✦ You have different pages for different browsers; with the appropriate JavaScript code (see Trick #90, in Chapter 9), users can be redirected to the page specially designed for their specific browser.

✦ Your site isn't up and running yet, or has been closed down for one reason or another; visitors can be redirected to an alternate site until your site is up and running.

In other words, any time you want visitors to go somewhere other than the original address, using a redirect script isn't a bad idea.

How not to be annoying

The unexpected nature of this trick is what makes it particularly annoying. If you want to reduce the annoyance of a redirect script, tell users what you're doing. That means posting a message on the original page to the effect that users will be redirected to an alternate page in ten seconds (or whatever). If you have an urge to be especially informative, you can even tell users *why* they're being redirected.

Trick #98: Nag Users to Bookmark Your Page

If you're like me, you don't like to be nagged. Whether you're being "reminded" to take out the trash, fold the laundry, or have that report on the boss's desk by the end of the day tomorrow, nagging is major-league annoying.

Nagging someone else is a lot more fun than being nagged yourself, of course, so the last two tricks in this chapter examine ways you can nag your site's visitors.

One of the more common ways to nag your site's visitors is to suggest, gently, that they add your page to their favorites or bookmark list. There's nothing inherently wrong with that — unless you do it every time they visit your site. Even if they've already bookmarked it. Even if they never want to visit again.

How to do it

There are two parts to this particular trick, because Internet Explorer and Netscape handle their favorites and bookmarks, respectively, slightly differently.

For Internet Explorer users (version 4 and later), this trick pops up an Add Favorite dialog box (shown in Figure 10-6) when users leave your page. Users are forced to either click OK (to add your page to their favorites) or click Cancel (to continue merrily on their way); being confronted at all is terribly annoying.

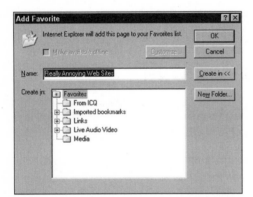

Figure 10-6: Annoy Internet Explorer users by automatically popping up the Add Favorite dialog box whenever they leave your page.

Unfortunately, there's no similar way to bookmark a page automatically within Netscape (or with versions of IE prior to version 4), so you're limited to annoying users via a dialog box message. When Netscape users choose to leave your page, this trick pops up a confirm alert box (shown in Figure 10-7) that nags them to return to your page to bookmark it.

Figure 10-7: Netscape users will be irritated when they see this confirm alert box when they jump to another page.

You activate this trick by entering the code in Listing 10-4 into the head of your HTML document; replace *url* with the address of the current page.

Listing 10-4: JavaScript code to nag users about bookmarking your site; insert in the head of your document

```
<script language="JavaScript1.2">
<!--

function netscapeAlert()
{if (confirm("Do you want to return and bookmark the previous
page?"))
{location.href = "url";}}

function savetoFave()
{if ((navigator.appName == "Microsoft Internet Explorer") &&
(navigator.appVersion>="4"))
{window.external.AddFavorite(location.href, document.title)}
else
{netscapeAlert()}}

//-->
</script>
```

You also need to add the onUnload event to the document's <body> tag, like this:

```
<body onUnload="savetoFave()">
```

Practical uses for this technique

If a user bookmarks your page, that user is more likely to return at some future date. For that reason, you want your site bookmarked by as many users as possible—and some percentage of visitors will click OK automatically just to close the confirm alert box. That makes this trick a decent way to increase your site traffic.

How not to be annoying

While being nagged once is bad enough, being nagged every time you leave a site is downright maddening. If you're good with cookies (see Trick #110, in Chapter 11), you can adapt this trick's script to *not* trigger for repeat visitors. Even better, you can eliminate the automatic pop-up altogether and replace it with a reminder link that users have to click. Assuming you left the JavaScript code in the head of your document, you'd remove the onUnload event from the <body> tag and use this code for the manual bookmarking link:

```
<a href="javascript:savetoFave()">Click here to add this page
to your Favorites.</a>
```

Trick #99: Nag Users to Make Your Page Their Home Page

While I'm on the subject of nagging, what about a page that nags you into making it the default home page for your browser? This is every bit as annoying as being nagged to bookmark a page and has even more exasperating consequences if the user actually clicks OK.

How to do it

This trick works pretty much like the previous one, in that it actually performs the action for Internet Explorer users (version 4 or later) and merely pops up a confirm alert box to nag Netscape users. Actually, the trick is polite enough to ask IE users before it switches the home page, via the message box shown in Figure 10-8.

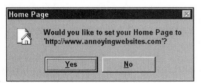

Figure 10-8: Why *wouldn't* users want to make your page their default home page?

Because the action part of this trick is Internet Explorer–specific, there's a bit more coding involved than what you're probably used to seeing.

First, you have to change the normal <html> tag at the top of your document to read as follows:

```
<html XMLNS:IE>
```

Next, add the code in Listing 10-5 to the head of your document.

> ### Listing 10-5: **HTML and JavaScript code to nag users into making your site their home page; insert in the head of your document**

```
<style>
@media all
{IE\:HOMEPAGE {behavior:url(#default#homepage)}}
</style>

<script language="JavaScript">
<!--

function netscapeAlert()
{if (confirm("Do you want to return and make the previous page
your home page?"))
{location.href = "url";}}

function setPage()
{if ((navigator.appName == "Microsoft Internet Explorer") &&
(navigator.appVersion>="4"))
{thisPage.setHomePage("url");}
else
{netscapeAlert()}}

//-->
</script>

<IE:HOMEPAGE ID="thisPage" />
```

Finally, add the following `onUnload` event to the `<body>` tag, as follows:

```
<body onunLoad="setPage()">
```

Make sure to replace both instances of *url* with the full address of your current page.

Practical uses for this technique

You find this trick used by a number of commercial Web sites, particularly portals. These sites want to be the first thing you see whenever you log onto the Internet, in order to command higher advertising rates — based on the increased site traffic from users too lazy to change their browser's home page manually.

How not to be annoying

This trick is less annoying if the user has to take a deliberate action to make the change. To change the activation from automatic on page unload to manual on a link click, return the <body> tag to normal and add the following code at the appropriate place on your page:

```
<a href="javascript:setPage()">Click here to make this page
your default home page.</a>
```

The Annoying Summary

As you can see, bewildering organization and navigation can totally bumfoozle even the most sophisticated visitors to your site. While simply being disorganized is a good start, if you truly set your mind to it, you can deliberately misdirect users in such a way that they'll never be able to find their way home.

When you're considering the concept of retaining users by keeping them too lost to leave, you shouldn't forget the approach of adding your own frames to other sites' pages, as discussed in Trick #48 (in Chapter 4). This approach, as you remember, ensures that any site linked to from your site will appear within a framed page that also includes some sort of frame designed to remind users of where they've been. (Your site, that is.) The nice thing about combining this trick with the techniques presented in this chapter is that after users *finally* figure out how to escape from your site, they're not totally released; your branded frame will continue to follow them, no matter how far they try to distance themselves from your site from hell.

✦   ✦   ✦

CHAPTER

Rage-Inducing Registrations

I f you understand how annoying it can be to be denied entrance—to a club, or a function, or whatever—then you can appreciate the particular annoyance of being denied entrance to a Web site. Whether it's an annoying Flash animation (discussed in Trick #88, in Chapter 9), a request for a user ID or password, or the need to complete some long and complicated registration form, anything that blocks your entrance to a Web site is a source of major irritation. With more than four billion pages on the Web, it's easy enough to skip those that include some sort of pre-entry watchdog—unless, of course, the site behind the locked door contains something that you really need.

So, in the spirit of presenting as many different ways to annoy users as possible, this chapter shows you all sorts of tricks to keep visitors from accessing your site, from simple passwords to blocked IP addresses. Have fun implementing these techniques—and get ready to watch your traffic count drop to near zero!

Trick #100: Force Users to Click OK Before They Enter

You enter the URL for a Web site, and instead of the site's home page, you're presented with a dialog box containing some sort of message. Maybe it's a welcome message ("Welcome to my Web site! Click OK to enter!"); maybe it's some sort of terms and conditions agreement. In any case, you have to make a conscious effort to click the OK button before you can enter.

It's a little thing, but it's really irksome.

◆   ◆   ◆   ◆

Annoying Things in This Chapter

Force users to click OK before they enter

Force users to choose a browser before they enter

Force visitors to click a banner ad before they enter

Force users to provide a password before they enter

Bomb their browsers if they don't know the password

Force users to register before they enter

Require that certain fields be completed

Make users complete the form within a specified time limit

Don't provide any help if users forget their password

Don't use cookies to track repeat visitors

Block underage users

Block users who come from certain IP addresses

◆   ◆   ◆   ◆

How to do it

There are several different ways to force visitors to click OK before they can enter your site. The simplest is the basic alert box, which you learned about in Trick #50 in Chapter 5, "Pointless Pop-ups and Worthless Windows." This technique is ideal if you merely want to display some sort of welcome message; all you have to do is insert the onLoad event handler and the alert box code in your document's <body> tag, like this:

```
<body onLoad='alert("message-text")'>
```

You should replace *message-text* with your personalized greeting, of course.

A slightly more complicated technique involves a confirm alert dialog box, which was also discussed in Trick #50. (Good old Trick #50 — pretty versatile!) This technique requires that your index.html page be blank, except for a few specific lines of code. (You'll have to name your site's main page something other than index.html.)

Begin by entering the code in Listing 11-1 into the head of your blank index.html document. Replace *next-url* with the address of the real main page of your site, *other-url* with the address of an alternate page to which to send anyone who clicks Cancel instead of OK, and *message-text* with your personalized greeting.

Listing 11-1: JavaScript code to display a confirm alert box before users can enter your site; insert in the head of your document

```
<script language="JavaScript">
<!--

function nagAlert()
{if (confirm("message-text"))
{location.href = "next-url";}
else
{location.href = "other-url";}}

//-->
</script>
```

You then call this function by inserting the onLoad event handler in the document's <body> tag, like this:

```
<body onLoad='nagAlert()'>
```

A more advanced entry blocker requires that users read your terms and conditions and select an "I Agree" check box before they can enter. This technique requires that your `index.html` page contain your terms and conditions, as shown in Figure 11-1, along with the following code. (If you want to be really annoying, make sure that your terms and conditions are as long and as obtuse and as totally irrelevant as humanly possible.)

Begin by inserting the `onLoad` event handler into your document's `<body>` tag, like this:

```
<body onLoad="termsAccept=true;">
```

Next, insert the code in Listing 11-2 into the body of your document, below your terms and conditions.

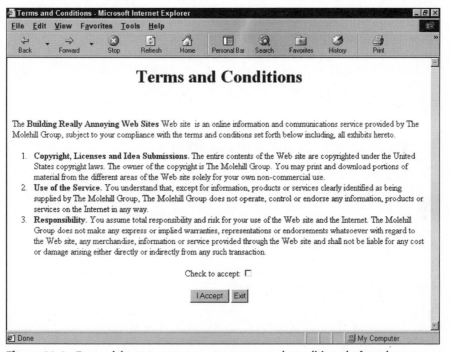

Figure 11-1: Force visitors to agree to your terms and conditions before they can enter your site.

Listing 11-2: HTML code for terms and conditions agreement; insert in the body of your document

```
<form name="myTerms" action="next-url" method="get">
Check to accept:
<input type="checkbox" name="yup" value="ON">
<br>
<br>
<input onclick="if (termsAccept)
{if (document.myTerms.yup.checked)
{document.myTerms.submit();}
else {window.alert('You must check the box to continue.')}}
else {window.alert('Please wait...')}"
type="button" value="I Accept">
<input type="button" value="Exit"
onclick="document.location.href='other-url';">
</form>
```

Replace *next-url* with the address of your next page (your site's real main page), and *other-url* with the address of the page where you want to send anyone who has objections.

Practical uses for this technique

If you have terms and conditions that you want users to agree to (involving the copyright of your content, for example), then this trick is a good one to learn. While this "click if you agree" approach probably won't stand up to real legal scrutiny, it's better than nothing, and it might make some users think twice before they agree to enter. (But, hey, what do I know? You should probably ask a real lawyer just to make sure.)

How not to be annoying

If all you want to do is greet your site's visitors, you can do so in a way that doesn't require that they click a button to enter. Consider one of the animated greetings discussed in Trick #88 (Chapter 9) — either a Flash animation or a faux-Flash JavaScript text greeting.

If you have terms and conditions for the use of your site, you should realize that most users don't read them — even when you display them right in front of their faces. You're probably better off just including a link at the bottom of your main page to a separate terms and conditions page, and forget about asking for explicit approval from your site's visitors.

Trick #101: Force Users to Choose a Browser Before They Enter

There are many different ways to force users to take some sort of action before they can enter your site. An oldie (but a goodie) revolves around the fact that some JavaScript and HTML codes work differently in different browsers. Because of this fact, some Web site developers create separate versions of their sites for Internet Explorer and for Netscape. While you *can* have your site automatically detect which browser is being used, it's more fun to force your users to select which browser they're using before they can enter your site.

How to do it

For this trick to work, you should create three separate Web pages — an index.html page (*not* your real main page; this page will contain all the "choose a browser" stuff), a main page for Internet Explorer (call it main-ie.html), and a main page for Netscape (call it main-netscape.html). Next, insert the code in Listing 11-3 into the body of the index.html page.

> **Listing 11-3: HTML code to force a browser choice; insert in the body of your document**

```
<table border="0" cellspacing="1" width="90%">
<tr>

<td width="50%" bgcolor="#0000FF">
<p align="center"><font color="#FFFFFF" face="Arial">
Click here to view this site with Internet Explorer:
</font></p>
<p align="center">
<form>
<input type="button" value="Internet Explorer"
onClick="window.location.href='main-ie.html'">
</form></td>

<td width="50%" bgcolor="#008080">
<p align="center"><font face="Arial" color="#FFFFFF">
Click here to view this site with Netscape Navigator:
</font></p>
<p align="center">
<form>
<input type="button" value="Netscape Navigator"
onClick="window.location.href='main-netscape.html'">
</form></td>
</tr></table>
```

The result is shown in Figure 11-2. When users click the Internet Explorer button, they go to your IE-specific main page; when they click the Netscape Navigator button, they go to your Netscape-specific page. (And if they click the wrong button, whatever happens next is their own fault!)

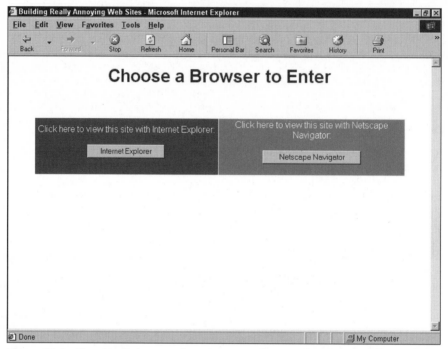

Figure 11-2: The simplest way to force users to choose a browser-specific version of your site before entering

If you really want to pull a fast one on your users, don't create separate IE and Netscape pages. Create a single site and link both the IE and Netscape buttons to the same page. Now you've forced your visitors to make a conscious choice and click a button, for no reason whatsoever!

Practical uses for this technique

If you include a lot of Internet Explorer– or Netscape-specific effects, it may be worth your while to create separate versions of your site. Otherwise, users of the other browser might miss out on some of the fun — or be faced with some nonworking site elements.

How not to be annoying

There are actually two ways to address the differences between browsers that don't require users to click a single button.

The first approach is to automatically detect users' browser types and then redirect their browsers to a browser-specific page. This technique was discussed in Trick #90; Listing 9-5 contains the specific code you want to use.

The second approach is the one followed for most of the code in this book — make all your code as cross-browser compatible as possible. (You can't do this with 100 percent effectiveness, but you can come close.) That way you don't need separate IE and Netscape versions of your site, which is a lot more convenient for your visitors — and a lot more convenient for you.

Trick #102: Force Visitors to Click a Banner Ad Before They Enter

Forcing visitors to choose a browser is irritating in its own way, but forcing them to click on an ad will frost even the most tolerant users. Most Internet users have trained themselves to ignore banner ads, so when you force them to look at and click an ad before you let them into your site, you're going to get some really ticked off visitors — if, in fact, they don't go elsewhere out of spite.

How to do it

This trick presents a page containing a banner ad *before* users reach your main page. Users must click on the banner ad to gain admittance to your site.

To make this trick work, you have to name your real main page something other than `index.html` and use the `index.html` page to contain your banner ad, along with the code in Listing 11-4. (Obviously, for this trick to be effective, you need to include some text on the `index.html` page alerting users that to enter your main site, they have to click on the banner ad first.)

Begin by entering the code in Listing 11-4 into the head of the `index.html` page.

Listing 11-4: JavaScript code for a must-click banner ad; insert in the head of your document

```
<script language="JavaScript">
<!--

function mustClick(ad, site)
{window.open(ad);
window.location = site;}

//-->
</script>
```

Now surround your banner ad (or sponsor's link) with the following code:

```
<a href="javascript:mustClick('sponsor-url', 'next-url');"><img
src="ad-image"></a>
```

Replace *sponsor-url* with the URL of the sponsor's Web site, *next-url* with the URL of your second home page, and *ad-image* with the URL and filename of your banner ad graphic.

Practical uses for this technique

This technique is useful for making sure that your sponsors get visited — and that you get compensated for those visits. If users have to click the ad to proceed, then you're likely to generate a lot of click-throughs — or reduce the resulting traffic to your site, one of the two.

How not to be annoying

Forcing users to view and click an ad is extremely annoying, to the point of causing a majority of potential visitors to bypass your site completely. If you're more interested in traffic than ad revenues, use regular (nonmandatory) banner ads at the top of your normal pages. You can encourage users to visit your advertisers' Web sites, but you shouldn't force them to do it.

Of course, if you want to be extremely unannoying, don't use banner ads at all. Everybody hates them and nobody clicks them anyway — unless you force them to!

Trick #103: Force Users to Provide a Password Before They Enter

Maybe your site is so important that not just anyone can enter. Maybe you require users to enter a secret password before you'll let them see what you've developed. Maybe you figure that requiring a password is just an easy way to irritate people. In any case, password-protecting your site is a good way to keep the riff-raff out while annoying pretty much everybody else in the process.

How to do it

There are many ways to password-protect your page. The simplest is to create a single password that all visitors must use.

Note The drawback to this — and any other — form of JavaScript password protection is that anyone with a modicum of JavaScript savvy can view the HTML source for your page and find your passwords. You'll need to employ a more sophisticated password scheme if you want more foolproof protection.

To implement this simple form of password protection, enter the code in Listing 11-5 into the head of your HTML document.

Listing 11-5: **JavaScript code to password-protect a Web page; insert in the head of your document**

```
<script language="JavaScript">
<!--
var yourPassword;
var pass1="password";
yourPassword=prompt('Please enter your password to view this
page',' ');

if (yourPassword==pass1)
alert('Password correct -- click OK to enter!');
else
{window.location="other-url";}

//-->
</script>
```

Replace *password* with your password, and *other-url* with the address of an alternate Web page you want to present to unwanted guests. (If you don't have an alternate page, just send them to a generic portal.) Whenever your main page loads, users will be prompted for the password. If they enter the right password, the page is displayed; if not, they're sent to the other page of your choice.

As I said, this initial technique is fairly simple, both to create and to use. A more sophisticated technique requires that users enter both a password and a distinct user ID. All you have to do is insert the code in Listing 11-6 into the head of your document.

> **Listing 11-6: JavaScript code to accept multiple user IDs and passwords; insert in the head of your document**

```
<script language="JavaScript">
<!--

var goodURL = "this-url"
var badURL = "other-url"
var userID = prompt("User ID:","")
var password = prompt("Password:","")

if (userID == null || password == null)
{alert("Incorrect user ID or password")
window.location=badURL;}

else
{var combo = userID + password
var total = combo.toLowerCase()
if (total == "id1password1" || total == "id2password2" || total
== "id3password3")
{alert("User ID and password recognized -- click to enter.")
location = goodURL;}

else
{alert("Incorrect user ID or password")
window.location=badURL;}}

//-->
</script>
```

You need to master several tricks within this trick. First, replace *this-url* with the URL of the current page, and *other-url* with the address of an alternate Web page for those users without the right ID/password combination.

Next, create your user ID/password combos and enter them as *id1password1*, *id2password2*, and so on. Just take your user ID and your password and crunch them together into a single word. For example, if the user ID is "tom" and the password is "swift," then you'll enter "tomswift" for *id1password1*. You can create as many ID/password pairs as you want; just keep extending the line of code with more of the following:

```
|| total == "idpassword"
```

Practical uses for this technique

You use passwords to limit access to your site. If you use a single password for all users, you control access by controlling whom you give the password to. If your security slips, however, the only way to deny access to a formerly approved visitor is to change the single password—which means handing out that new password to all accepted users.

When you assign separate passwords to each user (as in the second example), you can cut off access to any specific user by deleting that ID/password pair from the code; all other users will retain their access, along with their original IDs and passwords. You also make users think they're unique by assigning them IDs as well as passwords; it's a nice touch.

How not to be annoying

This particular trick revolves around user IDs and passwords that you create and then dole out to approved visitors. The users don't have any say in creating their own IDs or passwords; they have to take what you give them.

A more user-friendly approach is to let each user choose his or her own ID and password, as described in Trick #105.

Trick #104: Bomb Their Browsers If They Don't Know the Password

Forgetting a password isn't the worst thing most users will do in the course of a day. Still, you can really get their bells ringing if you treat this sort of thing as a capital offense and deliver harsh punishment when it happens.

Most sites will simply send you somewhere else if you forget your password—which isn't much punishment at all. A more severe approach is to "bomb" the users' browsers with a barrage of annoying pop-up windows when the wrong password is entered. This is a particularly cruel and unusual punishment, as the only way to escape the browser bombing is to shut off your computer!

How to do it

The script in Listing 11-7 builds on a simple password script but adds the nasty browser bombing twist at the end. (This is the same browser bomb I presented in Trick #56 in Chapter 5, by the way.) This particular code allows the user three tries to enter the right password; if the third attempt fails, multiple pop-up windows are launched . . . and launched . . . and launched.

Note Do *not* test this code on your computer—you'll be bombarded with an unending barrage of unwanted pop-ups!

If you're feeling really evil, all you have to do is enter the code in Listing 11-7 into the head of your HTML document.

Listing 11-7: JavaScript code to bomb users who enter the wrong password: insert in the head of your document

```
<script language="JavaScript">
<!--

var goodURL = "this-url";
var password = "password";
var numTries = 3;
var x = 0;
var y;

while (x < numTries)
{y = x+1
var trigger = prompt("Enter your password to proceed"
+" ("+ y +" out of "+numTries+" tries)","");

if (trigger == null) x++;
else
{if (trigger.toLowerCase() == password)
{alert("Password correct -- click OK to enter");
location = goodURL;
break;}
else x++;}}
if (x == numTries)
{while(true) window.open("alternative-url");}

//-->
</script>
```

Note In case you're wondering, it's the `while(true)` that opens the infinite number of pop-up windows. (The condition is always true, so the windows keep opening.) And, yes, you can use this code with other event handlers to bomb users just for opening or closing your page, as discussed in Trick #56 (Chapter 5).

Replace *this-url* with the address of this Web page, and *alternative-url* with the address of the page you want to appear in the pop-ups. Naturally, you should also replace *password* with the password to this page—and you can increase or decrease the number of tries each user gets by changing the value of the `numTries` variable. (The default is 3.)

Practical uses for this technique

The only reason I can think of to commit this sort of attack is if you suspect some rival of trying to hack into your private pages. In that instance, you should apply the bomb to a page where the URL is not widely known, so that you don't have unsuspecting users stumbling over it and then having their systems crash.

How not to be annoying

One could make the case that if you warn users about what can happen to them (after three tries), they'll get only what's coming to them. Still, this is one really mean trick — whether one knows it's coming or not.

Trick #105: Force Users to Register Before They Enter

In Trick #103 you learned how to insert a user ID and password between users and your main page. That trick was predicated on your assigning the IDs and passwords, although there are other ways to approach this situation.

A more time-consuming approach is to ask each and every user to register before you allow entrance to your site. While this approach does enable users to choose their own IDs and passwords, if you create an overly long and complex form that asks for the right combination of confidential and irrelevant information, you'll annoy the heck out of anyone dedicated enough to see the form through to the end.

How to do it

To use this approach, you need to know how to create Web forms, how to send form results to a database, and how to check future user logins against entries in the database.

While all that is beyond what I can present in this book, I can show you how to create the type of registration form shown in Figure 11-3. All you have to do is insert the code in Listing 11-8 into the body of your HTML document, where you want the registration form to appear; replace *server-url* with the address of the query server where you'll send the form results.

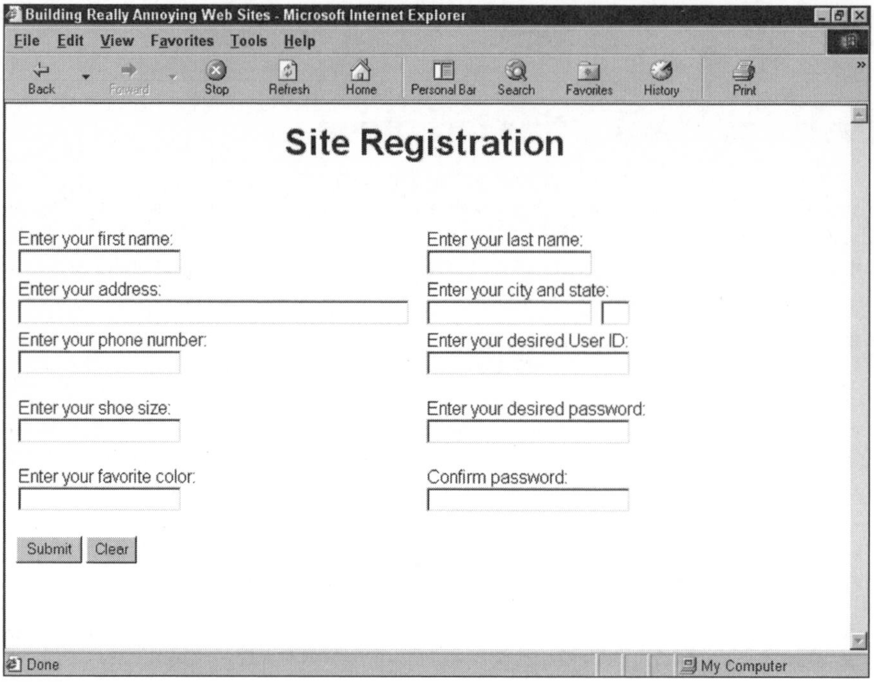

Figure 11-3: Make users register before they enter.

Listing 11-8: HTML code to accept user registration; insert in the body of your document

```
<form action="server-url" method="post">
<font face="Arial">
<table border="0" cellspacing="1" width="100%">

<tr>
<td width="50%">Enter your first name:<br>
<input type="text" name="formFirstname" size="20"></td>
<td width="50%"><p>Enter your last name:<br>
<input type="text" name="formLastname" size="20"></td>
</tr>

<tr>
<td width="50%">Enter your address:<br>
<input type="text" name="formAddress" size="50"></td>
<td width="50%">Enter your city and state:<br>
<input type="text" name="formCity" size="20">  <input
type="text" name="formState" size="2"></td>
</tr>

<tr>
```

```
<td width="50%">Enter your phone number:<br>
<input type="text" name="formPhone" size="20">
<P>Enter your shoe size:<br>
<input type="text" name="formShoe" size="20"></p>
<p>Enter your favorite color:<br>
<input type="text" name="formColor" size="20"></p></td>
<td width="50%">Enter your desired User ID:<br>
<input type="text" size="25" maxlength="256" name="userID">
<p>Enter your desired password:<br>
<input type="password" size="25" maxlength="256"
name="Password"></p>
<p>Confirm password:<br>
<input type="password" size="25" maxlength="256"
name="PasswordVerify"></p></td>
</tr>

</table></font>
<p><input type="submit" value="Submit"> <input type="reset"
value="Clear"></p>
</form>
```

Note   To learn more about creating and programming the results from Web forms, check
out the forms tutorial at WEBalley (`www.weballey.net/forms/`) or take a look
at *Creating Web Pages Bible* (Hungry Minds, 2001).

Practical uses for this technique

Forcing users to register enables you to collect valuable information about them.
You can then use that information for your own nefarious means (or even to help
you better target your site and services to your users' tastes), or try to sell that
information to interested third parties.

How not to be annoying

The shorter the registration form, the better. (User ID and password only is best.)
The more personal information you ask for, the fewer number of users will complete the form. In fact, if you want to truly minimize your site traffic, devise a form
that stretches over multiple pages.

If you do ask for personal information, be aware that many users are concerned
about their online privacy. These users will look for a privacy policy before they
submit any information, to determine what you intend to do with the information
you collect. While it isn't illegal to sell customer information (that's how mailing list
companies have stayed in business all these years), it's good form to tell users if
you're going to do so.

Trick #106: Require That Certain Fields Be Completed

One way that lazy users get around filling out an annoying form is to not fill in all the fields. You can't allow that sort of cheating, so let's look at a trick which requires that some or all of a form's fields be completed before the form can be submitted.

How to do it

This trick lets you mark specified fields in your form as must-completes. For the purposes of this example, I'll assume that you're tacking this code onto the form you created in Listing 11-8.

Begin by inserting the code in Listing 11-9 into the head of the document that contains your form.

Listing 11-9: JavaScript code to require completion of selected form fields; insert in the head of your document

```
<script language="JavaScript">
<!--

function mustComplete(which)
{var pass=true;

if (document.images)
{for (i=0;i<which.length;i++)
{var tempobj=which.elements[i];
if (tempobj.name.substring(0,8)=="required")
{if (((tempobj.type=="text"||tempobj.type=="textarea")&&
tempobj.value=='')||(tempobj.type.toString().charAt(0)=="s"&&
tempobj.selectedIndex==0))
{pass=false;
break;}}}}

if (!pass)
{shortFieldName=tempobj.name.substring(8,30).toUpperCase();
alert("Please complete the "+shortFieldName+" field!");
return false;}
else
return true;}

//-->
</script>
```

Now change the `<form>` field of your original code to read as follows:

```
<form onSubmit="return mustComplete(this)">
```

Now you need to go through your code and add "required" to the front of each field name that you want to be a must-complete. For example, if you want the field `formShoe` (in Listing 11-8) to be a must-complete field, you should rename the field `requiredformShoe`. Now, when a user tries to submit the form without filling in the indicated fields, the alert box in Figure 11-4 will be displayed.

Figure 11-4: Nag users to fill in all the form fields on your registration page.

Practical uses for this technique

If you need certain information to properly register new users, you have to employ this or a similar must-complete technique. The alternative is to assemble an incomplete database, which doesn't do anybody any good.

How not to be annoying

At the very least, you can alert users ahead of time as to which fields must be completed and which are optional. You can do this by marking the must-complete fields with an asterisk, or by using color text for the field's description. Alternately, you can add the phrase "(optional)" to the description of any optional field.

Trick #107: Make Users Complete the Form within a Specified Time Limit

Did you ever have to take a timed test when you were in school? Didn't the pressure of completing all the questions within a short period of time really stress you out? Didn't you *hate* that experience?

Well, now you can apply a similar time-pressure to your site's new visitors. Give them a registration form to fill out and then require that they fill it out within a specified period of time—or else!

How to do it

Here's how this one works. You decide what time limit to set (in seconds), and then users see a countdown as they fill out the registration form. If the time limit is up when they submit the form, they are presented with the friendly alert box shown in Figure 11-5.

Figure 11-5: Sorry—you're too slow to register at this site!

This trick will work with any form you create; for the purposes of this example, I'll assume you're working with the form you created in Listing 11-8. Begin by inserting the code in Listing 11-10 into the head of your form document.

Listing 11-10: JavaScript code to set a time limit for form completion; insert in the head of your document

```
<script language="JavaScript">
<!--

var i = 0;
var done = 0;
var timeLeft = 10;

function formTimer()
{if(timeLeft != null) timerId = setTimeout("formTimer()",
1000);
if(i < timeLeft)
{i += 1;
document.clock.seconds.value = timeLeft - i;}}

function timeAlert()
{if(i < timeLeft)
{done = true;}
else {alert("Registration time limit exceeded. Please repeat
the registration process.");
done = false;}
return done;}

//-->
</script>
```

Next, insert the `onLoad` event handler into your document's `<body>` tag, like this:

```
<body onLoad="formTimer()">
```

Now you have to change the `<form>` tag in the body of your document, to add the `onSubmit` event handler. Use this code:

```
<form name="clock" onSubmit="return timeAlert();">
```

Finally, add the following code directly after the `<form>` tag; this inserts the count-down timer at the top of the form.

```
Time Remaining: <input type=text name="seconds" value="0"
size=3>
```

The default timer is set to 10 seconds; you can increase or decrease the length of the timer by changing the value of the `timeLeft` variable.

Practical uses for this technique

Maybe you don't want users just sitting at the front door of your site, an empty form idling on their computer screens. Maybe you want to admit only users who possess a sense of urgency. Maybe you just like the fact that you can give users sweaty palms. Whatever the case, I'm sure there's a practical use for timing-out users who don't complete your registration within an acceptable time limit.

How not to be annoying

If you must limit the time allowed for registration, be sure to provide a reasonable amount of time to get the job done. Forcing users to fill out a complex form in ten seconds or less won't win you any friends.

Trick #108: Don't Provide Any Help If Users Forget Their Password

Let's say you took the less-annoying approach and let users choose their own user IDs and passwords, as described in Trick #105. What happens when users forget their passwords — or their IDs?

The nice thing about users' forgetting their own personal information is that while they get annoyed, they get annoyed at *themselves* for having such a bad memory. After all, what fault is it of yours if some guy in Mayberry can't remember all his passwords?

Where you start to take some blame is if you don't offer any help in remembering that forgotten information. If the user can't remember a password, and you won't help him recall it, that user can never again access your site. (Unless he registers with a new ID and password, of course.)

How to do it

This is really simple. Offer no means to recall the forgotten information — which also means eliminating all means to contact you or the site administrator. That means no e-mail contact links, or else you'll start getting e-mails from your more forgetful users. Cut off all means of contact, and those users will never again sully your virtual doorstep.

Practical uses for this technique

If the password to your site isn't important enough to commit to long-term memory, then that user doesn't deserve to get in, anyway. Leaving users completely on their own is a rather draconian way of weeding out less-desirable visitors.

How not to be annoying

The best sites offer a variety of help for forgetful users. This help can include:

✦ **Secret questions.** When users join the site, they're asked to enter a question to be asked of them if they forget their password. (They also enter the answer, of course.) Then a user who enters an incorrect user ID or password is asked the secret question; answering that question correctly (it's typically something like their mother's maiden name or their city of birth) grants them access to the site.

✦ **Passwords via e-mail.** If users can't remember their passwords, they click a link or a button to have their password e-mailed to them, using an address they provided originally.

✦ **Technical support.** If all else fails, provide a link to e-mail–based customer support, or a phone number for users to call if they have problems. Passwords can then be requested and supplied via these alternative contact methods.

Trick #109: Don't Use Cookies to Track Repeat Visitors

Entering a password or filling out a registration once is annoying enough; being forced to fill in the same blanks every time you enter a site cranks up the annoyance factor several levels higher than most people can tolerate.

The reason some sites keep asking you the same questions over and over again is that they're not tracking your visits. Every time you access their main page, it's as if it's your first time there — even if you visit every day.

The accepted mechanism for storing user information is called a *cookie*, and you probably know all about them, at least from a user's perspective. A cookie is nothing more than a text string, stored in a small text file on your computer's hard drive. Each cookie stores information specific to a given Web site. The text for a cookie looks something like this:

```
name=value;expires=date;
```

The *name* field is the name of the data being stored; *value* is the value of the data. The expires field is the date that the cookie expires; this field is optional. (Additional fields can be added for the path, domain, and secure status.)

You can use JavaScript both to create cookies and to read cookie files — and then use that stored data to perform additional functions on your page. For example, you could create a cookie that stores a visitor's user ID and password. You can then read that cookie the next time the user visits your page and use that information to automatically admit the visitor without requiring that he or she manually reenter an ID and password.

Note   To learn more about cookies, go to the Cookie Central Web site at www.cookie central.com or see *JavaScript Bible, Fourth Edition* (Hungry Minds, 2001).

How to do it

To create a cookie on a user's computer, insert the code in Listing 11-11 into the head of your HTML document. Replace *name* with the name of the cookie, *value* with the value you want to store, and *expires* with an optional expiration date for the cookie.

Listing 11-11: JavaScript code to store a cookie; insert in the head of your document

```
<script language="JavaScript">
<!--

function SetCookie(name,value,expires,path,domain,secure)
{document.cookie = name + "=" + escape(value) +
((expires) ? "; expires=" + expires.toGMTString() : "") +
((path) ? "; path=" + path : "") +
((domain) ? "; domain=" + domain : "") +
((secure) ? "; secure" : "");}

//-->
</script>
```

To return the value of a cookie, use the script in Listing 11-12.

Listing 11-12: JavaScript code to return the value of a stored cookie; insert in the head of your document

```
<script language="JavaScript">
<!--

function GetCookie(name)
{var arg = name + "=";
var alen = arg.length;
var clen = document.cookie.length;
var i = 0;
while (i < clen) { var j = i + alen;
if (document.cookie.substring(i, j) == arg)
return getCookieVal (j);
i = document.cookie.indexOf(" ", i) + 1;
if (i == 0) break; } return null;}

//-->
</script>
```

Let's look at a real-world (although not necessarily practical) example of how to use a cookie on your Web page. This script displays the number of times a user has visited your page. Begin by inserting the code in Listing 11-13 into the head of your HTML document.

Listing 11-13: JavaScript code to set and get the visit counter cookie; insert in the head of your document

```
<script language="JavaScript">
<!--

function getCookieVal (offset)
{var endstr = document.cookie.indexOf (";", offset);
if (endstr == -1)
endstr = document.cookie.length;
return unescape(document.cookie.substring(offset, endstr));}

function GetCookie (name)
{var arg = name + "=";
var alen = arg.length;
var clen = document.cookie.length;
var i = 0;
while (i < clen)
{var j = i + alen;
```

```
if (document.cookie.substring(i, j) == arg)
return getCookieVal (j);
i = document.cookie.indexOf(" ", i) + 1;
if (i == 0)
break;}
return null;}

function SetCookie (name, value)
{var argv = SetCookie.arguments;
var argc = SetCookie.arguments.length;
var expires = (2 < argc) ? argv[2] : null;
var path = (3 < argc) ? argv[3] : null;
var domain = (4 < argc) ? argv[4] : null;
var secure = (5 < argc) ? argv[5] : false;
document.cookie = name + "=" + escape (value) +
((expires == null) ? "" : ("; expires=" +
expires.toGMTString())) +
((path == null) ? "" : ("; path=" + path)) +
((domain == null) ? "" : ("; domain=" + domain)) +
((secure == true) ? "; secure" : "");}

function ResetCounts(name)
{visits = 0;
SetCookie("visits", browserVisits, expDate , "/", null, false);
location.reload();}

//-->
</script>
```

Now insert the code in Listing 11-14 into the body of your document.

Listing 11-14: JavaScript code to display number of visits; insert in the body of your document

```
<script language="JavaScript">
<!--

var expDate = new Date();
var browserVisits;
expDate.setTime(expDate.getTime() + (24 * 60 * 60 * 1000 *
365));

if(!(browserVisits = GetCookie("visits")))
browserVisits = 0;
browserVisits++;
SetCookie("visits", browserVisits, expDate, "/", null, false);
```

Continued

Listing 11-14 *(continued)*

```
document.write("You have visited this page "
+"<font color=#FF0000><b>"+browserVisits+"</b></font>"
+" time(s).");

//-->
</script>
```

The result of this cookie is shown in Figure 11-6. It's not particularly annoying (although it's a fairly useless trick), but it does show a bit of what you can do with cookies.

Figure 11-6: The result of the visit-counter cookie

Practical uses for this technique

There are many practical uses for cookies. You can use cookies to tell you if someone has previously visited your site, to store passwords and user IDs, to store any personal information you obtain from user registration forms, to track what sites users come from, to track their activities while on your site, and so on and so on. In fact, many user privacy groups decry the use of cookies to track what they feel is sensitive data, and newer Web browsers enable users to delete stored cookies or turn off cookies completely.

How not to be annoying

If you're a conscientious developer, you probably should make minimal use of cookies; track only the most essential data, and don't track anything that could offend hyper-sensitive privacy hounds. You can also add a blurb about your use of cookies to your site's privacy policy; this way, interested users will at least be aware of what you're tracking.

Trick #110: Block Underage Users

Who needs kids?

You don't, especially if you have adult content on your site. If you need to keep underage users away from all or part of your site, use this trick to ask their age— and then send the youngsters elsewhere.

How to do it

This trick creates a form that asks users their age, like the one shown in Figure 11-7. If their answer is 18 or less, they're sent to another page of your choosing. (Disney.com or Yahooligans! is always good.)

Start by entering the script in Listing 11-15 into the head of your HTML document.

> ### Listing 11-15: **JavaScript code to weed out underage visitors; insert in the head of your document**

```
<script language="JavaScript">
<!--

function ageCheck(form)
{if (form.value < 18)
{alert("Sorry, you must be 18 to enter this site");
window.location="other-url";}
else
window.location="next-url";}

//-->
</script>
```

Figure 11-7: Ask for the user's age — and admit only legal adults to your site.

Replace *next-url* with the address of your next, adults-only page; replace *other-url* with the address of a suitable page for underage visitors.

Finish up the trick by creating the age-check form. To do so, enter the code in Listing 11-16 into the body of your document.

Listing 11-16: HTML code to create an age-check form; insert in the body of your document

```
<form>
<p><font face="Arial">Enter Your Age</font></p>
<p><input type="text" size="4" name="age"></p>
<p><input type="button" value="Submit"
onclick="ageCheck(this.form.age)"></p>
</form>
```

Practical uses for this technique

This type of age-checking mechanism is absolutely mandatory if you have adult-oriented content on your site. In fact, the honor-system technique employed here might not be strong enough to keep you out of legal trouble (you should probably check with a real lawyer); you may want to subscribe to an age-check service or require that users submit a credit card number (because credit cards aren't issued to minors) before allowing admittance.

How not to be annoying

This trick gets particularly irritating if you *don't* have adult content behind the age-check firewall. It's also annoying if you change the age barrier in the code to something well above 18, so that you keep out everyone except octogenarians. Use this technique when you truly have content you don't want kids to see, and you should be all right.

Trick #111: Block Users Who Come from Certain IP Addresses

For the last trick in this chapter, it's time to get personal.

What do you do if there's a particular user or group of users you don't want accessing your site? The answer is simple—block 'em!

How to do it

This trick is remarkably easy to implement. All you have to do is create a special CGI file and insert the addresses (either full or partial) of the users or domains you want to block.

What you want to do is create a text file named `.htaccess`. (Note the dot before the name and no dot or extension afterward.) You can create this file in any ASCII text editor.

The contents of the file are detailed in Listing 11-17.

Listing 11-17: Contents of .htaccess CGI file

```
<Limit GET>
order allow,deny
deny from address-1
deny from address-2
allow from all
</Limit>
```

Replace *address-1* and *address-2* with specific addresses. If you know the complete IP address (in the form of xxx.xxx.xxx.xxx), use that. For example, to block the address 207.158.255.213, you'd enter the line:

```
deny from 207.158.255.213
```

If you know a partial IP address, enter that (making sure you end with a period—which forces the script to block all subaddresses). For example, to block all addresses starting with 207.158., you'd enter the line:

```
deny from 207.158.
```

If you know only the domain name, then enter that—but with a *leading* period. For example, to block anyone from the aol.com domain, you'd enter the line:

```
deny from .aol.com
```

You can enter as many deny from lines as you want.

Once you've created this file, upload it to the root directory of your Web site (or to the specific directory to which you want to block access). When users from the named addresses try to access your site, they'll find their access blocked.

Note   If you're using FrontPage extensions on your site, note that FrontPage creates its own .htaccess file. While you can edit that file with the code for this trick, you should know that any modifications to an existing .htaccess file can corrupt your FrontPage extensions and render your site inaccessible. For that reason, you should make a backup copy of your .htaccess file before you make these changes, just in case.

Practical uses for this technique

If you have important information on your Web site, you might not want your competitors to have easy access. If this is the case, just enter the address of your competitor's domain, and all their employees will find that they're blocked from your site.

(This actually happened to me once when I was working for a large corporation. One day we found that a competitor had blocked our access to their site — pretty mean-spirited, we thought. Of course, I could still access the site from my home PC, so I'm not sure how effective it was — but it *was* fairly annoying!)

How not to be annoying

Rejection is rough. There's really no way to make it any easier. That's just the way it is.

The Annoying Summary

It's kind of fun to have a guardian at the gate. Granting permission to enter your site — or withholding that permission — gives you a feeling of power, even if it's somewhat virtual. For that reason, these access-blocking or access-delaying tricks are among some of the most popular on the Internet. It never fails to amaze me how many otherwise-rational Web developers find totally convoluted ways to rationalize what is really nothing more than a power trip for passive-aggressives.

Yes, *you* can enter. No, *you* can't.

It's great to be the one who decides, isn't it?

✦　　✦　　✦

Painful Purchasing

This final chapter is a little different from the previous chapters in this book. First, it's about commercial Web sites, not the personal or semi-pro sites discussed previously. Second, there's not a lot of hands-on code associated with these tricks; the information here is more strategic in nature, so that you can implement it as appropriate to your site.

That said, the tricks in this chapter are some of the most-used of all the irritating techniques found on the Web. For some reason, e-tailers — both big and small — are particularly adept at ticking off their users. This might seem counterproductive, given that the traditional goal of traditional retailers is to turn casual visitors into paying customers, but for some reason e-tailers go out of their way to make their sites extremely hard to use. Maybe it's the fascination with new technology, maybe it's a lack of real-world retailing experience, maybe it's some kind of mean streak that runs through commercial Web site developers. Whatever the reason, my hat goes off to the annoying accomplishments of today's crop of commercial Web sites. We can all learn from their irritating techniques.

Trick #112: Hide the Most Popular Items on Your Site

In traditional retailing, there are two differing philosophies regarding the bread-and-butter items that drive the majority of sales. One philosophy is to put these popular items right out front, because window-shopping brings so many people into the store. The other philosophy is to put the most popular items in the rear of the store, to force customers to walk by all your other merchandise (and maybe buy some of it) to get to the products they came in for.

Neither of these philosophies says "Hide the good stuff."

Many e-tailers, however, do a fairly decent job of making it hard to find the items that are in the most demand. When you're shopping online, if you can't find the items you want — fast — you're going to leave that site and shop elsewhere. So if a site makes it too challenging to find and buy their most popular items, they're going to annoy a lot of customers — and lose a significant number of them to competitors.

How to do it

To hide your best-selling items, you first have to know what your best-selling items are. This means tracking your sales — or, more accurately, tracking customer demand — on an item-by-item basis.

Once you know what items are most in demand, then you can work to make those items harder to find. If you're trying to keep your best-sellers a well-kept secret, here are some things to try:

✦ Don't put the item on your main page.

✦ Don't feature the item as a special or on-sale item.

✦ Don't feature the item within its category — or don't put it in the proper category to begin with.

✦ Don't list the item first within its category — list it last, on some page after the initial page.

✦ Don't give the item a descriptive title — in fact, if you can, give it a deliberately misleading title (try calling a blue long-sleeved sweater an "azure full-length jumper").

Probably the most important thing to do is to not treat your bestsellers any different from your worst-sellers. Don't highlight the items at all; don't give any indication that these products are special or popular or otherwise out of the ordinary. Just hide them among the other product listings, so they get lost in the pack and customers will likely skip right over them.

With this kind of nonspecial treatment, you're sure to reduce the sales on this formerly fast-moving merchandise.

Practical uses for this technique

If you're having trouble keeping your best-selling items in stock, there may be benefit in artificially lowering demand. Likewise, if your best-sellers return the least profit — or are loss leaders — you may want to keep them to yourself. By reducing the visibility of the high-demand items, you can shift sales to other (perhaps more profitable) items that you're more interested in selling.

How not to be annoying

The proper way to deal with high-demand items in an online environment is to give those items prominent placement, ideally on your main page or on their main category page. Because a large number of customers are coming to your site specifically for those items — and because there is substantially less impulse purchasing online than there is offline — there is no sense at all in making it hard to find this merchandise. Help customers get in and out of your site as fast as possible by making it easy to locate and purchase the items that are most in demand, and your customers will turn into repeat customers.

Trick #113: Use Slow-Loading Product Photos — and Lots of Them

Because shopping online is not a tactile experience — you can't pick up an item, look at it closely, feel it, smell it, and so on — the temptation is to replace physical examination with really large and detailed photos of the item. In fact, some sites display multiple photographs (from different sides and angles) in an attempt to provide a 360-degree look at the product. The thinking is that the more you can see (from photographs), the more comfortable you'll be buying something essentially sight unseen.

This logic, however, is faulty — and results in irritated customers who have to sit through the long load times associated with multiple large graphics.

The reality is that those customers who are already comfortable buying outside of traditional retail (via catalogs and direct mail) are accustomed to operating with less sensory information than are traditional retail customers. Your core customers don't need the extra visual handholding, and you only stand to annoy them by clogging up their connection with slow-loading pictures. Those customers that need to see and touch and feel won't be buying online, anyway.

How to do it

The most annoying approach is to devote an entire page to each product, and then to include multiple photos — as large as is physically practical — of that product. Consider including both front and back photos, and (if the product is offered in multiple colors and sizes) separate photographs of each color or size variation. The goal is to load up a very long Web page with as many large graphics files as you can get away with — so that customers give up and go away before the page has a chance to finish loading.

Practical uses for this technique

There is benefit to showing *some* picture of each item you offer for sale. In fact, the more unusual or rare your item is, the more important a picture of that item is to potential purchasers. It's also important to show all the color variations, because not everyone knows the difference between mauve, lilac, lavender, and light purple.

How not to be annoying

Strike a delicate balance between showing enough detail to be useful and providing so much visual information as to be annoying. One approach to this dilemma is to make the pictures optional; provide a link to a larger picture but display only a thumbnail or a text link. In addition, you can make one picture do the work of many by showing a single picture of multiple products; for example, you can include all your different colors in a single photograph. By using fewer photos (even if each photo displays multiple products or variations), you keep the page size down and increase loading speed.

Trick #114: Make Visitors Watch Bad Flash Animations

Everybody loves product demonstrations — right? Well, okay, not everybody does, but they're still a good way to show off everything that your products can do.

The online equivalent of a product demonstration is a Flash animation. Not only can you use Flash to produce pre-entry greetings and commercials for your site (as discussed in Trick #88 in Chapter 9), you can also use Flash to provide animated demos of your key products. In fact, why not set these product-demo animations to play automatically whenever a customer accesses that product page? There are few things that can quell the buying urge than being forced to watch a boring demonstration of the product — even if you've already made up your mind to buy.

How to do it

You learned all about Flash animations in Trick #88, so I won't rehash that info here. The key thing is to produce a Flash animation that is long and boring (you wouldn't want to actually inspire an impulse purchase, would you?) and that plays automatically with no way to turn it off. Set the animation to play whenever the product page is loaded, and you've just placed a very effective roadblock between customer and checkout.

Practical uses for this technique

Some products need to be shown off. Products that do something—slice, dice, drill, buff, rotate, whatever—are tough to present in a static photograph. Flash provides a way for you to demonstrate what a product does, without the product's actually being there for the customer to operate on his or her own. If you do the animation right, it will serve as both a demonstration and a commercial, holding the customer's interest and answering key questions.

How not to be annoying

As with all things that move, providing some way of turning them off goes a long way toward reducing the annoyance level. Even better is to make the animation optional, so that it plays only when the customer intentionally clicks a link or a button. This way you avoid annoying everyone who visits the page while still providing the additional visual information for those customers who want to see it.

Trick #115: Require Uncommon Plug-ins

Imagine walking into your favorite department store and heading down the product aisle but then being stopped by a salesperson.

"I'm sorry," the salesperson tells you, "in order to shop in our store, you have to wear our special proprietary rose-colored glasses."

"I don't have any glasses," you reply, somewhat confused.

"That's okay," the salesperson continues. "We can provide you with a pair of your own. Just follow me into the rear of the store to be fitted."

"I really don't want to be fitted," you start to object. "I just want to buy that item right there . . ."

"And you can," the salesperson reassures you, "*after* we fit you with the proper glasses."

"I don't *need* glasses!"

"Yes you do."

"No I don't!"

"You *do*—if you want to shop here."

"Look, I have a $20 bill in my hand. I just want to buy that thing, right there . . ."

". . . which you can do *after* you're wearing the proper glasses."

"Just take my money!"

"After you get your glasses."

"Take my money—*please*!"

"I'm sorry, but I can't. Not until you're fitted with the appropriate eyewear."

You can also imagine what comes next. (It involves storming out of the store in a huff.)

As stupid as this scenario sounds (what retailer in their right mind would refuse to sell a product to a willing customer?), this sort of thing goes on all the time in the world of e-tailing. Think of all the ways that technology can thwart even the most persistent potential purchasers:

✦ A site might accept only users with a specific browser—or a specific version of that browser.

✦ A site might require that your browser have Java support installed and activated.

✦ A site might require a more specific plug-in or add-on, such as a particular type of movie viewer, or a viewer for 3D "walk-throughs."

Whatever the case, the more dependent a site is on a particular technology, the less likely it is that all potential customers will have the appropriate technology installed on their systems. Which means that users will be forced to leave the e-tail site to go to another site and download and install the appropriate utility (all of which takes time and skill and is prone to problems), and *then* return to the e-tail site and start the shopping process from scratch. It's a sure-fire way to drive away customers!

How to do it

The key to this trick is to embrace every bleeding-edge technology you can think of—especially those technologies least likely to be supported by a majority of users. (I'm a big fan of that 3D viewer—few if any browsers have this technology installed by default.) Then make sure that your site isn't usable unless that technology is implemented (by using JavaScript to detect plug-ins or browser versions) and refuse admittance unless the proper software is detected.

Practical uses for this technique

Some of these optional viewers are pretty neat. If you're selling something big, like a house or an automobile, the idea of a 3D walk-through is actually fairly useful. I particularly like the use of the 3D viewer at the Microsoft Carpoint site (carpoint.msn.com), or the QuickTime VR viewer used at some of the manufacturers' sites; you get a good sense of how the insides of selected cars look and feel.

How not to be annoying

Naturally, the less dependent your site is on esoteric technology, the more accessible it is by all types of users. (Think Yahoo!—there's nothing there that won't work on even the oldest text-based browser.) If you insist on forcing technology down your customers' throats, at least be considerate enough to include a direct link to download the plug-in; don't make users search the Web to find the utility you require for admittance.

Trick #116: Recommend Totally Irrelevant Items

Many e-tail sites attempt to personalize the shopping experience by recommending items to you when you visit their sites, presumably based on your past purchases. While this seems like a good idea in theory, in practice it tends not to be.

Here's why.

First, your purchases at that site don't always reflect your total purchases in that category. Let's say you buy half your compact discs at Online Disc-o-rama and the other half at a traditional bricks-and-mortar store. Online Disc-o-rama can track only those CDs you purchase from them online; all the CDs you buy elsewhere won't figure into the equation. (This gets particularly iffy when you use online stores to purchase more obscure items you can't always find in the real world; the e-tailer will think you have really obtuse tastes when you don't make your "normal" purchases online.)

Second, most e-tailers can't differentiate between items you purchase as gifts and items you purchase for your own use. So if you did all your Christmas shopping at Online Disc-o-rama, and that shopping included a Britney Spears CD for your teenage niece and a greatest polka hits collection for your Uncle Lester, the e-tailer is going to come back with some really bizarre recommendations for your future purchases. (My guess is you'll get a recommendation for the latest Weird Al Yankovic CD, which may or may not suit your particular tastes.)

Third, the online site doesn't know what items you already have in your possession. If you buy a copy of the Beatles' *Anthology*, for example, you might get a recommendation to purchase *Abbey Road*—which you probably already own. The site doesn't know this, and thus has wasted a recommendation.

Finally, many of these so-called recommendation engines just don't work, period. Ever buy an Elvis Costello CD and get a recommendation for a Carl Perkins collection? That's an engine that isn't doing its job right. (Wrong Elvis, in that case.) These things aren't perfect, after all.

Which makes just most of these recommendations amusing at best and highly irritating at worst. Still, there's no harm in trying — or is there?

How to do it

If you're making recommendations on your site, here are some things you can do to ensure the lowest level of accuracy possible:

✦ Track all customer sales, even those specifically marked as gift purchases.

✦ Don't allow any means of customer customization — don't let customers add or subtract items based on the accuracy of the recommendation.

✦ If you can, fine-tune your recommendation engine to recommend as broad a range of items as possible — which should result in a higher level of irrelevant recommendations.

✦ If you're feeling particularly malicious, program your recommendation engine to suggest items totally at random — otherwise known as the "serendipity setting."

Practical uses for this technique

Some users like having items recommended to them. If your recommendation engine is working well, it will occasionally suggest items with appeal to certain customers. After all, the only way to broaden your horizons is to open yourself to new experiences.

How not to be annoying

The least annoying of these recommendation engines let the user fine-tune the results. If the engine recommends the Beach Boys' *Pet Sounds*, for example, you can respond that this is a good match or a bad match, or that it's an item you already own. The engine will then "learn" your likes and dislikes and (theoretically, at least) deliver better suggestions in the future.

Trick #117: Don't Offer One-Click Ordering

Many users shop online because it's quicker and easier than shopping in the real world — no traffic to fight, no cars to park, no malls to walk, no lines to endure. For that reason, fast checkout is a highly valued quality for e-tailers; you don't want to keep your customers waiting any longer than you have to.

One way to speed up the purchasing process — among repeat customers, at least — is to use a one-click checkout. (You know, like the kind that Amazon has a patent on.) If the customer's credit card and shipping information is on file in your system, when the customer finds an item to buy, he or she simply clicks a single button and the item is automatically purchased and scheduled for delivery. The customers enter their information once, and that information is reused whenever the one-click button is pushed.

Not offering one-click ordering on your site forces users to go through the entire checkout process with every order they place. They have to enter their name and address, phone number, and credit card number and expiration date, and then choose a shipping method and address. That's a lot of information to enter once, let alone every time — and you'll drive users away from your site and toward competitors who simplify the repeat purchase process.

How to do it

Not offering one-click ordering is as simple as not offering one-click ordering. Don't store customers' information, and don't recognize past customers on future visits. Start fresh with every visit, and you're guaranteed to reduce the number of repeat customers on your site.

Practical uses for this technique

You could actually make a big deal over not storing customer information by playing the privacy card. If you don't store personal information, you're respecting your customers' privacy concerns. After all, it's those sites that offer services like one-click ordering that store all that customer information — and then what do they do with it? If the information is stored, it can be sold or stolen. By not storing the information — and not offering one-click ordering — you're ensuring that your customers' private information remains private.

How not to be annoying

Okay, so you don't want to (or can't) offer one-click ordering. You can still store customer information for future ordering convenience. Just assign each customer a customer ID and password, or track their user names via cookies, and then use that ID/password combination or cookie to pull up their ordering information on future visits. You may still display a traditional checkout order form, but you can at least "pre-fill" most of the forms based on the customer's previous orders.

Trick #118: Make Your Checkout as Confusing as Possible

While I'm on the subject of checkouts, how complicated does this really have to be? After all, what does a retailer really need to complete the sale — the customer's name, address, and credit card number and expiration date should do it. Oh, it might be nice to have the customer's phone number, so you can call if something goes screwy. But that's pretty much it.

Why, then, do so many online checkouts ask for so much more information than this? Why do so many checkouts stretch out over multiple pages? Why are you required to fill out shipping and billing information separately? Why do you have to make so many choices (shipping method, order consolidation, priority handling, gift wrap, and so on)?

The best checkouts are the shortest ones. The longer and more confusing you can make the checkout process, the more you can irritate your customers — and force them to exit your site before their checkout is complete.

How to do it

When designing the perfectly confusing checkout form, begin by thinking of every possible piece of information you might ever want to know. Don't stop with name, address, e-mail address, and credit card; consider asking for both home and work phone numbers, fax number, company name, purchase order number, separate shipping and billing addresses, preferred shipping method, and so on. And, in as obtuse a manner as possible, make the customer choose whether to ship the entire order at one time or wait until all items are in stock.

Now you should take all this desired information and throw it on a Web page in a completely illogical fashion. Make sure that pressing the Tab key takes users somewhere they don't expect to go (instead of to the next field), and split the information up into multiple pages to enhance the confusion factor. If you make it tough enough to fill out, it's bound to be annoying!

Practical uses for this technique

Asking for all this information in advance ensures that you'll always have what you need, no matter what happens to the customer's order. After all, if you don't have both a daytime and nighttime phone number, you won't be able to call the customer at dinnertime to say that the order is being delayed.

How not to be annoying

The rule is simple — ask for what you need, and nothing more.

And, it goes without saying, ask for it in a polite and logical fashion.

Trick #119: Make Visitors Complete a Questionnaire

"Excuse me, sir or madam, do you mind if I ask you a few questions?"

No one likes to hear that line, especially if you're waiting on line to pay for your latest shopping spree. The gall of someone to ask you to fill out a questionnaire before they'll let you pay for their merchandise!

Well, now you can employ this time-proven technique to annoy customers on your Web site. While you have them captive, ask them to fill in a page or two (or three or four) about their likes and dislikes, their education levels, their purchasing intentions, and how often they have sex each week. Then, and only then, let them proceed to checkout. After all, they probably wouldn't stick around to complete the questionnaire if you asked the questions *after* they've checked out!

How to do it

This trick is as easy as inserting a few extra pages before your checkout. That is, when customers click the Checkout link or button, they're redirected to your main questionnaire page. From there you can include as many fields and pages as you wish — more of which is more annoying, of course.

For extra credit, you can also use this opportunity to force customers to opt out of receiving future promotional offers from you and other companies. (Opting out means that the "Send me lots of annoying spam" option is automatically checked and must be manually deselected for customers not to get e-mailed to death.) If you use this trick, make sure you're prepared to follow up with daily or weekly e-mails about totally unrelated products and offers, and to sell your customer list to the most offensive spammers on the Web.

Practical uses for this technique

Market research is an accepted way to find out more about your customers — and the better you know your customers, the better you can tailor your site and services to their needs. And it's a lot less costly to ask your questions online than it is to hire a market research firm to phone or mail customers after the fact.

How not to be annoying

If you have to ask, have the common courtesy to first ask if it's okay. (That is, give customers an opportunity to opt out of the survey.) You should also consider asking the questions postsale, so your probing interrogatories don't interrupt the purchasing process. Or, as an incentive to answer the questionnaire, you could offer some sort of discount on future purposes. (In other words, bribe 'em!)

Trick #120: Require Credit Card Info *Before* Shoppers Order

Of *course* you need to ask for your customers' credit card information. What's annoying is when you ask for it *before* they place their orders. (After all, how many traditional retailers ask for your credit card as soon as you walk in the door?)

How to do it

The accepted way to do things is to ask for credit card information after users enter your checkout. Instead, rejig your site's code to require a credit card before customers can view your product selection. If they don't supply the numbers, redirect them to another site—maybe one of your competitors'?

Practical uses for this technique

It could be argued that you want to save your site's bandwidth for those customers who have a proven means to pay. There might actually be something to this argument if you're selling rare or high-priced items and you want to discourage window shopping. Use the credit card ploy to filter out the riffraff and keep your site free for the big spenders.

(For extra credit—no pun intended—you can actually check the customer's available credit before you allow admittance; if they don't have a high enough credit line, you don't let them in.)

How not to be annoying

If you honestly don't want to annoy your customers, don't ask for their credit card numbers (or other personal information) until they've made their selections and are ready to check out. Or, if you insist on prequalifying your purchasers, ask only once—and use cookies or user IDs to keep the information on file for future visits.

Trick #121: Make Visitors Start from the Top if They Screw Up

There are few things as bad as starting from scratch after you screw something up. So when an e-tail site sends you all the way back to the home page when you make a mistake filling out the checkout form, you're apt to get *extremely* annoyed—annoyed enough to not want to go through that whole process again.

Surprisingly, a lot of e-tail sites adhere to the "do it all again, and get it right this time" philosophy. I'm not sure why this is the case; it's just as easy to send customers back to the first checkout page, or to a product page, or even to Yahoo! than it is to send customers back to the home page. Still, that's the way some e-tailers do it, no doubt with a resultant lower order rate. If nothing else, it keeps them from worrying about low or nonexistent inventory in the warehouse.

How to do it

This one is so simple that anyone can do it — and it's derived from the code in Trick #106 (Chapter 11). In the `if (!pass)` line, which tells the browser what to do if a required field isn't filled out, replace the `alert` code with a `window.location` event. Insert the URL for your site's home page as the `window.location` value, and whenever users don't complete the entire form, they're sent all the way back to your home page.

It's that simple.

Practical uses for this technique

This one baffles me. I don't know why anyone would want to cancel out everything a customer has done and send them back to the shopping equivalent of square one. The only possible result is one ticked-off customer.

How not to be annoying

The better way to deal with customer mistakes (and they happen all the time) is to return the user to the form where the mistake was made — accompanied by an alert box that spells out what went wrong, and what the user should do to correct it. You can use the code in Listing 11-9 as a good starter script and modify it as appropriate to your site.

Trick #122: Don't Let Visitors Continue Shopping

Tell me if this has happened to you.

You're shopping at your favorite online store, you pick out a few things to buy, you go to the checkout, you enter your shipping information and credit card number, and the site displays a screen thanking you for your order. Then, for whatever reason, you decide that you need something else from the site. You scroll down the page, looking for some kind of "continue shopping" or "back to our site" link, but find neither. If you're dead set on doing some more shopping, you're forced to either enter the site's main URL in your browser's Address field, or to click your browser's Back button enough times to return you to the site's main product listing.

Definitely not a recipe for add-on sales.

While most customers are done shopping when they're done shopping, not all are, and you'd think a savvy e-tailer would want to encourage any additional purchases. Instead, many sites assume that the customer is all spent out and won't be back for a while; it's the online equivalent of rolling over and falling fast asleep at the conclusion of the evening's carnal activities. There aren't any second helpings if you're not prepared for them!

How to do it

As with most techniques that annoy your most profitable customers, this one consists of doing nothing. More specifically, it means displaying a Thank You screen that includes nothing more than those words — no links, no buttons, no nothing that would lead back to your shopping site. Because if you can't easily get there from here, most users won't take the trip.

Practical uses for this technique

Why wouldn't you want customers to return to your site? Maybe you're all sold out of the item the customer wants. Maybe the customer's credit line is all used up. Maybe you're in the process of reducing prices, and you don't want the customer to discover that he or she overpaid for recent purchases. Or maybe you just don't like your customers very much and don't want to deal with them any more than you have to. What other reason could you have for making it difficult for them to resume shopping?

How not to be annoying

Okay, it's fairly easy to make your customers happy. When you flash the Thank You screen, include a Back to Our Site or Continue Shopping button that links back to one of your site's main shopping pages. (If you want to be especially proactive, you can even present a page of "related items" that customers might want to add to their original purchase.) Even better, program your shopping cart so that any additional orders (placed within a specific — and relatively short — time frame, of course) are automatically added to the customer's original order, so the customer won't have to pay double shipping and handling for two separate orders. In other words, do whatever you can to encourage customers to keep shopping — until they spend *all* their money!

Trick #123: Don't Tell Visitors an Item Is Out of Stock Until After They Order

This trick really frosts my buns. I go through all the trouble of shopping and selecting and filling out the checkout form. Then, *after* I click the Submit Order button, the site lets me know that the item I wanted is out of stock. Not while I was shopping. Not before I ordered. Not before I filled in all my shipping info and credit card numbers. No, I wasn't informed of the inventory status until *after* I spent all that time and did all that work.

That's *exceedingly* irritating.

After all, I wouldn't have ordered that item if I'd known it was out of stock. I might have picked another item instead, or jumped to another site to see if they had it in stock, or just decided not to order that thing today. In any case, I wouldn't have spent all that time filling out the checkout form and acting like I was completing the order.

Which means, of course, that this is a perfect technique with which to drive away your customer base.

How to do it

Again, this is a simple one. All you have to do is complete the handling of the order form *before* checking to see if the item is in stock. It's kind of like putting point B before point A, but in this case it results in an extremely maddening situation.

Practical uses for this technique

Let's be honest. If a customer knows that a particular item is out of stock, there's a good chance that customer is going to leave your site and go elsewhere. If your goal is to retain customers on your site for as long as possible, it's in your best interest to delay the delivery of bad news until the last possible moment. And, if you're in the bait-and-switch business, you can display the Out of Stock page (after the order is completed, of course) alongside a suggestion that you have a similar item — "for a few dollars more," of course — in stock and ready to ship, and you'd be glad to switch the customer's order over to this other item, no problem. You'd be surprised how many suckers — um, excuse me, *valued customers* — will fall for this little scheme.

How not to be annoying

If you want to avoid angry customers, be up front with them. If you're out of stock on an item, tell them. At the very least, you can tell them as they're placing their order. Even better, tell them on the product page whether the item is in stock or out of stock. Even even better, tell them how many units you have in stock, or when you expect an out-of-stock item to be replenished. Even even even better, offer to ship the next best product for the same price.

Be honest, be open, and your customers will love you for it.

Trick #124: Don't Waste Time with Confirming E-Mails

Most people like a little handholding. They want to know if they did something right, they want to know what to expect, and they want to know that there won't be any big surprises.

Which is why most people are uncomfortable buying from most online merchants.

When you buy something at a traditional retail store, you know what's going on. You hold the merchandise in your hands, you carry it up to the checkout register yourself, you watch with your own eyes as the clerk rings up the sale, and you are given a receipt (and the merchandise!) to confirm the successful completion of the process. Lots of handholding, lots of feedback.

You even get a lot of feedback when you buy via catalog or mail order. You pick up the phone, you dial a number, you get a real honest-to-goodness human being on the other end. You tell this person what you want to buy, and he or she repeats your selections back to you, tells you whether the items are in stock or out of stock, tells you your total, takes your credit card number, tells you when the order will ship, and thanks you for your business. Again, lots of handholding, lots of feedback.

Now, let's examine the typical online merchant. You find the site (if you're lucky), you click through the pages (not really sure if you're heading in the right direction), you find something you want to buy (even if its picture is awfully hard to see), you click through to the checkout (or shopping cart or whatever the site calls it — are you sure that's the right button?), you enter all sorts of personal information (not quite comfortable with what they do with it all), and you click the Submit Order button. Nobody tells you if you've done everything right (or if you've made a mistake), nobody confirms that you entered your information correctly, no one tells you that the item is in stock or when it's going to ship, and no one thanks you for your business. It's just you and your browser, and you proceed on faith that you've done everything right and that you'll get the merchandise you ordered, in a timely fashion.

Granted, some sites are better than this, but not all — and not even a majority. It gets even worse when you consider how easy it would be for the site to confirm your sale. An order confirmation page isn't that hard to put together, nor is it rocket science to automatically send out an e-mail containing the details of an order and confirming the successful completion of the process.

We're not aiming for rocket science, however, so if you want to keep your customers in the dark, don't tell them what's going on. That means no thank you page, no order confirmation page, and no confirming e-mails. After all, following up on an order is a lot of work—and what's in it for you?

How to do it

This one is simplicity itself. You perform this trick by not sending out any e-mails.

That's all.

Practical uses for this technique

Think how nervous most customers will be if they get *no* feedback whatsoever regarding their order. (They'll get even more nervous as more time passes—which is a good reason to adopt extremely slow shipping practices, as discussed in Trick #127.) Now think how relieved they'll be when the product actually shows up at their door. They'll think a miracle has occurred—especially if they've mentally written off the order as already lost!

How not to be annoying

As I noted in the previous trick, open communication is one of the keys to satisfied customers. Use as many e-mails as possible—they don't cost you anything, after all—to keep your customers informed during the entire order process. That means a confirming e-mail directly after the order is placed, another e-mail when the order is processed and the payment approved, and a third e-mail when the package is shipped. If you're particularly well meaning, you'll include an internal tracking number with the first e-mail and a shipper tracking number with the last, so that the customer can easily access your Web site (or the shipper's Web site) to determine a more precise status.

Trick #125: Don't Give Shoppers a Way to Contact You

One of the joys of operating an online business is that you don't have to personally deal with the great unwashed that you call your customer base. Back in the real world you had to stand behind a counter and listen to their stupid questions and petty complaints, but thanks to the Internet you can distance yourself from all that. Let them complain all they want—you don't have to deal with it!

This is especially true if you don't provide any way for them to contact you. Hey, you're a virtual business—you're not expected to have a street address! Or a phone number! Or even an e-mail address!

That's right—you're under no obligation to provide any contact information whatsoever. If you don't list your address, your customers can't write you. (Or, heaven forbid, get into a car and visit you!) If you don't list your phone number, they can't call you. If you don't list your e-mail address, they can't even e-mail you.

There is joy in isolation.

How to do it

Even though a dedicated customer can find out where you work (you can find *any-thing* on the Web, thanks to search engines and online business directories), most customers won't go to all that trouble. If you don't list an address or a phone number on your Web site, they won't look any further, and you'll retain your virtual anonymity. Just leave out the About Us and Contact Us sections of your site, and only the most obsessed customers will go to the trouble of contacting you offline.

Practical uses for this technique

If you're trying to scam your customers, you want to remain as anonymous as possible. Anonymity is also good if you're running several businesses under different names; if there's no contact information, customers won't be able to put two and two together and find out that the same company runs all those sites. Plus, if you make it difficult for customers to contact you, you don't need to invest in an expensive customer support department; if there aren't any phones to ring, you don't have to hire anyone to answer them!

How not to be annoying

More reputable e-tailers provide the same type of contact information as do traditional direct mail and catalog merchants. That means that a street address, phone number, and e-mail address (or a `mailto:` link) should be listed *somewhere* on your site—preferably where they're easy to find, such as through a Contact Us link. If you want to go the extra mile, include a Web-based form in addition to these other contact methods, and spend the additional bucks for a toll-free phone number—and staff it 24/7. (Not all your customers live in the same time zone that you do.)

Then, of course, you have to ensure that your customer questions and complaints get answered in a timely fashion—which leads us to our next trick.

Trick #126: Ensure Unresponsive Customer Service

Sometimes things go wrong. Sometimes orders aren't shipped in a timely manner, or to the correct address. Sometimes items go out of stock. Sometimes customers have questions.

In other words, sometimes customers need to — or want to — contact you.

The handling of customer questions and complaints is called customer service. From the customers' perspective, they want to ask a question and they want a timely response. Ideally, they want to talk to a live human being and get an immediate response. If that isn't feasible, they might settle for submitting their questions via e-mail — as long as a real human being responds to their message, within a reasonable period.

Of course, customers want more than just a response — especially if it's a canned response. ("Thank you for your inquiry. Most orders ship within 2–3 weeks. You should be receiving your order shortly. Please shop here again.") They want *answers*, and they want *action*. They want someone to personally look into their situation and clear up any confusion or fix whatever has gone wrong.

In short, your customers want service.

Providing good customer service, however, is costly. You have to hire people to answer the phones and answer the e-mail. You have to provide those people with the information they need to answer all manner of customer questions, and the access to other people in your organization who can fix all manner of customer problems. Depending on the size of your organization, you may need to staff a customer call center from early in the morning until late in the evening, at least five days a week — with 24/7 operation expected from some types of businesses.

One guy sitting next to a phone for a few hours in the afternoon won't cut it.

Unless, that is, you never intended to provide decent customer service. After all, you didn't get into this dot-com thing because you liked dealing with people. One of the joys of working online is that you don't have to deal directly with other human beings unless you really want to. People calling on the phone and firing off e-mails at all hours of the day might not provide the most stress-free working environment; who wants to deal with all those whiny troublemakers?

The problem is, you pretty much have to provide *some* level of customer service. (Providing you don't take the advice in Trick #125, that is.) There's nothing that says, however, that your customer service has to be *good*.

How to do it

What is the bare minimum amount of customer service you have to provide? If you've given out your phone number, expect to get phone calls. You have to answer these calls — but you don't have to answer them *promptly*. You can let the phones ring for quite a long time before you answer them, or before the customers give up and hang up. Even better, you can invest in a phone hold system, so that your callers are automatically put on hold — where you can leave them for hours at a time. (Be sure to provide the most annoying background music as possible — I'm partial to old Barry Manilow tunes — and the occasional message telling callers that their call is important, but all operators are busy right now, so please hold for the next available operator.)

Even when your callers get through to a real live person, make sure that that person is relatively new and completely untrained, so that he or she can answer few if any customer questions. It also helps to overwork that person until he or she gets all cranky, thus virtually assuring that they'll talk rudely to your customers. And, no matter how much they ask, do not—I repeat, do *not*—allow your customer service staff to interact with the rest of your staff or have access to your order-shipment or inventory systems. It's important to treat your phone staff like lower-class citizens and not involve them in any company activities, especially training. Chances are that they're short-timers, anyway; why waste resources on a bunch of undedicated transients?

Of course, you'll also get some customer service inquiries via e-mail and snail mail. You should handle both these types of requests in the same fashion—ignore them. Print them out, set them aside, even file them, but definitely don't answer them. There's a certain satisfaction in watching frustrated customers send repeated e-mails to your contact address, that slight glimmer of hope that they'll receive a response slowly dimming with each new message sent. If you ignore them enough, chances are they'll go away.

Practical uses for this technique

If you provide lousy or nonexistent customer service—if you never answer a question or solve a problem—then customers will quit trying to contact you, which means you can probably reduce the number of customer service representatives on your payroll. Oh, your future sales will probably decline as well, but that may be a small price to pay for a little peace and quiet.

How not to be annoying

It's amazing the amount of management attention some companies devote to customer service. Not only do they provide toll-free phone numbers and 24/7 customer support, they also spend time and money to train their customer support staff and provide that staff with access to all the resources they need to handle even the most unusual customer complaints. Some companies even use the customer service lines as a form of market research, tracking call data to find out what products and features are giving customers trouble. Above all, they assign distinct and measurable goals to their customer service reps—minimum number of rings before answering a call, minimum number of minutes customers are kept on hold, minimum number of time elapsed before completing a call, minimum number of complaints unsolved, and so on.

In other words, to ensure their success, they treat customer service with the same level of attention and importance as they do any other part of their companies.

Incredible, but true.

Trick #127: Pack It Poorly and Ship It Slowly

Let's say a customer actually navigates to a live product page and manages to place an order. Assuming there are no customer service issues, the next step is to pack up that product and ship it out to the customer.

How can you manage the packing and shipping operation in a way that ensures a high level of customer annoyance?

How to do it

First, consider your inventory levels. To really annoy customers, try to keep as little stock on hand as possible, so that, more often than not, you'll be out of stock on what the customer wants to buy. If possible, make sure that your reporting systems are poor enough so that the correct inventory level is not reflected on any order status page that the customer sees; it's always fun to tell the customer you have something in stock when you really don't.

If you don't have an item in stock, set up your systems so that it takes as long as possible for you to replenish your inventory. That means no special orders from you to your suppliers and waiting as long as possible before placing your regular restocking orders. Weekly reordering is much too frequent; strive for monthly, at the fastest. (Of course, you shouldn't tell your customers how long it will take for their backorders to be filled; "soon" is as good a time frame as any to promise.)

Once you have an item in hand, you have to put it in a box or envelope and send it on its way. It's important not to have custom packaging materials, so that you're always trying to fit a small round peg into a big square box. Packing should be as shoddy and haphazard as possible, especially if you're shipping easily breakable items — and special care should be taken to drop, bend, fold, spindle, and mutilate the packed items as often as possible.

Note Unfortunately, spindling (which involves skewering an item on a thin, sharp spike) is a lost art — as is defenestrating, which is the act of throwing something out a window. (They both have a similar effect on fragile merchandise.)

Assuming that the package makes it to the end of the conveyor belt in one piece (your people aren't doing their jobs!), it's time to ship. Given all the different shipping alternatives available to you these days, take the special effort to find the slowest, least reliable method possible. If you can, inject a few misspellings into the shipping label, and don't place the label in a protective envelope or cover it with clear tape. (Without protection, the ink on the label will run in the rain, or get smudged by heavy handling — making it more difficult to read.) Remember not to insure the item, nor to obtain a tracking number. Just throw it on the truck and kiss it goodbye.

Practical uses for this technique

You can save a lot of money by using cut-rate shipping services. Savings are also to be had by reusing old boxes, cramming too-large items into too-small packages, and scrimping obsessively on peanuts and other packing materials. If you try hard enough, you may be able to turn your shipping department into a profit center — especially if your cost cutting is accompanied by absurdly high shipping and handling charges to your customers.

How not to be annoying

It's funny. The more care you take in packing and shipping, the fewer complaining calls you'll get to your customer service department. It's almost as if spending a little more time and money in shipping reduces costs elsewhere in your organization!

How do you reduce the number of customers annoyed by your shipping operation? Start by using the right shipping and packing materials, and by "overpacking" more fragile items. Then spend a few bucks on first-rate label-generation software; get a program that automatically generates 5+4 zip codes and prints trackable bar codes on all the labels. Finally, go with a reliable shipping firm, one that will work with you if you have any problems. Add at least the option of shipping insurance to your order process, and you're all set.

Trick #128: Make It Impossible to Return a Product

Sometimes you make mistakes; sometimes customers make mistakes. Whoevers fault it is, sometimes your customers get items that they don't want — which brings up the issue of returned merchandise.

Naturally, customers will want to return merchandise for a full exchange or refund, no questions asked, no additional charges made. For your part, you want to discourage returns — or, if forced to take something back, be compensated for your efforts.

When it comes to what you want versus what your customers want, that's a huge gap to bridge.

How to do it

The most draconian return policy is to take no returns at all. "All sales are final" should mean what it says. It doesn't matter if the customer changed his mind, if the product doesn't work, or if you shipped the wrong item — once it's left your warehouse, it's not coming back.

Next-best is a policy that both limits what can be returned and charges the customer for the privilege of sending something back. You don't want those shifty customers to give you the shaft, so limit returns to defective items or wrong sizes only — "Items can be returned for like items only." Then make sure that you invoke a restocking charge; 10 percent is a good number. And top it off by making the customer pay for all shipping back to your company — or, if you can get away with it, for all shipping in both directions.

Practical uses for this technique

If you make it difficult for customers to return items, you'll get fewer returns. This will help to reduce your overall costs and keep your obsolete inventory costs low.

All joking aside, this is a real issue for those who deal in rare or high-priced items. It's not unusual for some collectibles to be sold on a no-returns basis, as the items are unique and can't be duplicated. It's not like stocking legal pads and paper clips; taking back a high-priced rarity can cause a real financial hurt for small dealers.

How not to be annoying

Remember that old motto "The customer is always right"? Well, that's how the least-annoying retailers handle returns. They'll take anything back, no questions asked, and cheerfully issue a full refund or exchange. (Think Nordstrom, here.) The result is an extremely satisfied customer base and a reputation for first-class customer service.

After all, it's hard to get annoyed at a store that bends over backward to make you happy.

The Annoying Summary

As you can see, there are so many ways to frustrate potential paying customers that it's a wonder anyone buys online at all. Every obstacle you place in front of your users keeps them from spending their money at your site; these tricks are the online equivalent of a bricks-and-mortar store's blocking the aisles, gluing the products to the shelves, and locking the cash registers. No real-world retailer in their right mind would want to impede paying customers from spending their hard-earned money; why this happens so frequently online is one of those little mysteries of life that keep us awake at night. Still, maybe there's something to be learned from all this — or maybe commercial Web site developers are mean-spirited recluses who take perverse delight in irritating the average Joe. The result is still the same, of course; when customers get annoyed, they quit shopping.

And that is that. This is the last paragraph in the last chapter of this book, which means that it's time for you to close the covers and get back to work on your Web site. There are a lot of people out there to annoy, and the clock is ticking. Remember, if you want to see online examples and code listings — as well as additional annoying tricks — head to the *Building Really Annoying Web Sites* Web site at `www.annoyingwebsites.com`. And don't feel reticent about e-mailing me with your questions and comments (my e-mail address is `annoying@molehillgroup.com`); all those messages might get annoying, but I'd like to hear from you anyway!

✦   ✦   ✦

Index

Continued

Continued